The Fabulous Girl's Guide to

Grace Under Pressure

Also by Kim Izzo and Ceri Marsh

THE FABULOUS GIRL'S GUIDE TO DECORUM

The Fabulous Girl's Guide to

Grace Under Pressure

Extreme Etiquette for the Stickiest, Trickiest,
Most Outrageous Situations of Your Life

Kim Izzo and Ceri Marsh

Broadway Books
New York

PRINTED IN THE UNITED STATES OF AMERICA

BROADWAY BOOKS and its logo, a letter B bisected on the diagonal, are trademarks of Random House, Inc.

Visit our website at www.broadwaybooks.com

First edition published 2004

Illustrated by Roxanna Bikadoroff

Library of Congress Cataloging-in-Publication Data
Izzo, Kim, 1967–
    The fabulous girl's guide to grace under pressure : extreme etiquette for the stickiest, trickiest, most outrageous situations of your life / Kim Izzo and Ceri Marsh.— 1st ed.
        p.   cm.
    1. Etiquette for young women.   I. Marsh, Ceri, 1968–   II. Title.

BJ1857.Y6I993 2004
395.1'44—dc22   2003069578

ISBN 0-7679-1548-8

10   9   8   7   6   5   4

For Meredyth

Contents

INTRODUCTION ix

1. THE WORKPLACE 1
Fabulous Workspace 9
The People in Your Workspace 12
Bad Business 22
Sex in the Workplace 36
Down and Out 40

2. SOCIETY 47
Your Reputation 53
The Art of Conversation 60
Fabulous Girl as Bad Girl 70
Private Moments (or What Should Be Private) 74
The Party 78
Fabulous Girl on the Lam 85

3. MONEY 93
The Rich FG 98
The Poor FG 107
Criminal Money Matters 116

4. FRIENDSHIP 121
Meow 126
Competition Among FGs 128
Friends' Fortunes and Misfortunes 134
Health Issues 140
Extreme Friends 144
Friends and Men 149

5. SEX AND COURTSHIP 161
Sex, Sex, Sex 166
Courtship 181
The Men 190

6. COUPLEDOM   201
Relationship Woes   205
Break Up and Make Up   219
Ex Marks the Spot   233
Other Women   242

7. WEDDINGS AND DIVORCES   249
The Proposal   253
The Planning   256
Fractured Families and Your Wedding   265
The Event   267
Fabulous Girl as Friend of the Bride   273
Second Marriages   282
Divorce   287

8. HOME AND FAMILY   293
The Home Front   299
Family   306

9. ENTERTAINING   337
Fabulous Girl as Hostess   343
Whom to Invite?   356
Fabulous Girl as Guest   361

EPILOGUE   373

ACKNOWLEDGMENTS   381

Introduction

Two wise women once said that manners make you sexy. Oh, yeah, that was us. In our first book, *The Fabulous Girl's Guide to Decorum*, we set out to create a primer for women who crave both style and civility. We wanted to declare that far from making you a retiring bore, manners will make you a better and more socially desirable person. In our own lives, there were so many women of great charm, wit, and decorum that we wanted to celebrate the type: the Fabulous Girl. FG to her friends. She's that stylish, witty, and caring friend you rely on to make parties more fun and disappointments less painful. She is not interested in the much more traveled road of bad behavior. Rather, she chooses to set off down another path, that of civility. The FG knows how to get the most out of life while still remaining a caring part of her society.

But it's hard. Everyday we all encounter countless acts of selfishness and bad behavior. Whether it's a friend who is always late, a mate who forgets to introduce you at parties, the stranger who cuts you off on the road, or a colleague who takes credit for your work, etiquette is at an all-time low. At a time when we so desperately need civility, we find an intense focus on personal satisfaction in its place. Although bad manners are not appealing, they are increasingly common. And who wants to be common?

Not the FG. Rather than become cynical as a result of the rude old world she lives in, she rallies to the cause of decorum. The Fabulous Girl is passionate. She may be well mannered, but she is never mild mannered. Her zest for life is one of her most charming attributes. It also means she often finds herself in extreme situations. Despite the best-laid plans (or because of the best-laid plans), sometimes life spins out of control. An FG does not live to avoid these sorts of adventures. In love and work and in her friendships, the FG throws herself in deep—which can bring her big success as well as, sometimes, big disappointments. The FG knows that her word to live by is *decorum*, not *doormat*, so she tackles these ups and downs with equal vigor. An FG never shies away from this challenge. She knows that these adventures are the very fabric of her great big life.

The Fabulous Girl's Guide to Grace Under Pressure is geared toward this very Fabulous Girl. The one who uses her style and social decorum to cope with life's inevitable roller-coaster ride. We can all behave beautifully when things are going our way, can't we? But an FG wants to maintain her grace even under extreme circumstances. Some crises and turning points will come as a result of her evolving life—bigger jobs, bigger relationships. Also, some crazy and uncomfortable moments—cash windfalls, getting fired, discovering a philandering spouse—will arise in ways that are beyond her control. These are the moments that really count—when it's hard, when you'd rather be selfish or rude than extend yourself for another person, when you just feel like stamping your little foot—and they are true tests of character. But it is this ability to behave with grace under pressure, as well as her style, manners, and wit, that sets the Fabulous Girl apart, and, yes, makes her sexy and irresistible to all who know her.

The Fabulous Girl's Guide to

Grace Under Pressure

CHAPTER ONE

The Workplace

"What did you do to your hair? It looks good," Cheryl, a senior editor at *Smack!* magazine, squealed at me as she ran past my desk. Despite the backhanded compliment, I had to admit that I was having an unusually good hair day. Normally my hair misbehaves a few times a week, generally when I have a can't-miss cocktail party to attend. But that day my tresses looked fab. I chose to take my good hair as an omen.

I loved my job as associate editor for the magazine. *Smack!* is known in the rag trade as a general-interest magazine, but I'd been hired to give it specific interest: young and hip. In other words, it was my job to tell our middle-aged readership about what the pretty young things were drinking and shopping for, where they went to listen to music and get their hair done. I'd been at it for over a year. And while I was happy, I was beginning to want to move my work in another direction—upward, that is—but unfortunately I couldn't yet grasp exactly where up was.

Whack! Something walloped my desk with a mighty slap.

"Do you read Dudley's page?"

There stood John Bradley, *Smack!*'s editor in chief, the big boss, with a wad of rolled-up newspaper in his hand. I wondered if he was now going to swat me on the nose with it.

"He's funny. Your writing should be more like his. You know, chatty."

"But he's a gossip columnist."

"And?"

"And I'm not." I tried not to sound annoyed, but lately Bradley seemed to find fault with whatever I did or didn't do.

"Well, if you'd rather have dull copy. Did you dye your hair?"

"No, it's just a good—"

Bradley hurried away, leaving the offending paper on my desk. Dudley's gossip column ran in a national newspaper. Since being on the job, I'd become an observer of sorts. Being out many nights a week gave me plenty of opportunities to people-watch. I'd met Dudley on many occasions and he was not what you'd call gentlemanly. I wasn't really on his radar—he would barely say hello to me. And now there was Dudley's sucky face sneering at me.

Truth be told, I hated his column. It was brash, tacky, and rude. He was not the sort of gossip columnist who lived to suck up to local celebrities, he was the kind of creep who wormed his way into parties thrown by the well known only to turn around and mock their choice of wine or fashion sense in his next column. But like the dutiful worker bee, I read Dudley's words, most of them meaningless drivel. Meaningless, that is, until I got to the last paragraph, which was horrifying: "TV producer Bingo Jones was all hot and bothered with local celeb news babe Muffie (first name only, please) at last night's opening of the so-hip-it-hurts eaterie Spanks. If Bingo's regular chica, mag art director Elenor Brown, had eye-spied the duo giving each other a good tongue-lashing, it would have been spanks all right."

Now, I've never been a fan of Bingo. He was an ill-mannered lout, the kind of guy who took cell calls at dinner parties, was rude to waitresses, and, worse, was a terrible boyfriend. I knew this last fact to be utterly true because Bingo was in a long-term relationship, off and on, off and on, with one of my two best friends, Elenor. And the fact that Bingo was now a confirmed cheating bastard (during a supposed "on" moment) really riled me. As did Elenor's public humiliation at the keyboard of Dudley.

My first reaction? Poor Elenor! My second—I would never stoop to those depths in my writing! Bradley would have to find another writer to dish the dirt. The fact that I wanted to keep my job, however, prevented me from marching into his office to tell him so. I was hoping he'd just forget the entire conversation and continue with his latest idea for making over *Smack!*, which was more sex and gardening.

But first and foremost, I had to reach Elenor. She would need her friends. I called her work, her home, and her cell. No answer. Which meant one thing: Elenor had read Dudley's column. There was only one other person who might have known her whereabouts, our other best friend, Missy. I dialed.

"She's here."

I must admit Missy's revelation caught me off guard. Sure, we're all equally close, but I was mystified as to why Elenor would choose refuge in the suburbs over me. Why was Missy her first call?

At this point I should explain: Missy lived on the outskirts of the city. In a very big house with a 4-car garage. But Missy didn't drive. Her husband, Joe, had struck it superrich and Missy was still adjusting to her newfound wealth. This was becoming a bit of an issue with me. Along with the fatter wallet came a fatter head. In any case, it had taken a lot of effort for Elenor to get to Missy. I was a mere bike ride away.

"Elenor doesn't want to talk right now. Can she call you later?" Missy sighed.

I hung up the phone, still unsure of why Elenor didn't want to talk to me and further irked by Missy's tone.

"Did you change your hair?"

The question shook me out of my pondering. I contemplated shaving my head. A few more of my colleagues hovered around my desk.

"Just a good hair day."

Bradley hustled over with his coat on. "We're all going to lunch. Want to join us?"

I was dumbfounded. I mean, never once since my first *Smack!* day had I been invited to one of Bradley's lunch things. Naturally, I couldn't say no, no matter how ticked I still was at the Dudley incident—perhaps I was finally being let into the inner circle of senior editors. Don't get me wrong; people have been nice to me, but seeing as I'm so junior, the so-called real journalists had kind of kept their distance from me. I knew that they considered my pages the necessary but shallow fluff that kept advertisers happy. My out-and-about pages and the fashion and decor pages were the cute ghetto of the magazine. But then, an invitation to lunch. This was serious. We all headed out to Bradley's regular diner. Although my mind kept obsessing about Elenor, I tried to fit in with the group.

"We have to get that piece on John Daly in before next week."

"Who's John Daly?"

Bradley looked at me like I had asked him how to spell my own name.

"Um, he's probably going to be elected mayor," said Cheryl.

"Oh, that John Daly!" I lied.

For the rest of the walk to the restaurant I tried not to feel excluded from the conversation, but I was afraid to say anything else. I was positive that they were questioning Bradley's judgment in hiring me, let alone inviting me. I consoled myself with the knowledge that I was at the very least charming, and I vowed to be bright and witty at lunch.

Arriving at the restaurant, we were led to a large round table and began to fan out. I walked around the entire circumference and ended up sandwiched between Cheryl and the arts writer, Marshall, with big boss Bradley straight across from me.

We ordered. I assumed Bradley was picking up the tab and so went for a slightly larger lunch than I would normally have. Besides, half the table were eating steak, so my salmon wasn't the end of the world. But still, I was too intimidated to speak.

"I was thinking of giving the movie roundup piece to Stella," Marshall announced.

Bradley simply nodded. There was only one film critic in town named Stella, Stella DuBois, and I thought she sucked. She hated everything she saw, and her writing was grossly self-indulgent. Every review she wrote somehow came back to herself and some formative experience in her life. Finally, a topic I could get in on.

"No, you're not giving work to that hack?"

Marshall just looked at me in disbelief. I took this as a sign that few people challenged him, but I was aiming to prove I could hold my own in this merry group. I'd show Bradley I was no dummy.

"I mean she hates everything but has no critical eye. I read that she once tried to make a film but her script was so bad no one would touch it. She's just a frustrated filmmaker who takes her own disappointment out on the real artists. And don't get me started on her writing!"

I had never seen people so silent. Cheryl and Marshall smiled meekly. Everyone else stared down at their plates. Everyone except Bradley.

"She happens to be my wife," Bradley announced, as he stabbed his steak and tore it apart.

I wanted to quietly swallow my own head. How had I not known this? I mean, sure, Bradley kept to himself, and I was hardly his confidante, but no one had ever mentioned Stella and Bradley in the same sentence. I had a vague memory of seeing Stella at the Christmas party, but she had drunk too much and left early.

"I'm so sorry, I had no idea."

"They like to keep their personal lives private. You couldn't have known; only industry types would know." Marshall tried to make me feel better, but I was stung by the implication that I wasn't even in the same industry as the rest of them. It didn't really matter what I said now, my stiletto was in my big mouth and deep down I knew my days at *Smack!* were numbered. There would be no upward mobility for me. I finished my salmon in silence.

Back at my desk, I listened to my voice mail, trying to recover from the lunch debacle by being busy, too busy to listen to my colleagues' whispered comments. Most of my messages were from PR people pushing products that were of no interest to me. I dubbed these annoying phone calls "sevens," the number I pressed on my phone's keypad to erase them. This was also true of mean and nasty reader calls. "What do you know from a good bar? I read your piece on Dino's last month and you suck. It's the best place. My brother-in-law owns it so I know it's good. I think you should be standing under a cliff during an avalanche." Definitely a seven. But not a single call from Elenor. I looked at the clock: 4:57 p.m.

I was so glad it was quitting time. Despite my sunny outlook at 9 a.m., I was feeling deflated. I looked in my compact mirror. Even my hair had become limp. So much for having a good hair day.

∞

∽ *Fabulous Girl as Big Girl* ∽

FINALLY, AFTER YEARS OF Jill Jobs (those easy and meaningless jobs a girl does on her way to future fabulousness), the FG has made it. She's gotten to where she wants to be, or at least a lot closer than that temp job was. The Fabulous Girl with a career has to navigate a whole new professional landscape. Work is still one of her highest priorities and where she spends most of her time and mental energy. But if she's lucky, she's spending it doing something she loves. As a wise FG once said, "Find a job you love and you'll never work a day in your life."

In the early days of her career, a young woman's burdens are most likely to be boredom and frustration. She may get stuck with tasks that she feels are beneath her abilities. As her work life takes off, she'll have different pressures: keeping up a level of performance she has established for herself, the added responsibilities of her seniority, and dealing with the office politics that accompany a rise through the ranks. Even an FG at the top of her professional game can have a Bad Hair Day or a Fat Day. And while the FG thinks these are prime reasons to call in sick, her boss probably won't. But for truly bad days, the FG may have to pull out all the tools in her decorum arsenal or else risk turning into the angry, bitter, depressed type she shrinks from.

∽ *Fabulous Workspace* ∽

Assembly lines aren't exclusive to factories churning out widgets. In past decades the standard office environment consisted of row upon row of uniform desks and chairs situated in one large room. If that seems barbaric to the Fabulous Girl aesthetic, consider the current equivalent for cost cutters in corporate America—the open-concept workspace. Here the "cubicle dwellers" sit at their desks toiling away at their jobs. Love them or hate them, the little cubes are here to stay. For the FG, however, there are ways of coping with grace.

YOU'RE STUCK IN CUBE COUNTRY

Privacy—you really don't have any, do you? Staunch supporters of cube country suggest that what the cubicles lack in privacy they make up for in team building. Collaboration, it seems, is easier when you don't have to waste precious seconds picking up a phone or strolling to someone else's office to speak with them. Hey, we thought that's what boardrooms and luncheons were for. Apparently it is downright inspiring to have colleagues overhear your sales pitch or see what your presentation looks like on your computer screen so they can give you their two cents without your needing to ask. How convenient.

However, what all cube-country residents need to understand is that just because you don't have any privacy doesn't mean you shouldn't respect the illusion of it. Don't give your opinion on your colleagues' work unless you're asked for it; they may not be ready to share their work yet and may resent your butting in. Likewise for personal problems. If you hear Sue fighting with her boyfriend, you cannot say, "So sorry you're having problems, do you need to talk about it?" Pretend you heard nothing! Sue will confide if and when she wants to.

Did you hear that?

A voice that is obviously speaking quietly is one that wants to avoid detection. Take this as a sign to distract yourself with something else, say, your own work. And while no one really wants to hear you whisper sweet nothings to your accountant, sometimes it cannot be helped. If a call is very private, it's time to take your cell to the parking lot or use a boardroom phone instead.

Why shout? No matter how eager you are to express your enthusiasm to a new client over the phone, raised voices are very distracting to your colleagues in cube country. If you sense that coworkers are stuffing cotton into their ears, turning up their desk radios, or sneering at you, take these hints to pipe down.

Noisy neighbors

Sometimes you may have to address a colleague's habits in order to carry on with your own work. If you are slaving over this month's bottom line but your cube buddies spend all day talking about Saturday night plans, feel free to bring it up with them. Chances are they weren't aware that you could hear them, and this reminder will embarrass them enough to keep it down—and they may also be a bit worried that you'll squeal to the boss about their work ethic. Either way, the problem should be solved. On the flip side, music is nice, but not everyone will appreciate your love of opera or Eminem. Really, boom boxes and radios shouldn't be played without headphones.

Desk hovering

Just because there aren't any doors on the dam things doesn't mean it's all open concept all the time. If your teammate is on the phone or eating her lunch, you cannot just stand there in her tiny space waiting for her to finish so that you can talk to her. Come back when she's free. At most, stick a Post-it down to inform her of what you need and she'll find you when it's a better time.

If you are a victim of desk hovering, ask the person you're speaking on the phone with to excuse you for a moment, place your hand over the mouthpiece, and firmly but politely tell the desk hoverer that you will come over and see him when you are finished with your call. People in your office may think you are being overly picky about boundaries initially, but they'll soon stop assuming that your cubicle is their cubicle or at least part of the common space in the office.

⁓ *The People in Your Workspace* ⁓

Loutish Behavior from Male Colleagues

Some types of work environments are still dominated by men. The FG does not try to be "one of the guys." She relishes her femininity, and since she acts with grace, the men around her will respond in kind. However, if you are the sole female in a workplace, you can expect the men to be on their guard. And that's just fine with an FG. She has no problem being a civilizing presence. Hopefully, the guys will take into account that an FG doesn't want to listen to PMS jokes or constant sports talk (unless she's in a sporting field). If one or two gents seem to be behaving in an ungentlemanly fashion, the FG would initially much rather deal with the issue on her own, perhaps asking the guilty party to refrain from his off-color humor or constant belching, with subtlety first: "You really should stop eating that chili every day, Bob." Fortunately, most men are acutely aware of the PC attitudes that permeate the modern workplace and will be hyperaware of potential problems.

If the man or men do not cooperate after her polite request but continue in a loutish mode, an FG should stand her ground and give fair warning. Tell him or them explicitly to quit with the sexist comments or to remove the centerfold tacked up in the lunchroom. If this doesn't work, an FG will need to take it up with her manager. Of course, if bad behavior turns into out-and-out harassment, then there are other, legal, courses of action.

SEXUAL HARASSMENT

Bingo's behavior has gone beyond annoying, yet basically harmless, flirting and entered the harassment zone. Because FGs are independent minded, they are inclined to deal with these things on their own. The FG has the confidence to tell a man, even her boss, when his stupid lewd "jokes" are unwelcome. Usually a straightforward warning, disguised as a talk, will suffice. Many employers and male coworkers are so attuned to sexual harassment that they will stop their behavior. FGs also will not use one off-color remark as an excuse to ask for a raise or more vacation time. These types of moves do not further the cause of women in the workplace.

However, if the harassment continues and/or gets physical then you will need your company's support. You should document what's going on by writing down the incidents or saving strange messages. But you should talk to your boss and the human resources department as well. If Bingo spends a staff Christmas party groping your ass while no one is looking, it's time to bring out the big guns. Consider it your part in making your workplace safe for everyone, not just solving what is an extremely unpleasant situation for yourself. In plain terms let those in a position to help (and frankly, with an obligation to do something about it or face the music themselves) know exactly what is going on. Many firms will have in place a process that must be followed in situations of alleged harassment. And if they don't you may want to consider introducing them to the concept via your own lawyer. This is a large and difficult task and an FG may feel that her time is better spent working for and with people where these problems don't exist. Either way, she knows that it is her right to work in an environment where she doesn't doubt her own safety.

BITCHY FEMALE COLLEAGUES

Working with women can be great. There can be plenty of bonding and fun in an all-female workplace. The FG thrives in estrogen-strong situations, being a girlie-girl herself. However, she does occasionally experience a downside. Workplaces staffed entirely by women can have the double-edged sword of surplus sensitivity. This is welcome when you get dumped and your chickmates understand why you're a wreck for two weeks. But the flip side is that feelings can easily be hurt within this feminine office. You may find that you need to—or think you need to—watch your tone of voice more carefully. This can be tiring and can make jobs take longer than they should. Gossip can also be more rampant with a female majority, and again this is unavoidable, for if you don't spend some time gossiping the other "girls" will think you unfriendly. It's all about balance. Remember that you are not obligated to become BFFs (summer camp lingo for Best Friends Forever) with every woman in the office. There's nothing wrong with having a friendly yet professional tone with many of your workmates. You don't have to spend every coffee and lunch break analyzing each other's relationships. Naturally some close friendships will develop at work, but it doesn't make sense for all your work relationships to be up close and personal. Don't offer up details of last night's argument with your mom to all and sundry and don't encourage the woman in the next cubicle over to stop by every morning for a coffee-and-confession session. Keeping a slight professional distance from coworkers will keep you out of the hardcore gossip loop, which is what you're after.

Since the FG is so poised and stylish she may find herself confronted with jealousy—a sure sign she is not working with other FGs, who never hold poise and style against a girl. If this is the case, the FG must bide her time and continue to be her friendly, warm self. Eventually, all but the most hardheaded bitches will be won over by the FG's obvious charms.

If an FG works in a predominantly female office where one or two men also work, the conversations need to be sensitive. That's right—male-sensitive. When women discuss bad dates or mean boyfriends, things can easily devolve into male bashing, which is very impolite. Conversely, trying to get them to explain why your boyfriend is a jerk is also not fair.

COMPLAINING COLLEAGUES

It's one of the great myths that complainers actually want someone to fix their troubles. What's far more likely is that the complainer wants the person they're whining to simply to listen and sympathize. (This is a particularly difficult one for men to wrap their minds around.) There she is again. Fifi is standing in your office for the umpteenth time complaining about her unappreciative boss. What to do? Most of us have been tricked into giving unwanted advice. Work troubles can be complicated because many people have ongoing problems that they may need to vent about. Passive-aggressive assistants and undermining coworkers are the kinds of problems that tend to need chronic airing. As the friend of someone with a problem, you must be careful not to fall into some of these traps.

Don't give pat answers. If you've heard your friend whine about how undervalued she is in her job for the past year and a half, you understandably will want to recommend that she do something about it. Don't. Any advice that starts with "just," as in "Just tell your boss you're not working on the weekends and nights anymore," will not be appreciated. It may seem clear what the answers are, but most people will be insulted if their troubles are reduced to one-line fix-ups.

Don't encourage confrontation. Workplaces are complicated systems. Assume that you don't understand the lay of the land. Therefore, think twice before encouraging your friend to have it out with the guy sitting next to her who may be taking credit for your friend's work but who also has lunch with the boss and is more powerful than he seems.

Instead

What does she want? Ask your friend what she wants out of her bitch session—probably just a chance to vent her irritation over work troubles, and possibly some help in analyzing the psychology of the people in her office. Do not immediately assume that she is looking for you to solve her problems.

If the complainer has been upset by a work situation for a long period of time, it is fair to gently point this out: "Wow, you've been unhappy with your boss's attitude for the past year, haven't you?"

Listen and ask, don't tell. Listen with care and attention—that's what she really wants. And ask questions such as, "Do you want to quit your job?" so that she can arrive at her own conclusions.

YOUR COWORKER IS A SUCK-UP

This person kisses your boss's ass at every opportunity, even if it means insulting or undermining colleagues. The Suck-Up will pass the buck on his own mistakes or tell the boss how he loves an idea but behind the boss's back tell you how stupid it is. The only solace for the Fabulous Girl is that chances are the boss knows a simpering sycophant when she sees one. The FG never falls for the charms of such a person, nor does she seek favor by acting in kind.

YOUR COWORKER IS INCOMPETENT

Bingo is a boob. Everyone knows it, right? He's so obviously incompetent that it's difficult not to let your lack of respect for him show at work. But at an absolute minimum you must treat him—even behind his back—with decorum. Remember that someone hired him, and that person likely is your boss. Any slag you make against Bingo is an indirect slag against his superior. Many bosses are extremely defensive about the hires they make and will take personally any criticism of them. Most managers also have a lot of problems to solve each day, so don't make Bingo two problems. His incompetence is the first and most obvious hassle, but then your unhappiness about it becomes another. If you are in a position where you must complain about Bingo to your boss or in front of your boss, be very careful. Stick to the facts and make no personal remarks: "I found my job difficult this month since Bingo delivered his reports three weeks late. I was able to compensate for the lost time, but it wasn't an ideal situation." It behooves you to go out of your way to seem reasonable and accommodating when dealing with the Incompetent, as you will come off as the star of the situation. You will also do much more to change your boss's opinion of Bingo the boob.

YOUR COLLEAGUE IS A PRIER

She's friendly, a great listener, and she seems very, very interested in your personal and work life. Every time she comes near you she has a salacious tidbit about someone else in the office. Which means her prodding questioning about how much overtime you put in last month isn't so she can sympathize, it's ammo to take to the next person and say, "She's just rancid about having to work all weekend; she really thinks she's doing more than anybody." If you've been burned by the Prier, or see her doing it with others, then you simply must keep quiet about your opinions, especially those concerning the job and company, and make it clear to her that you're not interested in the opinions of others when she tries to share.

YOUR COLLEAGUE IS A BACKSTABBER

You bump into your close work pal Janey at the coffee shop under your office and just as you're about to launch into a rhapsody on the beauty of her shoes, she breezes by you without even a smile. You're dumbfounded. When you finally corner her in the ladies' room and insist on knowing what is going on, she confesses that Fifi told her what you said about her after the staff meeting yesterday. You search your memory to think what you possibly could have said and then it comes back to you. You mentioned to your boss on the walk to the elevator that you were concerned about the deadline on a project you and Janey are working on together. And guess who was standing behind you? Fifi then worked it into a conversation with Janey but in her telling of it, you were whining to your boss that Janey couldn't keep up her half of the work. Meet the Backstabber. This is inevitably someone who has been very friendly (bordering on prying behavior) to you in the past. This person lives to divide allegiances between others. So, of course the first thing you must do is put Janey at ease that no such thing happened and that you're sympathetic that Fifi went out of her way to hurt her in this appalling way. The only good thing about the Backstabber is that she does respond well to confrontation. Of course, when you first have it out with Fifi she will deny any responsibility. It doesn't matter. This is a person who sees the world in terms of whom she can push around and whom she can't. So go ahead and get tough. "It doesn't matter what you're telling me now, Fifi. Janey is someone I trust. If she says you phoned her at home last night to run me down and make her feel terrible then you did. I'm telling you don't ever do it again. You never have need to repeat my conversations. You're obviously out to cause trouble and I won't have it."

YOU WORK FOR A REAL SLAVE DRIVER

We all need a bit of a kick now and again to meet deadlines. But somehow there is always one person who sets about it in a manic fashion, driving everyone else so hard that the work actually suffers. Granted, some people respond well to added pressure or being spoken to like children, but the Fabulous Girl is not one of them. She doesn't see the need to get spastic about a report that is due, she just does it. So when the Slave Driver rants and raves and tells the FG ten times that she has only three days to complete her report, the FG needs to calmly repeat to the SD that all is under control. When she sees the SD coming her way, she may cut her off at the pass by saying, "Yes, I know it's due. Is there something else I can help you with?"

You Have a Condescending Boss

You know that you're twenty-nine, it says so right on your birth certificate (and if you're honest, it's starting to show a little around your eyes as well, but that's another matter). So why when your boss speaks to you does it suddenly feel like you're twelve years old again? When she explains tasks, she repeats herself five times as if you may not have heard her the first four. When you do something that displeases her she lets it rip in front of your coworkers. And when you do accomplish the smallest task she responds as if it were a small miracle or at least a great relief to her. These are usually the ways of a very new manager. Your Condescending Boss doesn't trust herself yet in her role as leader and so passes on to you a sense of distrust. Make an appointment with this kind of boss as soon as possible. Clarify that you both understand what your role is and ask if she's satisfied with your performance. You may unwittingly not be meeting her expectations and she will appreciate that you've come forward to clear things up. If she is happy with the work you're doing, then let her know that you've been worried in the past that this hasn't been the case. On the other hand, just having this conversation may be enough to make her conscious of your abilities and drop the babying tone.

You Have a Disapproving Assistant

The qualities that make good leaders are not the same as those that make good administrators. Good leaders are usually people with vision—they are not necessarily good with details. It is often confusing for those who toil in support positions to work for leaders who are not good at coping with minutiae. In fact, an organized and efficient assistant can find her boss's haphazard way with schedules or paperwork extremely annoying. This classic role reversal can result in the assistant's developing a disapproving, tsk-tsking attitude toward her boss.

When an FG boss finds herself in this situation, she needs to address it. If she feels in any way guilty being in charge of someone else's time, it may be tempting to fall into this codependent relationship. It's sort of an "I feel bad that I'm your boss, so let's both pretend that I'm incompetent without you" mode. This dangerous game can end up with the boss being pushed around by her assistant. An FG boss needs to make it clear that it does not matter a whit that she is bad about entering info into her electronic diary because that isn't her job and she is busy with the things that are. Remember, your assistant will often have more contact with the rest of the staff than you will, and so how she treats you and talks about you is important. When your whereabouts are inquired after and your assistant rolls her eyes or sighs before answering, she is undermining your authority in the workplace.

An FG may feel uncomfortable about getting tough in this situation, but she must. She's worked hard to earn her position and the right to an assistant. She may need to pull back from a palsy relationship with her assistant, be a bit more formal, to right this imbalance. Nip it in the bud as soon as you notice disapproval creeping into your assistant's tone. When she teasingly reprimands you about the state of your desk, raise your eyebrows, pause (the pause is very important), and tell her, "Yes, I see that you haven't had a chance to organize my mail yet. I'll be going out to a lunch meeting shortly so you'll have some time and space to sort that out." In the sweet mind of the FG this may seem like a bitch slap but it will also remind the disapproving assistant of the actual structure of the workplace. Just make sure that when you do come back from lunch you stop by her desk and thank her for tidying things up.

☜ *Bad Business* ☞

YOU DISAGREE WITH YOUR COLLEAGUES

If a colleague's suggestion doesn't sit right with you, say so immediately—especially if it affects you personally. Of course, you need to express your concern in a diplomatic and controlled way: no temper tantrums. But don't assume that speaking up puts you in conflict with your colleague. Know that you are just adding information to the discussion. If Bingo's pitch to create a new department means that you and everyone else in the office will end up having to work Saturdays from now on, you need to pipe up. If your objections are ignored or dismissed without proper debate, take the person or your boss aside and make your point again. Go on the record if you feel passionate about it; send a memo to the interested parties. It's possible you won't alter the course of events, but your "told you so" moment is assured if their plans fail. And let's face it—sometimes we love to say, or at least think, those three words. Once your boss has decided which course of action she prefers, you must get on board. Take solace in the knowledge that at this point the responsibility for the choice rests with your boss. But remember, the FG picks the battles that she can win or that she feels most passionately about, not just disagreeing because she feels bitter that her idea wasn't chosen.

You Disagree with Your Boss

The situation is more sensitive if the bad idea comes down from the boss. Your only recourse is to present alternatives, again on paper, and then keep quiet. If the situation becomes too ridiculous, it may be time to hit the want ads for another gig. But then, if the idea's really bad, your boss may be looking for work too.

Everyone Disagrees with *You*

Halfway through your presentation you can feel like you're losing the room. By the end you know you have. In fact, did your boss actually nod off for a minute there? And as soon as you finish talking the half of the room that stayed awake for your proposal attacks it like so many sharks. We're not talking about suggestions here; they really hated your idea. The proposal that you thought was so brilliant has just been killed. Naturally, an FG is shattered. Unfortunately, you can't show it. You must at the very least give the appearance of being interested in the criticism you are receiving. The worst thing you can do in this situation is get defensive. Part of becoming a Big Girl is putting your ideas out there and taking the risk of rejection that comes along with that. If you don't feel that you can hold it together and engage in a reasonable dialogue with your detractors, simply thank everyone for their input and say that you'd like to consider their remarks before moving forward. If there's no salvaging enthusiasm for your project, let it go and don't grumble about it. To avoid this situation in the future, it's always good to have a dry run of any big presentation with a good work buddy (hopefully, someone who will be in the room when you actually make it). Ask that person to be brutally honest and tell you what you may have missed yourself or where your delivery may need some polishing. Many great ideas run aground because the person hasn't thought through her presentation carefully enough.

Your Boss Is Tanking

When you got your job she was on top of the world. She was successful and her career was on an upswing. No wonder you were so enthusiastic about hitching your wagon to her star. Now things are beginning to look a little different. You can see it in her boss's eyes: she's on her way out. As someone closely associated with her, what do you do? Assuming that you still respect your boss, you can do one of two things. If your boss is the talented and intelligent person whom you've always admired, it won't take much for you to stand up for her in a down time. Not necessarily covering for her, but if need be, that too. You may consider having a heart-to-heart to let her know in a subtle fashion what others may be thinking of her. Ask her what's troubling her and see if she is simply unhappy and is in fact contemplating a change of jobs.

If the situation is indeed a lost cause and you find you're on a sinking ship, it is more complicated. Although an FG is a loyal person, she needs to play this situation very carefully. How happy are you in your job? If you love your job but have to admit that your mentor isn't what she used to be and doesn't seem open to help or advice, then you need to make some strategic moves now.

1. Start distancing yourself from your lame-duck boss. Let people in your company know that you are independent. Avoid

lunching together or even sitting next to her in meetings. Don't spend as much time in her office as you used to.

2. Try to find out if the powers that be see the two of you as a team. If you are thought to be her right hand, then you should probably start looking for a job. The seniors in your company may never be able to think of you as a separate entity, and if your boss is replaced, her successor will certainly have a hard time getting over your relationship with your old boss. Even if they don't fire you, they may begin to weed out your responsibilities.

3. If you think there's room for change, do what you can to distinguish yourself from her. Work on solo projects. Put it out there that you did it on your own.

4. Spend some time with different people in your company.

5. Complain to her boss. This is a most extreme move, only to be employed as a very last-ditch effort. It comes with considerable risk. You may never know what management is really feeling about your boss—hey, they hired her in the first place. Even if things don't look so good from the outside, you don't know if they intend to support her through thick and thin. If so, they will certainly turn you around and recommend that you deal with your boss on your own (before picking up the telephone to tell her what you've done). Only go over her head if you are willing to leave the company over it. If you feel, for instance, that she is doing you professional harm through her manner and that you'll end up leaving because of it, you have nothing to lose in going to her boss. Be as neutral as possible in your tone and let him know you trust him to do what's best. He may feel as you do that the boss is on her way out and hope to keep you instead.

HOW TO SURVIVE A MERGER

If your company gets bought by a bigger one, you'll be seeing the landscape change pretty quickly. Try not to get caught up in the panic that can set in during a merger. Get information. Listen to gossip. Ask for a meeting with your boss and have a frank conversation. What does she know about what is going to happen? Is your job secure? What can you do? Make sure to meet the new bosses as soon as you can. Introduce yourself and make it clear that you're excited to be working with them. This may seem simple, but it's amazing how many people don't make it through a power change because they didn't have the sense to pledge allegiance to the new regime. New bosses who are taking over an old staff often worry about the old staff's loyalties. Don't get involved in office gossip focusing on what your old boss did that this new fool doesn't. It almost always gets back to the new boss.

YOU'RE THE COMPANY WORKHORSE

FGs hate to let others down. They are therefore easily guilted into accepting too heavy a workload. In the early years of her career, an FG may decide that she wants to make an impression on those around her by working like a demon. She will take on many tasks and complete them brilliantly, never complaining. By working hard like this, an FG is sure to gain a reputation as, well, a hard worker. She may not, however, make the move up the ladder in this way. Hard work is not always what is most prized in the professional world.

After you have paid your dues for a few years, you need to change your status from workhorse to show pony. Now's the time to switch strategies and be more choosy about how much work you do yourself and how much you delegate. Tackle a few key projects that will allow you to shine. Because that's what leaders do. They make important choices and then gather people around them to help execute their plans. So when your boss is heaping an unreasonable amount of work on you, you don't have to wimp out and say you can't do it. Instead, say that you'd love to manage all the projects she has in mind, and present her with your plan to oversee some of the work that others will do.

You Have a 24-7 Office

You're just settling into the evening of your dreams—a stack of new magazines, order-in Thai food, and a new bottle of bubble bath with your name on it—when the phone rings. It's Bingo from work. Without bothering to ask if this is a good time, he launches into a list of reminders he wants to give you about the project you're working on. You can barely get a word in edgewise he's on such a roll, and by the time he's wrapping it up, your dinner is cold and your mood is ruined. For some people without a developed personal life there are no boundaries separating work from play. But an FG is not someone who lives and breathes work; she needs time for her bustling social life and more important, she needs time to herself. If someone from your work life can't keep a thought until 9 a.m. the next morning, you should start screening your calls. If their message is truly frantic you can always call back but most things can wait until morning. This situation gets a little trickier if the person who can't wait until morning is your boss or client. It's hard to let someone know they don't own all your time when they may in fact feel that they do. But calls on the weekends and evenings are usually unnecessary. Get in the habit of screening your calls. You should return these calls but at least if you're screening you can call back with an idea of what your boss wants and have a quick answer ready. And there's nothing wrong with starting the conversation with "I'm just about to serve dinner to my in-laws but I wanted to get back to you with those numbers you needed."

You're Traveling Constantly

If your job involves travel, you must learn to suffer in silence. Everyone around you, and most of all your nontraveling workmates, will assume the work-related trips are the biggest perk going. And to some degree they are. But they are also a disruption of your life and home comforts, they are tiring, and they are work—often more than work done at the home office. You are necessarily spending longer hours on the company clock (even if your company does not want to acknowledge this). It's difficult to catch up on what you've missed once you return. But the only people you can really complain to about these hassles are fellow travelers. When you are getting ribbed about your glamorous job, it is best just to smile and say, "Yes, I'm very lucky." There's no point in explaining to people why it's hard—they'll never understand.

Time

If you travel frequently for work, you may want to work out a time traveling/time off arrangement with your firm. A day spent working away from the office almost always involves more hours than a day at the office. Really, the entire time you are away you are on company time. Discuss with your boss the possibility of taking at least a

day off (with pay) for every week you are away on business. Preferably, you'd like to take these days as soon as you get back.

The home office base

It's important to lay down some ground rules with the people you
work with if you are frequently away on business. First of all, you
must insist that they behave as if you are working. Somehow it is
difficult for people to believe that although you are in Paris, you are
not on vacation. (However, if you really were on vacation, they
would think twice about sending you ten or eleven e-mails a day,
wouldn't they?) Ask your assistant, or whoever will be in touch with
you most often, to try to call once a day with all the concerns of the
day rather than every time something comes up. Also, ask that he or
she be sensitive to how information is being translated. If there is
nothing you can do about a problem from where you are, it is more
disruptive than productive to receive hysterical calls about the situation. And remind people before you leave what the time differences
are. You'd think that grown-ups would know that California is three
hours behind New York, but sometimes they don't. More than one
FG has been woken up in the middle of the night while away on
business by a call from the office.

Expense accounts

Bless them. A corporate credit card is one of the nicest things in an
FG's life. She knows how to use it with respect and care, but she
loves it, loves it, loves it. A credit card that someone else pays for—
what's not to love? When you're away on business, it does pay to be
thoughtful about how you handle your expense account. Bring along
a bunch of empty envelopes to put each day's receipts into rather

than jamming them into your wallet until you get back home. You are not obliged to live like a pauper when you are away for work, but you shouldn't go crazy either. Wine with dinner is fine, but a round of champagne for everyone at the hotel bar is out of the question. Room service for breakfast is nice, but you can probably get a better and cheaper dinner away from the hotel. The key is balance. If you spend little on breakfasts and lunches while you're away, then the dinner that you treat yourself to—and somehow business trips are always in cities where everything is pricier—won't raise any red flags with the accounting department.

Hotel phone bills are always a robbery. However, it doesn't make sense to be self-conscious every time you need to make a call. You are working, after all. Also, since you are being separated from your regular life to be at work, it is reasonable for you to make calls home on the company bill. One brief call home to your mate or kids each day is well within reason. If you are traveling often, you should consider getting an international cell phone and billing your company for the calls you make on trips. It will be much cheaper than using the hotel line, and they are usually beautifully designed little things that look chic when whipped out of your handbag.

Boy Toy

There's not much that is nicer than being able to offer your boyfriend or husband a little trip to Los Angeles because you'll be there for business. By all means, ask him along. It doesn't cost your company anything to have your man stay with you. But you do need to be careful about how you handle your expenses if your man joins you. Obviously, your company is not going to pay for his trip as well. And just as obviously, you're not going to stop him from ordering breakfast from the room service menu when you do. Just make sure it comes out even. Go out for dinner or lunch, but don't include that receipt if there are a couple of breakfasts, including two stacks of pancakes. You might also include a note explaining the situation when you submit your receipts.

Make clear to your sweetheart that although you are thrilled to have him with you, this is primarily a work trip and you need to fulfill your duties before heading out on the town with him. If your love is the adventurous sort, this will not pose a problem. He will happily go off on his own to check out the new show at the Getty while you are in meetings, and then rendezvous with you at the hotel for an afternoon tryst. If your beau is not so independent, it may be better to leave him at home. It's straining to be worried about rushing back to entertain a sulking boyfriend when you need to be focusing on impressing a new client.

Welcome home

As was mentioned before, coworkers will not be entirely sympathetic to your jet lag. However, people should greet you with a "Hello, welcome back" or "How was your trip?" before launching into what you forgot to do before you left or what has to be done this very second. If they don't, jokingly reprimand them: "My trip was great, thanks for asking." Also, insist on having an hour of quiet to go through all your mail (paper, voice, and e-) before they start making demands on your time.

YOU GET PASSED OVER FOR A PROMOTION

A spot just opened up in your company and you know you are perfect for the job. You are more than qualified and you've had a lot of great conversations with the manager you'd be working for. Your interview goes brilliantly. And Fifi gets the job. Not only are you devastated by the rejection, you now wonder if you're appreciated in your current position. Hopefully when your would-have-been boss tells you the bad news, she also tells you a little bit about why you didn't land the job. If you're reeling too much in the moment to take it all in, make an appointment to talk it over a week later. As calmly as you can, ask what ruled you out of the job. Ask if you're seen as someone with a future with the company or if it was just that particular position that was the wrong fit. If you are passed over for more than one promotion, then no matter what is said in these postmortems, it's time to start looking for another job. It's often the case that you need to change workplaces to truly move ahead; it's hard for people to see you in a new light. When you do try to move up the ladder at your own firm, it's a good idea to keep it very quiet. You can be surprised and embarrassed if you've told too many people that you're up for the job that Fifi eventually lands.

You Get Too Drunk at a Company Function

Inevitably, the Fabulous Girl will find herself having to attend company functions. Say, an awards banquet or company retreat. While it all may seem like a party, getting rip-roaring drunk is not a wise or decorous move. Perhaps the FG is frustrated with her job, or is so stressed she feels the need to cut loose—regardless, her colleagues are really her colleagues and shouldn't be mistaken for college roommates. In other words, they will judge your behavior. If, however, you do down six martinis and wind up on the balcony of the five-star hotel tossing a roll of toilet paper onto the street while your entire company watches, you will have some sucking up to do.

If you're very lucky, a close friend you work with will escort you to your room or home, sober you up, and be there in the morning to help unravel the mystery in your head. But then it's damage control time. You must learn to be your own spin doctor. Set up a meeting with your boss pronto and tell him or her that you are sorry and make appropriate excuses: stress, family trouble, whatever.

When you face your coworkers for the first time, it is best not to mention the incident unless they do. They may make a joke, in which case you should laugh along, then change the subject. If they say nothing, which is really the polite response to another's transgression, then do not bring it up yourself. Unless you personally owe someone an apology, just move along. Something else will occur in the meantime to distract the gossips. But know that your colleagues will tell the tale of your escapades for years, longer than you will probably have the job. This last reason should be enough to follow the simple rule of company functions: do not drink too much.

SOMEONE IS TRYING TO UNDERMINE YOU

Great jobs are hard to come by. So when you have an awesome job, someone somewhere wants to take it away from you. It could be your assistant, or even a colleague with a similar job. But you notice that this person tries to "help" you out with your projects when you don't even ask for assistance. The FG will spot underminers by these signs:

1. They offer to go to that meeting or industry event so you can take a much-needed night off.
2. You discuss how a task is to be done, but by the deadline

they've done it an entirely different way without bothering to tell you until presentation time.

3. They've made contacts on your behalf but haven't passed them along to you.

4. They tell your boss how much they've done on your project because you're too busy.

5. They commit to helping you out but bail at the last minute, knowing you don't have enough time to complete the job.

Once the Fabulous Girl has spotted an Underminer, she needs to take action. Since this person can no longer be trusted, the FG needs to prevent her from being closely involved in the FG's work. If the Underminer is a colleague, the FG will to need to avoid working on projects with her, but also avoid her at work-related social events. The Fabulous Girl should also be more aggressive in the presence of the Underminer, never allowing this person to take over a project or to represent the FG's work in a meeting. The one thing the FG wants to avoid is being seen as paranoid. This can be achieved by not running to the boss or other colleagues and spilling her guts and woes. She needs to handle the Underminer solo, like a lone sheriff in an old Western film.

Everybody Hates You

On rare occasions, an FG will find herself the object of her employees' wrath. They hate her. They don't respect her and at any opportunity they challenge her authority. When she walks into a room, conversation stops. There is eye rolling going on in meetings when she makes presentations. Despite the FG's being the boss her employees are ruining her work environment. However, labor laws being what they are, big boss FG cannot simply hand out a fistful of pink slips. She has to work with her cranky crew.

In such an extreme situation, the first thing the Fabulous Girl needs to determine is whether her staff has a legitimate reason for griping. Was she once their colleague but in her promotion has grown bitchy and condescending toward them? Are they jealous because of the promotion, or is she simply new to the job and hasn't yet earned their respect? The FG may need to modify her own behavior by being more reasonable if she realizes she has not been a considerate boss. But if no discernable reason exists, then the FG must learn to distinguish between personal and professional attitudes. The Fabulous Girl wants to be liked by everyone—an impossible feat even if she's not the boss. So she will have to accept that as boss, she is bound to be disliked by some on her staff. She cannot punish a person who dislikes her in any way or treat that person differently from the others if he or she is performing the work adequately. Of course, if said person blatantly challenges her authority in front of coworkers, say, by whispering to a colleague in a meeting or rolling his or her eyes at the FG's suggestions, then a thorough one-on-one talking to is in order. Here the FG must be firm and put her foot down. "Bingo, I noticed you were whispering throughout the meeting and making faces. I expect everyone in the office to behave respectfully to each other. If you're having some kind of problem I'd be happy to discuss it with you but this is no way to make yourself heard." Or you can always rely on that old schoolroom method of stopping the meeting, turning to Bingo, and asking, "Do you have anything to share with the group?" She doesn't have to be liked, but big boss FG does have to be respected. In fact, the less she appears to be moved by her employees' malevolence, the more they are likely to give her respect. These scenarios are never pleasant and no one wants to toil in a tense environment, but the rotten apples may decide that they hate the FG boss so much they quit.

∞ *Sex in the Workplace* ∞

YOU HAVE A CRUSH ON YOUR COWORKER

The committed Fabulous Girl

You like the new man in marketing. You really like him. He's cute, funny, and sexy as heck. You can't help yourself when he's around— you giggle like a high school kid. You have a crush. Problem is, you're taken. You're Ms. Faithful, so it's not really a problem, but it does whiff of inappropriateness. Whether you're married, living with someone, or just plain going steady, your work crush may be harmless, but unless you follow certain rules of propriety you may end up sending the wrong signals. The Fabulous Girl can follow this "crush course" for playing it safe with the guy she can't take her eyes off.

Coming clean

Sure, you work together, but if the object of your affection happens to be a newbie, he may not know you're spoken for. He may, in fact, be attracted to you too. You both flirt and enjoy each other's company, so when do you let him know you're involved with someone? Before it becomes clear that the flirtations are not so innocent. In other words, before the two of you are groping in the copy room. And tell him yourself. Don't wait for him to ask after you've had après-work cocktails. It is best to mention your significant other as soon as you find yourself crushing. This will probably keep both of you in the right head space.

Affectionate stalking

In other words, putting yourself into your crush's path at every opportunity, hoping for a smile or quick chat to show him how charming and witty you are. It's easy to trick yourself into thinking there's nothing wrong with this kind of behavior. Sure, he seems to notice you too, but being there at his every turn will give him the message that perhaps it's an affair you're after.

Easy on the e-mails

E-mail is dangerous territory for anyone experiencing a crush. Not only will you end up flirting, you will use up half your day doing it. When composing an e-mail to your crush, you will obviously want it to sound cute and cheeky, which is much more time-consuming than you think. Not to mention the dangers of being caught sending personal, flirtatious e-mails on company time.

Keep it to yourself

There is something about having a crush that makes us need to talk about the person in his or her absence. Everyone will note if you're constantly talking about Bingo in Accounting, but not discussing work—rather, "Bingo really loved that movie, did you see it?" This is especially true of your boyfriend or spouse. He doesn't need to hear you sing the praises of your crush. If you mention Bingo more than three times in one week, your spouse will probably suspect something and may even ask you if you have a crush, which of course you'll deny. But it's just that Bingo is so brilliant . . . Get real.

Kissing is cheating

All you did was slip him the tongue at the company Christmas party—surely that doesn't count, does it? Yep, it does. A one-two peck on the cheek is one thing; swapping spit is another. You've now taken the crush too far—what you want is an affair. If you really think there is nothing wrong with an "innocent" kiss, then ask your husband/boyfriend his opinion.

The single Fabulous Girl

While many of the same rules apply—e-mail, affectionate stalking—the single FG can enjoy her crush in the knowledge that maybe it's mutual and perhaps can develop. First, she needs to determine if there is some company policy against dating between coworkers. If not, she is free to proceed, but should consider the consequences of a potential breakup. Can she work with a future ex? If the FG thinks she can handle it, then there is nothing wrong with this scenario. If, however, the company does ban interoffice romances, she is risking both her job and that of the object of her affection. Does she really want to sneak around? What may seem titillating at first may wear thin and create more stress than great sex.

You Kissed a Coworker

If you are single and so is Bob from Accounts Payable, then you may find yourself at an after-work lounge with one glass of champagne too many and Bob's hand up your skirt and your lips on his. If afterward you realize that (a) Bob is not really the intellect you took him for, (b) he's a lousy kisser, or (c) you really like Bill in Accounts Receivable, you may have to end it before it begins.

First of all, don't pretend nothing happened. It did, and both of you know it. No need to be high schoolers all over again. No silly notes, awkward glances, or silent treatment. Walk up to Bob and tell him the truth: "I think things got out of hand last night . . . I'm really not ready to start something."

Of course, you could find yourself in the situation in which you now love Bob, Bob is everything. But Bob is acting like he doesn't know you. You'll have to be the grown-up and confront him. Do it sooner rather than later. If you let it build up, you'll end up shouting at him in cube country when what you need is privacy. Even an elevator will do. It is not rude to ask him what is wrong and why he's being a boor. If he's just going to stammer at you and not give any reasonable form of conversation, then it is clear: you really did make an error of judgment, so move on and e-mail Bill.

GETTING CAUGHT

As a wise FG once said, you can never underestimate the thrill of sex with the boss. However, sex with a nonsuperior coworker can also add a bit of sass to your workday. It may be that the Fabulous Girl and Bingo have been at it for months unbeknownst to anyone. With your secret safe, taking greater risks may seem easy as pie—until you're half naked atop the photocopier when your manager strolls in with a stack of contracts. If caught in the buff or partial buffness, the FG can only cover herself and apologize. Tell the manager (who by now has fled the scene in shock) that it will never happen again. And hope that your company does not have a no-dating-between-employees policy. If it does, see "You're Fired!"

∞ *Down and Out* ∞

YOU'RE FIRED!

Getting fired is about the worst thing that can happen to an FG—particularly if she is accused of a wrong. If your boss is determined that it was you who stole the missing coffee money and tells you to pack up your desk, there's little that you can do about it at that moment. Take a deep breath, go to the ladies' room if necessary, and pull yourself together. Don't let anyone see you cry. Go to your boss's office and tell her in the calmest possible voice, "You are making a mistake. I did not steal anything at all. If you don't drop this accusation, you'll be hearing from my lawyers. I'm very sorry our relationship has to end in this way." And then head out the door.

No matter what you do, the phone lines will be burning up with news of your sacking. This kind of story is simply too juicy for people to do anything other than pick it apart with some amount of glee. This, too, will be a terrible blow to the FG. Even people she has known professionally, people who like and admire her, will be dissecting her fate. More than ever, she must keep her head held high. If you reply to questions with "It's a very disappointing situation. I'm not able to discuss it, but I'm confident that it will be cleared up soon," you will give the best impression possible.

Being fired does present another role for the FG spin doctor. When interviewing for new positions, be sure that you do not use the opportunity to rant about how awful your past job was or to cut up your former boss or other colleagues. This is only a poor reflection on you, and it will instantly result in having your name crossed off the short list.

You may not have to broach the subject of your being fired at all. Most prospective employers ask only why you left your last position and will not demand, "Were you fired?" It's fair to respond that you and your last job weren't a good fit. Be as honest as you can. "My previous employer and I had a misunderstanding from the beginning about what kind of work I would be doing, which naturally made it difficult for either of us to be satisfied." If your interviewer asks if he can phone your old boss for a recommendation, you are going to have to come a little clean. Explain that unfortunately you and your previous employer did not see eye to eye by the end of your job, and that you know that the reference will not be a good one. You can't stop him from calling your old boss, but also offer other references to balance what will certainly be a negative review.

FIRING SOMEONE

This is never pleasant, even if you despise the person. You'll be nervous, but you know it must be done. Before firing an employee, be sure to discuss it with the human resources department of your company, or if such a department or person doesn't exist, a lawyer. Labor laws concerning dismissals are very specific; make sure you've got all your ducks in a row before storming into a potentially litigious situation. Your own boss will know this is happening and will be prepared to back you up if need be. Tell the person the reasons it is not working out. Keep it brief, calm, and professional. Knowing that it's going to be difficult for the person being fired to act with grace, do it either early, before most people arrive at work, or at the end of the day, when most have left. Chances are she knows what you say is true, but she may have a hard time not lashing out in the moment. At least briefly, you should allow the person to show her anger. After all, you are firing her. These scenes can get ugly, which is why many companies use security to escort fired employees out of the building.

If Fifi starts to scream obscenities at you, it's time to call in the big boys and make your own quick escape.

YOU'RE BETWEEN JOBS

Even if you've lost a job through no fault of your own, it is still a devastating experience. Everyone will tell you not to take it personally, but of course you do. It's you. And your job. Well, it was your job. How you handle the change in public can determine how quickly you get back on your feet. You don't have to be a big faker, but you should try to stay upbeat, at least when you're describing the situation at a cocktail party. It's a sad fact of life that people don't want to be around sad sacks. Better to tell people that it's an unfortunate reality that many law firms are scaling back and that a few people at your company were let go, but that on the upside you're finally able to take that French immersion course you've been wanting to take for the past five years. Also, try to play down the financial duress you are probably under right now. Even if you go home and cry your eyes out, it's better to leave people with the impression that you are a fulfilled and vital person with or without a job. You are also much more likely to attract a new job with this reputation. Once you are out on the job market it's best to be discreet about your options. You may be so excited by the interviews you're landing that you end up spilling to anyone who will listen, "They loved me at over at Major Big Corp, they seemed really keen down at Really Big Shoo and then you won't believe who called me . . ." Not only do you seem to be overcompensating for what is probably a very real fear for your own future—which is never attractive—you will also feel and look foolish when things don't pan out. Best to smile and say, "I'm out there looking" than get into details.

Your Best Friend Lands Your Dream Job

You've only ever wanted the best for Janey. You were college room-mates, helped each other out through the years of Jill Jobs, and lately, listened to her complain about her job an awful lot. Then she calls you with the news that she's landed a dream job. Only it was your dream job. The one that everyone who knows you knows you've had your eye on for years. You can't believe it. Of course, you want to be happy for your best friend but this stings. A lot. You can't help but wonder how you didn't see this coming, how she didn't tell you she was even up for the job. You wouldn't be human if you didn't feel jealous and a little bitter. You must suck it up and offer her your congratulations. But it's perfectly appropriate, and probably necessary for your friendship, to discuss the awkwardness of the situation. Hopefully, Janey herself will offer this up. "I know you always wanted to be Queen of the World but when they asked me to interview for it I realized it was what I really wanted, too." She should also explain why she wasn't forthcoming earlier. Probably because she was afraid of your reaction, but as your friend she should have trusted you with the information. Once you're satisfied that she played fair in getting the job you must forgive her. Still, you may need some time to bounce back from this one, and that need to digest it should be understandable to Janey.

"Why didn't you tell me?" Finally I was speaking to Elenor, but I'd had to phone her again. She was still in the suburbs. I didn't know what to tell her. She accused me of keeping the truth about Bingo from her. Had I not been at the Spanks opening? Why didn't I ask Dudley not to write about it?

Elenor was right, I had been at Spanks. But I had to tell her that I didn't actually see Bingo doing anything with Muffie other than talking. As for asking Dudley anything, Elenor had obvious illusions about my relationship with the wretch.

"I would have warned you, but honestly, I didn't know that anything had happened, let alone that Dudley would write about it."

Elenor seemed placated when we hung up, but I couldn't stop thinking about her and Bingo. Not just how awful the entire situation was, but how Dudley had made it so much worse with his rude gossip.

Then I had a thought: why not write about it? I could write an article about the inherent rudeness of gossip. How it was bad manners to make nasty observations and to spread rumors. The piece could distinguish between innocent, fun comments and hurtful, backstabbing slander. I wanted to write a treatise on how a polite person would handle gossip and being gossiped about. Finally, something to sink my teeth into, something I really cared about that might make a difference. To my friend, anyway.

The next morning I was determined to pitch my manners article, but I had one huge obstacle: big boss Bradley. Before I launched into my pitch, I apologized again for what I'd said about his wife.

"Everyone's entitled to their own opinion," he said with a grimace.

I realized I was on thin ice suggesting a story about etiquette, given my blunder the day before, but I went ahead anyway.

"Manners are boring. No one would want to read that stuff," he spoke into his computer screen.

I gripped my chair. Bradley hated me now, and I guessed that he wouldn't care what I did. I took a chance.

"Can I pitch it to a newspaper?"

He smirked.

"Yeah, go ahead."

Permission granted, I dialed up Frank, the section editor at the paper. But not just any paper. If I was going to write this type of opinion piece, it had to run in Dudley's paper. The section editor liked my pitch, especially when I intentionally let it slip that it was inspired by Dudley's gossip column and that in a sense mine was a rebuttal.

"Can I get it by tomorrow, noon?"

After I hung up the phone I looked at my watch. How could I? But a funny thing happened at my computer. The words flowed, I typed like mad, and in only an hour and a half I had an eight-hundred word story. I read it and reread it. This manners thing came naturally to me. I had always been interested in decorum and in the social skills that could make life smoother—I had once joked that I could write a book about it—but I had never really given it serious thought. Until that moment. I handed in my copy early.

Two days later I pranced into the *Smack!* office with a copy of my article in the paper. It looked fabulous, and I loved seeing my name there.

"What's that?" Cheryl asked, a stack of old magazines in her hand.

"My piece I wrote on manners—it's in today's paper."

"Huh. Oh, that's nice. Now, can you photocopy this stuff for me? I've marked the pages."

She dropped the stack of mags onto my desk and walked away. That was the other part of my associate editor job, grunt labor. I didn't really mind—I just wished that after a year I wouldn't be asked to do that stuff anymore. Feeling chuffed about my article, I decided I would be more grown up at work. I delegated the copying to an intern.

I had to finish writing my usual restaurant roundup for *Smack!*, but I watched Bradley come into the office. He had the paper in his hand. I guess I was silly to think he'd be impressed with my work or would somehow value me more as an employee. After all, I had made an ass out of myself at lunch, and why should he forgive me? But that was no excuse for him to be rude, was it? Shouldn't he be gracious and congratulate me?

"I told you to photocopy the pages." Cheryl towered over me.

"Um, I was busy so I gave it to an intern."

"Next time, tell me if you can't and I'll find someone else. Really, when I ask you to do something, you should do it."

So much for my great story and moving up in the world. I settled into my work and later that day prepared for the other facet of my role as associate editor of *Smack!*—social butterfly.

CHAPTER TWO

Society

I did the party circuit when I was a freelancer,
but when I came on staff, my invitations to parties, launches, and events
doubled. Some were boring, but others were pretty fab.

The first big event of the social season had arrived, mere days after
the Bingo-as-lout outing in the paper. Missy and I were determined that
Elenor should not hide, and we pretty much forced her to attend the
party. It was an art opening at one of the city's swankiest galleries, and,
being an art director at a decor magazine, she would normally be there—
normally on Bingo's arm, but still, she'd be there.

Missy arrived at my place with her car and driver idling outside.
This was an added perk for me from Missy's new station in life. I did
drive, but having the chauffeur thing was admittedly irresistible: I didn't
worry about how much I had to drink, and I didn't need to pay for cabs.

Our priority for the night was simple: get Bingo. We wanted to
ensure that when he laid eyes on Elenor, he'd regret Muffie. Elenor, for
her part, was terrified of seeing him, but she knew she had to get that
first brush with him over with. She wasn't ever going to get back with
him again, but they hadn't spoken since the Dudley column so she
needed us for backup. In order to be fully prepared, we put the finishing
touches on Elenor's Fuck-Him Dress, a strapless cocktail number. Tight,
yes. Sophisticated, yes. Slutty, no. She looked positively vampy.

"Where's Nice?" Missy always wanted to know where Nice was.

"He should be here any minute." Nice was my lovely boyfriend. He was all things good: polite, kind, honest, and sexy as hell. We'd been together for almost a year and things had been going swimmingly. He was a real grown-up, not one of those dark brooders or superslick busy guys. He was simply Nice, and I loved him.

"Why didn't Joe come tonight?" Elenor asked.

Missy just shrugged. We didn't push it, but Missy didn't seem too happy.

"Can I join the party?" Nice had arrived. Kitty, my little ginger cat, raced to the door as always, wanting to sink her claws into him before I could.

"I'm so glad you're here." I kissed him long and hard.

The opening was swarming with people, which wasn't a bad thing as Bingo-and-Muffie sightings would be minimal. I was going to keep my eye out for Dudley, which wouldn't be hard—it was never difficult to pick him out of a crowd. He was tall and scrawny, and had a prematurely stoopy posture—very Ichabod Crane—but most remarkable was his near-white blond hair, which he wore perpetually greased back, exposing his abnormally high forehead.

In the meantime, I had another game plan to put into action. I had rehearsed Elenor and Missy in the art of the snub. Besides arming Elenor with her Fuck-Him Dress, we had vowed not to acknowledge Bingo, Muffie, or particularly Dudley. You see, neither Elenor nor I could yell at Dudley or respond to his column in person (and I doubted he'd discuss my manners piece with me). However, we could ignore him en masse, pretend he didn't even exist. We were simply not going to see him. But in order to maximize the effect, we had to make sure that Dudley saw us not seeing him.

· · ·

"I'll get us some cocktails," Nice offered.

"I'll help you." Missy trotted off beside him.

"I think someone has a crush."

I didn't respond to Elenor because ten feet in front of us, in the middle of the mix of scruffy painters and slick collectors, were Bingo and Muffie, and they were talking with Dudley. I couldn't believe my eyes. It wasn't as though Bingo was telling him off either—they were engaged in what appeared to be a social conversation. There were chortles. There were shoulder slaps. There was friendship.

"I have to go." Elenor abandoned me midsnub. Without their noticing, I too retracted into the crowd. I had to regroup—this social snubbing was trickier than I had thought. Elenor had found Missy and Nice and the four cocktails. Only one drink survived—Elenor had chugged back three flutes of champagne.

"Here he comes," warned Missy.

I turned around, trying to be casual. There stood the man, Dudley, rocking back and forth on his brogues, ready to speak. I scanned the room around his twiglike body, never looking directly at him, then turned my back to him as if I hadn't seen him at all. The girls and Nice fell into the act, and we all chatted and laughed. Dudley stalked away. We had succeeded in our plan. But I couldn't help wondering what Dudley had wanted to say. Was he going to apologize to Elenor? Had he read my article and regretted some of his actions?

I'd never know, for the rest of the evening became a veritable snub-a-thon, with Bingo, Muffie, and Dudley sightings every five minutes. But my main concern was Elenor. Knowing how difficult an evening this was, I wanted to distract her. Keeping her out of eye- and earshot was really the best medicine. I took her by the elbow on a tour of the art in the room. It was an unsettling show, with video panels blinking text and images, all revolving around the theme of anxiety. Elenor was miserable.

"I wonder if Bingo misses me."

"I think you've had too much to drink," I offered.

"Maybe you're right. I'm going to the bathroom." Elenor trundled off.

Nice came and put his arm around my waist. I leaned into him.

"Do you think that man Dudley will actually care that you're ignoring him? Aren't you making things worse?"

I stopped leaning and turned to face Nice. "He really hurt my best friend, and I won't stand for it. I'm not going to try and destroy the man, I just want him to know not to mess with us."

Nice nodded, and I hoped he understood. I also hoped my plan would work and that Dudley would leave us alone.

∞ *Society* ∞

AS TWO WISE WOMEN once wrote, "Society is a Fabulous Girl's best friend." She is both buoyed and shaped by society. She loves meeting new people and is open to new social adventures. Always stylish and civilized, the FG excels in communicating and socializing with everyone she meets in her days and nights. These are the vital players in her life, and in good times, dealing with them is a piece of angel food cake. But no matter how skilled the FG is, there will be situations that will spiral out of her control. Whether she's putting her foot in her mouth or attending a party alone or—worse—involved in a public scandal, she must try to navigate these turbulent moments as if they were well within her command.

∞ *Your Reputation* ∞

It may sound Victorian, but like it or not, a woman can still carry the social stigma of a bad reputation. She can be known as a "slut," "mooch," "man-poacher," or any other derogatory slang. While such labels are old-fashioned and silly, women still seem ready to hang them on each other, and some even enjoy spreading the bad word. Of course, one can have a good reputation too. In any case, the very notion of a woman's reputation as something that is decided not only by her but also by the society she moves in still packs a wallop. Nonetheless, the reality is that a woman can achieve any reputation she wants, and on occasion there may even be advantages to cultivating a bad one.

The Fabulous Girl wants her friends and colleagues to think of her as, well, fabulous. To ensure this opinion she needs to act the part. The Fabulous Girl is someone who is an integral part of her social set. She puts herself out there socially by attending parties, art openings, and other events. She plays host too. The FG is someone who values style and considers it part of her contribution to society. Included in her definition of style is an interest in the arts, literature, politics, and whomever she is conversing with. And, of course, she must be polite.

One thing that makes the FG stand out is her confidence. She does not indulge her shyness; she shares her opinions. She even talks about her commitment to good manners, for instance. Of course, we don't mean she should talk incessantly about herself or lecture others on how to behave, but certainly actions speak louder than words. So behave like an FG, and you will be one.

How to Change Your Reputation

But what of our FG who wants to dabble with danger? She's always been good—maybe too good. She frets that men find her too nice to seduce and her employer thinks her too meek to manage. Well, the solution is in the presentation.

With lovers or potential lovers, you may want to be more daring, in your dress and in your demeanor. When out socially, you may flirt a little more outrageously, wear something a bit more sexy. Maybe you'll invite him out for an after-party cocktail or make the first move on the guy who refuses to think of you in that way.

At work, put more polish into your delivery. You can start this by crisping up your wardrobe. In most work environments, people associate a pulled-together, even slightly formal wardrobe with seniority. Work this angle. More important, though, is your demeanor. Start speaking up at meetings, offering your thoughts and suggestions in discussions. If you've been a quiet member of the team, you will definitely get noticed if you raise your voice. Find ways to spend time with important people in your office and in your field. When you're at a work event, don't be too shy to go up to the people you admire and simply introduce yourself to begin with. Compliment them on a project they worked on recently. The next time you see them, you'll more easily fall into conversation and make an impression. These are the kinds of relationships you should build on—they allow you to get the word out in your industry that you want to be taken seriously.

One technique for changing one's reputation is to switch social circles. Creating a different image is easier if you're not surrounded by those who will only ever see you as your old self. This is not to say that you must cut everyone from your life; just expand your list of acquaintances and spend time with different sorts who won't question why you're suddenly discussing poetry so much. Then, as your confidence builds, even the old friends will come around and embrace the change.

The Fabulous Girl must realize that her reputation cannot be made in one day, week, or month. And all of these alterations to her behavior must be parceled out gradually so that she eases into this new attitude. They must also be repetitive or else it won't be a new reputation but a mere blip in her love life or career.

HOW TO SALVAGE YOUR REPUTATION

No amount of preemptive fabulousness can protect the FG in every crisis. And sometimes even good girls act badly. If you've actually done something to earn a bad reputation you're going to have work a little harder to come out clean. Even the most damaged reputation can be salvaged—if on such a downslide you behave with grace.

You're a man-poacher

If you had the reputation of being a nice, loyal friend but ended up stealing your best friend's husband, then understandably your reputation has been altered. How does an FG find herself in such a mess? She doesn't wake up one morning and decide, "Today I'm going to destroy my friend's marriage." She is not a man-poacher by design. Perhaps the man in question is in a very unhappy relationship, a fact confirmed for the FG by his wife. People fall in love with the wrong people all the time. The Fabulous Girl may find herself caught between her heart and her friendship. Naturally, this affair is not fabulous, but as a wise FG once said, "Life gets messy and complicated, but how you handle the mess can make or break your reputation"—not to mention your sense of self. In this instance, the FG wouldn't gloat about her new boy prize or defend herself to people by cutting up her old friend, no matter how the wounded friend may verbally attack her.

You're a party girl

If you have a reputation as a cokehead party girl and you want to play straight, be honest and tell people that you've cleaned up your act and are focusing on your career now (or art or whatever). Dump your friends from the party world and cultivate acquaintances with the people you wish to emulate. Change your manner, your wardrobe, your way of talking, and your bedtime. Be seen leaving the bar at 11 p.m. and not after it closes. You may be regarded with suspicion or even ridicule at first, but time will prove the deciding factor in your reputation makeover.

You're a mooch

You don't know how it happens, but you never seem to realize that you forgot to visit the ATM until the restaurant bill comes. And then sometimes you don't see the friend you borrowed the twenty dollars from to cover your half until a month later and gosh, doesn't it happen again! Guess what? You're a mooch. While this is not a personality tick that people read as pure evil, it is irritating in the extreme. If you know that you've been lazy about returning borrowed money, then your friends have definitely noticed as well. Always, always, always return money before the lender has to ask for it. The only way to recover your reputation as a mooch is to never ask for a loan from friends again. And don't ever show up at a restaurant with an empty wallet.

You're a flirt

You have lots of girlfriends who are crazy about you. Until their boyfriends are around, that is; then it's another story. If you find yourself in mixed company, but always with the male end of the mix, you are probably a flirt. There's nothing wrong with a little flirting in most social situations. You may think it's funny and sexy to give all the men in the room long good-night kisses but you can bet it inspires a name for you other than flirt. If you notice that even your friends seem uncomfortable with you around their mates, it's time to straighten up. Make an effort to spend more time chatting with women than men. When you are talking to the guys, tone it down. Go easy on the arm-touching and the ear-whispering. If you find it hard to know where to draw the line, pretend you are at work and talking to a coworker.

You're a slut

The single FG is the kind of girl who has sex when she feels like it, and with any single guy she feels like. She is not shamed into celibacy by uptight attitudes. Still, a girl can be her own woman while being discreet—just because she feels okay about her own sexuality doesn't mean she wants the world talking about it. And she realizes what people might say if they knew how often she gets the good stuff. The extreme scenario is a long line of public seductions and one-night stands. This may also seem like high school, as in "Lesley puts out," but if you still find your libido is getting noticed by colleagues and friends, it may be time to think about discretion. The FG should avoid sleeping with more than one man within the same social or professional group. For example, doctors at the hospital where she works. Or she will then become known as the hospital slut; believe it, people male and female will say, "Lesley is the hospital slut." Men will like her but not in a respectful way, and female coworkers, while perhaps amused, will tend not to be too warm. Of course she may often not even realize she has this reputation; she must just be going through a slut phase. What to do? If you are a "slut," then stop talking about your conquests and stop with any overt flirt moves and innuendo. You can still have fun—just spread the fun around in different social circles and keep it on the downlow.

In any such extreme situation, apologize to the friend or whomever your actions hurt, taking full responsibility for your bad deed. Then keep a low profile until the dust settles. Inevitably, people will move on and turn their attention to fresher gossip. It may also be time to work on new friendships while keeping your distance from the old group.

You're the Target of False Gossip

An innocent trip to the ladies' room midway through a party can turn into a trip to hell when you overhear a nasty conversation about yourself. "Did you see her swanning around here as if everyone doesn't know that she and Mr. Hunk were fooling around on Fifi for months before he finally ended things . . ." Their voices trail off as they leave the room and you're left shaking in the bathroom stall. Of all the . . . ! You hadn't even met Mr. Hunk when he was with Fifi, and you were both absolutely single when you met. In fact, you're not even sure who belonged to the nasty voices in the ladies' room so what could they possibly have against you? If something like this happens only once you can probably tell Mr. Hunk about it just to get it off your chest and let it go. But if you hear it more than once or if someone else hears it as well it may be time for further measures. Without spending too much time (these things are too poisonous to give much effort to), find out the source of this malicious gossip and by all means confront this person and set the record straight. "I did not have an affair with Mr. Hunk. You have no right to be discussing subjects you don't know anything about—I'll ask you to not talk to anyone about my personal life." Don't expect an apology from gossips like these; they've already shown you their true colors. Just keep a distance from them and hope that you've shocked them into leaving you out of their conversation from now on. And while you shouldn't run around making sure that everyone has the story straight, if the gossip's name does come up in conversation you can warn very close friends of your experience.

∞ *The Art of Conversation* ∞

It is an often-neglected art these days, but for the Fabulous Girl being a good conversationalist is a top priority. She needs to converse with people from all walks of life, from the plumber to the banker, with the same attention and politeness. Why? People will remember the FG who listens well and who treats them with respect. In turn, the FG is valued by those who feel her respect for them. She knows life runs better if you take the time to make conversation with all of the people in it. The banker will return her calls, the mechanic will fix her car while she waits, and the editor will give her the story assignment. Also, the Fabulous Girl will learn more about people, how the world works, and valuable facts and tips that may come in handy later (including as conversation starters).

This may sound simplistic or clichéd, but as anyone who has been a party to bad small talk can attest, the ability to strike up a conversation is not always a natural character trait. But it can be learned. It should be simple: you talk for a bit, then I talk for a bit, I ask you a question and wait for a reply, I show some interest in that reply, you reciprocate with some curiosity of your own. Instead, what passes for conversation in many sophisticated circles is more like a battle for air time: I sit through your noises until you need to inhale, then I jump in and make noise until you cut me off to make some more of your own. All this "me" and "no, me" just doesn't cut it in polite company. The FG has studied and perfected her own set of rules for giving great gab:

1. Listen. Don't just wait for your conversational partner to stop talking. By all means, add your thoughts to whatever it is he or she is saying. It's all too clear when people aren't listening, though.

Bingo is regaling a group at a cocktail party about his trip to surf school in Hawaii and Jessica jumps in and says, "Oh, that reminds me of the time I lived in Guam for the winter." If this is your conversational tactic, you can be sure everyone is thinking, "Huh?"

2. Be aware of whom you are talking to. Does everyone in the conversational circle know about medieval pig farming? You don't have to avoid your favorite topic if the entire group is not up to speed on it, but you do have to be sure to fill them in. Of course, if you find yourself in the middle of a topic you don't know anything about, it's your job to pipe up and ask questions rather than sitting there getting irritated. Likewise, beware of shoptalk in mixed company. Sticking for long stretches of time to conversational topics that necessarily exclude some people at a party is simply rude.

3. Ask questions. Nothing is more tedious than people whose idea of conversation is to outline their latest accomplishments. There's nothing wrong with filling people in on what you've been up to or sharing a piece of good news, but be sure to take a real interest in the other person as well.

FOOT-IN-MOUTH DISEASE

Everyone is capable of saying the wrong thing at the wrong time. The Fabulous Girl is no exception. You opine to your acquaintance, Bob, during a work event that you find the latest soft-drink ad campaign to be insipid and lacking in imagination. Later that evening, another colleague tells you that Bob was the creative force behind that very soft-drink ad. The realization that you've put your foot in your mouth is alarming. You secretly wish Bob had offered up the truth before you continued your critical tirade and made such an ass of yourself. But then you understand that Bob was trying to be polite. What to do? Damage control, of course. You must immediately find Bob and have a chuckle over your indiscretion. Apologize and explain that clearly you had no idea of the connection, but be light-hearted, even admitting what a dummy you are. Bob may not feel better, but he will accept your apology. Bob may now be plagued by self-doubt, but hey, who isn't sometimes?

If you find yourself on the other side of Foot-in-Mouth Disease, then it's most polite to let the ranter in on the misunderstanding as soon as possible. However, you must be able to make the person feel better about the mistake, so you can't then take the ranter to task for poor taste in soda commercials. You may think it's better to behave as Bob did and just keep quiet, but inevitably people will realize they've put their foot in it and feel like idiots—better to just get it over with.

If you notice a friend putting her foot in it, as discreetly as possible take her aside and fill her in on her gaffe.

YOU'RE A WALLFLOWER

If you are the shy, silent type, chances are you tremble in fear as you approach the door of the event or party you know you must attend. Your fear only increases when you enter and realize that, exactly as you thought, you don't know anyone, or at best you've had vague introductions to people who may or may not remember you. This is surely one of the most challenging situations for the Fabulous Girl as she moves through life.

But shyness is not an excuse for avoiding social situations. Rest assured that no one enjoys standing alone in a crowd feeling like the only stranger in the room. So take a deep breath and a sip of champagne, and introduce yourself. Make an effort by asking people about themselves and you may develop the reputation of being an excellent listener. Of course, you also run the risk of never getting a word in, but you can't have it both ways. If you do connect well with someone new, make sure that you do not monopolize him for the entire evening. Your new pal may find you fascinating, but he may also be eager to chat with others in the room. If you sense his interest is waning, it's time to make a break.

It may sound silly, but a trip to the ladies' room can be good for shy girls on two counts. First, it gets you out of the room for a few minutes and allows you to pull yourself together if you're feeling uncomfortable. But the other bonus is the mysterious atmosphere of a women's washroom, which allows perfect strangers to strike up conversation with each other. Ask the woman at the next sink for the time, and pretty soon you're chatting away.

It is also wise to give yourself a time limit. If you decide ahead of time that you're going to give the party forty-five minutes, then do so. Parties shouldn't be a chore. And when you've been at the party for forty-five minutes, had a couple of drinks, made a few conversations, and you've had enough, then head home with your head held high.

If you are the one speaking with a shy person, at least make one or two attempts at conversation. But if the person still won't say boo, it's time to move on.

YOU NEED A GOOD OPENING LINE

Banter. Chat. Repartee. Whatever you call it, witty and appropriate conversation at a cocktail party can make or break an FG's rank on the invite lists of many hosts. For example, on one occasion an FG invited a new acquaintance to a particularly swank party at an artist's loft in Santa Monica. A group of guests had been casually discussing the best boutiques in West Hollywood when the new girl interjected with "My boyfriend has a ten-inch cock." Everyone was stunned into silence. There's nothing wrong with making a provocative remark to rev up a dull conversation, but an FG stays within the limits of polite society.

However, even the Fabulous Girl can get rusty between social seasons. Fortunately, there are a few opening lines that never fail and aren't the least bit tacky. Remember, it is your job as a guest, be it at a house party or a charity ball, to be polite, friendly, and charming.

Introduce yourself

As soon as you realize you are standing next to someone you don't know, stick out your hand and say hello. This is particularly important if you're with people who are bad with names and therefore with introductions.

"How do you know Bingo?"

The easiest way to strike up a conversation with a stranger is to ask her about her relationship with the host or the guest of honor.

"I love your dress."

Shoes. Eyewear. Whatever. You can never go wrong opening a cocktail conversation with a piece of flattery. As long as you're sincere, there's nothing more socially lubricating. And it's nearly impossible not to find something praiseworthy.

"You had me at hello."

One of the most challenging conversation hurdles is what to say to the handsome man you're dying to meet. If you're lucky, a friend or colleague will supply the introduction. If not, keep it simple and try a smile, your name, and, sure, go for a compliment. But don't blurt out, "You're the sexiest man in the room," even if you think he is.

"Can I get you another drink?"

If you have nothing to say, a trip to the bar just might be the pause that refreshes. Come back with a few observations to share along with those martinis. And yes, all you Fabulous Girls out there, this means you. There's something just plain chic about offering to get a guy a drink (okay, beer not so much), and men appreciate that independent forties-film-star type. Lauren Bacall was forever fixing cocktails for Bogie!

"I'm between books—have you read a good one lately?"

A multiple-tangent topic. If he says he never has time to read, ask him how he does like spending his free time.

"How is work?"

While the first question out of your mouth should never be "What do you do for a living?" the old rule about avoiding shoptalk during the cocktail hour just doesn't apply anymore. People spend hours and hours at their jobs, and they are far more likely to have something interesting to say about their work than about their nonexistent hobbies. Be open-minded; while selling insurance may be a deadly dull topic, your new friend may have hidden talents and interests.

"How about that slide show?"

If you're trying to engage a stranger in conversation, it can be wise to comment on the evening's festivities, be it the silent auction items or the soprano who just wouldn't shut up about her latest CD before singing her aria.

"I haven't heard this music before—do you know what it is?" It doesn't really matter what the answer is. It's a gateway topic.

Be seasonal

Get a little more adventurous than "How 'bout all that rain?" In spring try, "Are you a gardener?" In summer ask, "Any holiday plans?" to get the conversation started.

CONVERSING WITH A BORE

You'd do anything to avoid spending even two minutes in conversation with Bill because he's such a bore. Sadly, boring Bill is your boss. He also doesn't like to be left alone at social functions. The best you can do in this situation is to introduce Bill to as many people as you can so that at least they can share your pain.

CONVERSING WITH AN EGOIST

The upside to talking to this self-centered person is that there never need be a lag in the conversation. It takes very little to get egoists going on their favorite topic, so on those nights when you don't feel quite up to being dazzling yourself, you can just feed them a couple of questions about themselves and sit back and watch the show. And don't wait for the reciprocal "And how are things at your work?" as you'll be waiting forever. Just move on.

Conversing with a Curmudgeon

This person can seem like the death to pleasant conversation but is actually a fun cocktail person in disguise. Unlike most people who happily agree with whatever opinion is being floated in a conversational circle, curmudgeons will argue and debate, usually with an amusing snarl. And they're used to people disagreeing with them so you can get into a playful fight without the worry of offending them. While you don't want to get too close to curmudgeons (eventually their negativity is exhausting), they're a good part of a successful party.

You're Cornered by Someone You Loathe

How Sally has missed all the signals that you can't stand her is beyond you. You didn't reply to her e-mail invitations to join her S & M poetry-reading group and surely she notices how tense you get when she talks to your boyfriend. Somehow she has remained oblivious to these hints and is now cornering you at a party filled with other people you actually like. Don't stand for it—life, even social life, is too short—excuse yourself to the ladies' room and find a friend who can help you avoid her for the rest of the night.

Someone Insults You

Being insulted—particularly in public—is something no FG tolerates. If after discovering that you are an interior decorator, Bingo tells you how stupid he finds an interest in decor, you may at first cut him a break. "Oh, you seem like a pretty stylish guy, Bingo," you gently tease. If he responds, "Sure, but I could never really take that kind of thing seriously. I mean, how could anyone take decorating seriously, it's so ridiculous," feel free to pat his arm with a touch of condescension and wish him a good night.

SOMEONE INSULTS YOUR FRIEND

Just because the rudeness wasn't directed at her doesn't mean an FG can watch silently while others are insulted. When she sees someone being treated badly, an FG commiserates with the victim. At the very least she makes eye contact with the person who has been treated rudely and shakes her head in sympathy. But a true FG sticks up for the underdog. Politely, of course. If you notice a pregnant woman or an elderly person standing on the bus—and you are standing yourself, of course—you can pleasantly ask someone to give up her seat. Very often people just aren't thinking and need only a little nudge to do the right thing. However, if the situation is more extreme, an FG ups the ante. If you witness a coworker being unreasonably snappish or condescending to his or her assistant, speak up: "Wow, you were really harsh with Linda there. If you've got a problem with her, maybe you should talk it over with her."

HOW TO SPOT—AND AVOID—A SOCIAL CLIMBER

There's a difference between wanting to meet interesting and successful people and being an obvious social climber. Many hostesses gain reputations for bringing together fab people, some of whom they may not know at all well themselves. This is not social climbing. Of course, there is also nothing wrong with wanting to better your position in society and to have new and interesting people as your friends. But you must cultivate them with subtlety and sincerity, not because you just want to be able to say you know them. Here's how to spot an SC and therefore not become one:

1. They name-drop. Literally. Climbers tend to use and say names more than normal people. They repeatedly mention the name of the musician they were seated next to at a dinner party as if the sound of that person's name uttered over and over somehow suggests a friendship. "And then Yo-Yo Ma said the funniest thing about wanting some more bread. Yo-Yo Ma really likes bread."

2. It's in the eyes. Social climbers are hungry, and it always shows in their big, wide eyes.

3. They're rude. SCs tend to look over your shoulder while in conversation—unless you're famous, that is—on the lookout for more desirable prey.

4. They're bold. SCs always ask to be introduced to the highest-status person in the room.

5. They ditch their old friends for bigger and better invites from the bigger and better people, and they won't ask their old friends along.

Someone who wants access to your Rolodex is not ever going to be a true friend—and needn't be treated as one. Those who ask social favors without offering themselves to you as a friend may quickly be done away with. Don't go out of your way for them—they certainly won't for you. When they ask to be invited someplace fabulous as your guest, decline. When they invite you (as long as you bring so-and-so) to a party, decline. They will soon learn to release you from their ambitious social takeover scheme.

∞ *Fabulous Girl as Bad Girl* ∞

SURVIVING A SCANDAL

However much style, grace, intellect, and wit she may have, the FG is still human and can make poor judgment calls. Or she may fail to consider the consequences before acting. Sometimes it's an affair of the heart, and in that particular scenario no amount of common sense will dissuade her. For in love, as in art, one can justify almost anything. Being a passionate person, the FG may find herself voicing unpopular opinions that will put her in conflict with powerful people or she may simply be close to an unlucky friend. However it happens, even an FG can find herself in the midst of a scandal.

The upside of being involved in a scandal, however small, is that in certain social circles you may be seen as an even more desirable guest. In this century, a person's cachet may rise out of her involvement in varied sorts of intrigue. "Good society" has been replaced with "celebrity society." People are always interested in innuendo and gossip and want to be on the inside track. Hoping that you may confess your "sins" or at least tell your side of it is very enticing to many a dinner-party host. Pick your invitations carefully and make sure, if need be, your legal counsel approves before the RSVP goes out.

The scandalized Fabulous Girl does not, however, spill her guts to this select group. On the contrary, she maintains her composure if prodded, politely changing the subject. The host should see to it that the conversation does not remain on the scandal. In other words, the elephant in the room should be ignored. The "fallen" FG may add spice to the table, but she is not there to be flambéed.

However, if you're not the one who's been scandalized but a friend or acquaintance of one, you may need to give some thought to social interactions with that person. If you do want to entertain your friend who is under investigation for insider trading or who left her boyfriend for her boss, you may still do so, but you should keep it simple. A dinner party for ten is fine; a cocktail party for fifty is too much attention for your buddy.

How to Snub and Survive a Snubbing

In the last decades, as social constraints have loosened, people have become increasingly reluctant to judge the character of others. The FG urges a reconsideration of this issue. Think of society as a big sandbox. Those who play nicely may stay, but those who kick sand in the eyes of the other kids must find their own playground. You must, of course, kick people out of the sandbox decorously. Here is the FG guide to snubbing and being snubbed.

1. Keep it quiet. Snubbing simply means that you behave as if the offender doesn't exist. It does not involve publicly haranguing or in any way drawing attention to the act of snubbing. You just don't see the offender.

2. Choose your snubbing moments carefully. Snubbing is an extreme social move and must be reserved for extreme situations. The offender must have wronged you in a serious way for snubbing to be considered. If a colleague ate the lunch you put in the office fridge, you might be cross but it is not grounds for the silent treatment. If an acquaintance spreads slanderous rumors about you (restraining orders, an affair with the babysitter) among your social set, snubbing may certainly be in order. A call to your lawyer may also be appropriate, but at a minimum, snub.

3. Apply preemptive snubbing. In most cases, the FG will give

all humanity the benefit of the doubt and avoid prejudging people. There are certain characters in society, however, who it is reasonable to assume will do you harm—gossip columnists, for instance. These types should not be welcome in polite company. Never assume that they won't use their friendship with you to do their terrible job or get you to say or do something compromising for use as a weapon later. They always do.

4. You may snub only those who have done you, or those extremely close to you, harm. Just because you heard a rumor that Bingo had an affair with his friend's wife five years ago, you may not snub him. It is not your business and you have no snubbing rights.

5. If you are being snubbed you probably know why. You will recall that, in fact, you did have an affair with your friend's boyfriend, and that's why she looks right through you at social functions. If you are being snubbed and don't know why, go ahead and approach the snubber. But don't try to get to the bottom of it at the party, where you risk a scene. Call him the next day and ask if you've slighted him without realizing it.

6. If you are the object of a snub and you know why, you may try to get back in favor by apologizing to the appropriate party. If, however, what you did was so horrid that an apology won't suffice, you may have to suffer the consequences of your actions. If you are snubbing someone and she apologizes, you must accept her apology, so ending the snub. While you don't have to be best friends again, you must acknowledge her in public.

You're Jealous

You're still struggling in your Jill Job but your best friend has suddenly landed her dream position. The ex-boyfriend who broke your heart has finally gotten his big break in show business. Sure, you're happy for him, right? Right? Admit it, this type of situation can make even the most stable FG recoil just a bit. "Why not me?" she may ask herself. And let's be honest, if the supersuccessful person happens to be someone you don't like, or whom you even despise, you're certainly not going to be happy for him. You're going to be rancid. You can't believe that Barbi got that weekly travel spot on your fave daily TV news show, and now she'll be jet-setting around the globe for free and you have to see her stupid face on the tube and hear how fab she is when really you know she hasn't an original idea in her head. Yada yada yada. Fine. Don't be happy for her. And let's face it, you're probably right and your opinion is no doubt shared by others you do respect. However, this is where you must up the fabulousness quotient and employ the "nicing" tactic, where you counter bad behavior or your own bad feelings with sweetness. You must congratulate Barbi, saving your critical musings for your closest friends. Nicing is very useful when you encounter someone in your social circle whom you are irrationally irritated by. You don't want anyone to see you behaving in a jealous manner, and sometimes you can even trick yourself into a more generous attitude this way.

When is it appropriate to criticize? It is not the intention of this book to brush aside all negative opinions or to hide all feelings that aren't "nice." But what an FG needs to do is make the distinction between bitchy banter and intellectual debate or constructive criticism. Back to Barbi the travel princess. Maybe the FG has a point. What if Barbi's TV spots are trivial drivel? An FG can extol her opinions in mixed company, and by that we mean the fans and nonfans of Barbi. But she needs to do it in a nonsnarky way. And she must hear out those who may retort, "I love Barbi, she makes me laugh . . ."

∽ *Private Moments (or What Should Be Private)* ∽

YOU NEED TO PRIMP IN PUBLIC

A simple rule: don't do it. It is never fabulous to apply a full face of makeup on the subway or at your desk (if you work in an open-concept office). While driving, it is both unfabulous (we can see you) and dangerous (mascara wand through the eyeball, anyone?) to apply makeup. There's something intimate about the act—all that touching of your face—that is simply not appropriate for public viewing. No one is so busy that they can't do this part of their routine at home.

This goes double for anything at all to do with hair. Do not brush your hair in a meeting. Do not brush your hair while waiting in line at the grocery store. Do not brush your hair anywhere in public except the ladies' room. If you find that you've forgotten lipstick one block away from an appointment, it's fine to discreetly apply some gloss in the back of the taxi or on the street—just make it quick.

USING PUBLIC WASHROOMS

This is a subject that the Fabulous Girl would rather not discuss at all. However, it is an area of life that every FG must navigate.

Togetherness

If you and a girlfriend skip to the loo together, it's polite to let conversation fade as you enter the stalls. Many people do not feel comfortable chatting while they use the facilities. Likewise, if you walk into your office's washroom and think you recognize a pal's shoes under the stall door, don't call over. And if you do notice that someone is lingering in a stall, allow her privacy and leave as soon as possible.

Sharing

If the person next to you does pipe up with her need for toilet paper, you must oblige if you can. Polite FGs do not reply that they "can't spare a square." And pass over more than you think your neighbor needs.

Keep it neat

While in the stall, please make sure that the toilet is flushed completely and successfully. Remember to wipe the seat before you exit. And at the sink, if you splash a gallon of water on the counter, take a few seconds to wipe up your mess.

Move over

While it is a part of women's culture to preen, make room for those who need the sinks while you are applying your lipstick. It's impolite to block them just because you were there first.

Sex

While it sounds like the stuff of rock-star legend, sex in a public washroom does happen. If you really can't wait until you get home, then at least try to have polite tawdry sex. If there are only two stalls and one is broken, use the broken one. Don't get down in the only working stall, leaving a line of crossed-legged women.

Comfort levels

Just because your last boyfriend had an open-door-while-peeing policy, it does not mean your new sweetheart will be open to it.

Always assume that people want complete privacy in the washroom. That includes talking through the door when they are in there. Even peeing in front of other FGs may not go over well.

Fab girl exception: despite the above rules of decorum, there are certain circumstances in which talking is vital, say, in the restrooms of nightclubs, bars, and restaurants. The washroom, ladies', toilet, loo—whatever you wish to call it—is the only place where secrets can be whispered or admissions made during a group outing. Many a decision has been made during lipstick application in a public restroom. What better time to tell your best pal that Bingo is eyeing her? Or to ask what should you do about Ivan, who can't keep his hands to himself? Or that you want to ditch Bert and go home? Use washroom time for these little issues and to basically assess the evening. Consider these moments the FG half-time show.

YOU REALLY NEED TO GO

Public peeing

A Fabulous Girl would, of course, never stoop to relieving herself in public no matter how small her bladder is. Answering nature's call outside in nature (that is, camping) is totally inappropriate. Okay, it's gross. Obviously, men are far more guilty of this than women. Men's peeing in public has become such an issue in Europe that monuments—doing double duty as urinals—are actually eroding. *Eeew.* An FG will strongly discourage any man in her life or her vicinity from behaving in this manner. (Likewise spitting.)

The men's room

You gotta go. Really, really badly. But the women's room is being used. Then you spot it, the oasis: a single toilet for men. First you must knock loudly before opening the door to the opposite gender's washroom, then open the door a crack and announce your intentions of entering. Great, no one is inside. Just be ready for that sinking feeling when someone from the outside tries to get in. A man. You're gonna have to face him. Hopefully, he will be a gentleman and smile and say hello—not, as has happened, swear and stomp and be all indignant (he who pees in public). If you are treated rudely by the unruly male, just ignore him and go back to your table. He's utterly wrong to berate you for this.

Jumping the queue

There are times when an FG knows that if she waits her turn in line there's going to be trouble. Pregnancy, bladder infections, or a too-long car ride can result in your not being able to hold it while you wait your turn. If the choice is between speaking up to your fellow washroom waiters and peeing your pants, by all means pipe up. Speak directly to the gal at the head of the line (even though it affects everyone, she's the one you must appeal to): "I'm having a situation here, do you think I could go next. I'm sorry, it really is an emergency." All but the most coldhearted will let you go ahead.

OTHER WASHROOM EMERGENCIES

If you get surprised by your period in a public washroom, you have two choices: you can, again, call on your fellow women and see if anyone has a tampon in her bag she's willing to part with or you can look after the problem yourself. That's right, it's time for the toilet paper pad. Wrap toilet paper around your hand a few times to make a small pad and place it where a real pad would go. It's not pretty and it won't last long but you can then make it home or to a corner store to get what you really need.

❦ *The Party* ❦

DRESSING FOR EXTREME MOMENTS

An FG understands that her fashion choices can set the tone for just about any moment in her life. Style speaks volumes for her. Sometimes it says the thing she's too much of a lady to say herself.

The Fuck-Me Dress

You're going out on the third date and you're pretty sure that tonight's the night. You don't need to be over-the-top sexy, but you should reach for a Fuck-Me Dress. Which doesn't necessarily have to be a dress at all. Depending on where you're off to, it could be a cashmere shell and a pair of jeans that give great ass, or a wrap dress that keeps you fairly covered but makes the ladies look great. The Fuck-Me Dress doesn't need to show a lot of skin. It's more about the fabric: this is a dress that should make you seem touchable.

The Fuck-Him Dress

If you know that your ex is going to be at a party, you're obviously going to pay a little extra attention to your outfit. Whether you go for that outfit he always loved on you or something brand-new (really, the better way to go since it implies that your fabulous new life is full of fabulous new things), what you're looking for is a Fuck-Him Dress. Go tight, short, or low-cut—but only one, whichever works best on you. You want to look sexy without looking slutty.

The Fuck-Her Dress

If the ex is going to be at a party or event with a new girlfriend, or perhaps a woman that you have other competitive issues with will be there, the FG pulls out the Fuck-Her Dress. FGs aren't catty by nature, but there are times when a girl needs a little extra armor to get her through the night. However, use restraint, as you would when consuming alcohol at such an occasion: avoid that micromini, cleavage-to-there dress that will only make you appear insecure. Remember, your outfit for feeling good and confident when in the company of this potentially troublesome new girl or definitely troublesome old nemesis should be sexy in a simple, chic, and sophisticated way. And remember, women notice details that men never do. Designer duds or fab knock-offs will get her goat, and if the dress itself is simple, punching it up with a killer bag, a great pair of shoes, or a piece of antique jewelry will give the effect you're looking for.

Shooting Her Video

An FG takes pride in her appearance. She loves clothes and keeps up with fashion and beauty trends. But she knows when to pull back. While dressing, the FG keeps in mind as a cautionary tale the girl who goes too far. The girl who goes too far wears the peasant blouse with the flounced skirt, the rustic sandals, and the turquoise jewelry, and carries a straw bag. All at once. This lack of restraint— the overly styling girl—is known as Shooting Her Video. As in, "Check out the girl in the head-to-toe Dolce & Gabbana. She is so Shooting Her Video." Don't go there.

COCKTAIL PARTY MISHAPS

There you are, having a lovely time at the cocktail party thrown by Mrs. and Mr. Fancy. Candles are floating in their backyard pool, the champagne is flowing, the conversation is flirtatious—and the dog is peeing on your Prada sandals. Yep. Their beloved dog, Rover, has escaped from his kennel, made a beeline for you and your most expensive shoes, and gone ahead and relieved himself on your left foot. These are the kinds of moments that truly test an FG's mettle in the decorum department. You love your Pradas, and even though you love animals you feel like hoofing Rover into the drink. At a minimum you'd like to screech and tear off the now-damp shoes. Alas, as a well-mannered woman you can do neither, particularly if your hosts have witnessed Rover's breach of etiquette. You need to act as if this is the most amusing thing that has ever happened to you. They will naturally feel terrible about it and your job is to make them feel better. Walk over to the pool, laughing, and say you just must know what the water is like; dunk your whole pee-soaked foot in the pool, give it a shake, and ask for another glass of champagne.

If you're the host and such a mishap occurs—say, your guest steps in Rover's "present"—then you must clean off his shoes. Don't just hand him a paper towel; offer to do it for him. If he refuses and wants to do it himself, let him, but by all means take him to another spot, away from the party. There is nothing sexy about watching a person clean dog shit off his sole.

EXTREME SPILLS

Some spills are impossible to ignore. As a good hostess or guest your usual method in coping with other people's blunders is to make as little of them as possible. Some people make this very difficult indeed. When a fellow partyer dumps an entire glass of red wine on your new, perfectly white shirt it's hard not to imagine she did it intentionally, let alone not to scream out for the loss of your new shirt. Instead, make your way to the kitchen to dry yourself off. Don't bother with dabbing yourself with soda water, you'll only turn it into a wet T-shirt contest. If the spiller follows you into the kitchen and offers her suggestions simply look her in the eye and say, "I think this is a job for the dry cleaner." She should offer to pay. If she doesn't, avoid her at parties in the future. If you're the spiller apologize immediately, and yes, offer up cash for the dry cleaner.

If you are the hostess of a party where wine is spilled on the furniture, try to react as little as possible. Of course, go ahead and douse the material with soda water but mostly you should deal with it in the morning. You should laugh it off and try to make the klutz feel better about his mishap. If you are having a lot of people over, look around your apartment first and remove breakables before guests arrive, rather than worrying that someone will smash your granny's crystal vase.

Another form of extreme spillage can come in the form of one great joke and a mouthful of wine. Yes, spit. If you're at a gathering and someone lets loose with a particularly witty remark and you have just taken a swig of cabernet, it is quite possible that whoever is nearest to you will get your wine spilled forth from you mouth. All you can do is apologize, and the poor sap whom you spat on should have the good grace to accept your apology and even laugh at the situation. After all, a well-mannered person possesses good humor in extreme scenarios; this includes both you and the victim.

BLURRY NIGHTS

Every once in a while—or for some, every night—we need to go out on the town and let loose. One, two, or five cocktails and a bottle of wine later, however, and you may end up saying or doing things you don't really want others to hear or see. For instance, an FG attends a birthday party wearing a striking pair of lace-up stilettos. She drinks a lot. A whole lot. She is barely able to stand up on her high heels. It's time to give the birthday toast. The FG grabs the un-opened bottle of champagne, insisting on opening it. The other guests watch nervously as the FG sways, her laces loosening. Just as the cork is about to pop, her laces give way and she falls over, sending the cork flying in the direction of the hosts' plasma television, cracking the screen. You can't help wondering if the next morning she'll be able to face facts, let alone the replacement bill for the TV. Of course, it is best not to get so drunk that you do things you later regret, but hey, whom are we kidding?

Therefore, in honor of all drunken blurs, the FG has a set of rules for coping with those harrowing realizations on the morning after.

1. The Backtrack. Okay, so you just confessed to your long-term pal your ardent love for him, but it was not reciprocated. Or you invited someone you actually despise to your upcoming dinner party. In situations like these, there is one fortunate fact: the person in question probably has as hazy a memory of the event as you do. In fact, if you were to pretend it never happened, he or she might actually be relieved. But an apology needs to be extended for the blurted words of love that made your friend uncomfortable. Let him or her decide whether to discuss the matter beyond that. The same

applies if you have shared too many personal details about yourself or someone else while tipsy. Be honest and ask the recipient to keep it to herself. As for the regrettable invitation to your dinner party—if you cannot cancel then you do have to suck it up. You can always make it a big dinner party, or even a buffet-style dinner, so you don't have to spend much face time. And who knows, maybe you'll find something to like about the person by the end of it.

2. The Blind Eye. Even if you haven't committed a drunken indiscretion, you might find yourself a witness to one. When you see someone do something you know is embarrassing, it's best to laugh and forget about it.

3. Passes. The most common blunders made while people are under the influence are of a sexual nature. Maybe you've had your eye on that handsome theater producer for a long time, or maybe you've just caught sight of that swivel-hipped young architecture student. But suddenly you're locked in an embrace. The next time you see him or her, you must acknowledge that some intimacy has passed between you. Just a note saying "Oops, we kissed. Thanks" is fine. If you realize that you used your tipsiness as an excuse to act on real feelings for someone, then you need to come clean, particularly if you think there's a chance your feelings may be reciprocated. Call your crush and tell him that although you're embarrassed by your behavior you'd like the chance to take him out for *one* drink sometime. Hopefully you'll be able to steer things into a more romantic (as opposed to purely lusty) direction. But if you suspect that your drunken attentions were unwanted, you must certainly apologize. And if you've made such a pass and you are not single, it may be time to reevaluate the soundness of your relationship.

4. The Repeat Offender. As mentioned, these situations can happen to the most polished FG. But if you repeatedly get so blitzed

at parties that you end up doing it in the bathroom with strangers, you've got a big problem, and something stronger than an FG's good advice is called for.

HOW TO CURE A HANGOVER

Be it during a long night or a long weekend, more than a few FGs have indulged enough to wake up the next morning to a searing headache (especially if all that alcohol was accompanied by a few cigarettes), a reeling stomach, and the occasional spinning room. Such experiences will motivate many women to proclaim, "Never again." And some may even mean it. But as long as there are hangovers, there will be etiquette issues involved.

1. Take your medicine. Remember, this is a self-inflicted illness, so you really can expect only so much sympathy. Your hangover is no excuse to cancel brunch plans or business meetings. You must graciously crawl to whichever event you are committed to. This, of course, underlines the fact that in accepting invitations or setting up meetings, you are obliged to avoid overindulging the night before.

2. Put a cork in it. Again, you did this to yourself, so cut out the whining. If you can't stop, then at least sequester yourself in a dark room until it passes.

3. Offer spousal support. While no one enjoys being around a hungover mate, if you are the clean and sober half of the couple (or a roommate) you must not sneak into the den and whip open the blinds. You will not snap the victim out of her misery. Likewise, this is not the time for lectures, especially in a loud voice. Wait until the next day to broach the subject of overindulgence.

4. Turn over a new leaf. It's not unusual, after a few weeks or

years of heavy partying, for the thought of detoxifying the system to enter some people's minds. With this choice come other measures, such as special diets. If it's a weekend juice fast, it's fairly simple to self-cleanse in private. But if you're after a longer-term diet-and-drink overhaul, you must warn your dinner companions in advance. Though many will do their best to accommodate you, don't expect that heavy drinkers will necessarily want to accompany you to a juice bar.

Fabulous Girl Hot Tip

The Bloody Caesar is the best "hair of the dog" to soothe the savage hangover. To make this delicious cocktail (which is yummy at any hour), fill a highball with ice and 1½ ounces of vodka, top with Clamato juice, and season with Tabasco and Worcestershire sauces, with a lime wedge on the edge. If you're not too bleary-eyed, you can first rim the glass with seasoning salt (very tasty).

∞ Fabulous Girl on the Lam ∞

Just as the FG doesn't plan to fall in love with a married man, she also doesn't aspire to be Bonnie Parker and lead a life of crime. However, without thinking, she may inadvertently end up on the wrong side of the law. This is a different kind of bad behavior, beyond the social scandals and love triangles.

YOU GET CAUGHT DRINKING AND DRIVING

So you have one too many martinis, but you still feel fine. You think you are fit to drive. But you are over the legal limit, and no one else at the party seems to realize it. You leave and get behind the wheel.

You take it slow. Too slow. A marauding tow-truck driver spots your tortoiselike speed and calls the cops. Next thing you know, Sheriff Junior has red-lighted you to the shoulder of the highway and you're standing there in your halter gown and strappy stilettos blowing into the Breathalyzer. At least you're trying to. You fail the test like your college calculus exam, and Junior plays by the book, snapping the handcuffs on and shoving you into the backseat of the cruiser. Now what?

This is one situation where being fabulous fails, try as you might to behave with grace. You inquire after the cop's family as he fingerprints you. Rather than being charmed, he writes in his report that your chatter indicates you're not taking the charge seriously. You are now a criminal. The FG in such an extreme circumstance will be scared, but she must not throw a diva fit, crying and screaming to be set free. She must be cooperative and polite. She must also call her lawyer and promise to never drink and drive again.

FRIENDS WHO DRINK AND DRIVE

If a Fabulous Girl spots someone unfit to drive, she should speak up. It is not rude to tell a stranger that he or she should call a cab. Or the FG could point out to the host that a guest is too drunk to get behind the wheel. However, if the FG is called to bail out a friend who has committed such an offence, she shouldn't lecture. The friend no doubt understands the seriousness of the crime and will thank the FG for picking her up from jail. The FG will not tell all her friends about buddy's adventures or that she lost her license. If this becomes a pattern in your friend's life you must have a serious conversation with her. She is risking her own life and the lives of everyone else sharing the road with her. Tell her she needs to stop her dangerous habits. When out with her socially you may need to monitor her alcoholic intake when you know she is driving. Once she's past the limit, try to encourage her to drink water. If this fails don't be afraid to call the police if you aren't able to stop her from getting behind the wheel; you could be saving her life.

YOU GET CAUGHT SHOPLIFTING

There is nothing fabulous about stealing (well, maybe if you play an art or jewel thief in a 1950s film set in Europe), yet there are known FG thieves. One very famous FG film star was caught red-handed in a Beverly Hills boutique. She didn't need to steal, she was rich. Some thieves are motivated by the simple thrill of it, others by some deep-rooted pathology. But if you do get nabbed by those nasty-looking plainclothes security guys or gals, then you'll have to turn on the charm to prevent them from giving you what you deserve—a trip to the police station. The standard excuse of "I just dropped it in my handbag to make it easier to carry, then I forgot it was there" may work the first time. But seriously, this type of behavior or mistake is only barely acceptable for teens in a rebellious phase. If you find yourself drawn to this kind of perilous high jinks, it is something you must discuss with a therapist.

YOUR SHOPLIFTING FRIEND

The store is packed with weekend shoppers, and the teenage staff can't handle the volume of merchandise and customers coming in and out of the changing room. You and your buddy share a dressing room. Nothing fits so you're ready to take off, when buddy notices that a skirt doesn't have a security tag. A skirt she likes. A skirt that fits her perfectly. She stuffs it into her purse and makes a break for it. Unfortunately, if you find yourself an unwitting accomplice to a shoplifter, there is little you can do outside of scolding your friend. It is not very loyal to turn her in. However, you should certainly guilt her about it, even letting it slip while in the company of other friends. This should embarrass her enough to not repeat the offense.

The party had thinned out. A group of artists and writers was going down the street for a punk rock karaoke night. So not our thing. Missy, Nice, and I were ready to go home. But Elenor was still missing in action. It had been twenty minutes since her trip to the bathroom. I volunteered to go find her while Nice and Missy got our coats.

As I passed the bar, I was sideswiped by a tall guy carrying two pints of beer. It was Bingo, too close to ignore.

"Hey, how ya doing?"

"Fine, Bingo. I read about you in the paper."

"Oh, that. Well, ya know, word gets out. Say, how's Elenor?"

"How do you think she is?"

He shrugged. Then, unbelievably, he slowly ran his eyes up and down my body. "You look foxy tonight. Still with that guy?"

"Yes, that guy is waiting for me."

I stormed away. What a jerk. Not only did he have the gall to ask about Elenor, but he checked me out as if I were auditioning for a live sex show. Yuck.

Enraged, I threw open the ladies' room door. It was empty. But I could hear a woman giggle, a woman who sounded just like Elenor.

"Elenor?" I wandered down the line of cubicles, but she wasn't there. Still, the Elenor-sounding woman was somewhere. She seemed to be on the other side of the wall. The men's room. Worried, I raced over, knocked first, then swung open the door. Lucky for me the urinals were unoccupied. But two of the stall doors were shut.

"Elenor?"

"Woohoo! That's me!"

One of the doors swung open and out flopped Elenor, half-naked, her dress up around her waist, and a total stranger in the cubicle, buttoning his trousers. Her Fuck-Him Dress had morphed into a Fuck-Me Dress.

"What did you do to her?" I asked stupidly. For some reason my anger was directed at this total stranger.

He ignored me and strode out of the men's room. Elenor was laughing.

"I needed that." She was too drunk to know what she was doing. She shoved her dress down to its proper place.

"Oh, Elenor. Did you at least use a condom?"

"I don't think there was time." This was from Dudley, who flushed the toilet and emerged from the second occupied stall. "But she did seem to enjoy it."

"I did indeed!" Elenor burst out laughing again and slapped Dudley on the back. I wanted to shove his head down a toilet.

"You can't write about this."

"I read your piece. All gossip and gossip columnists are rude, hey? I couldn't help but take it personally."

I couldn't bring myself to suck up to him. "No, I guess you couldn't."

"Now, what exactly is the etiquette of sex in a public washroom? See you in the funny papers, Manners Girl." He smirked out the door.

"I have a sudden headache," Elenor whimpered at me.

"You'll need a whole lot of aspirin tomorrow," I said, dragging her through the washroom door.

The next Saturday, Dudley's column came out, and there I was, dubbed "Manners Girl," all my exploits (not to mention Elenor's) served up in his characteristically snarky tone. Big boss Bradley would not be amused.

CHAPTER THREE

Money

"I really want to have breakfast in the hotel!"
Missy had resorted to foot stomping.

The three of us had decided to escape for a long weekend away. Besides being an exercise in bonding, it answered our need to leave town after Dudley's skewering of us in the press. So there we were, standing in the lobby of this five-star hotel arguing over breakfast food. You see, Elenor was a bit short on cash. After twice being publicly humiliated, she had gone on a shopping binge. And after splurging on $500 shoes and a $3,000 gown, she was now flat broke. Still, we needed to get out of town, so I picked up the tab for her. That's right, not rich Missy, me. Which brings us back to the foot stomping. I had suggested a greasy spoon down the street with a $3.95 breakfast special. Missy wanted the $15 eggs in the hotel. I had to be firm.

"I just think it's too expensive."

Though I kept thinking that Missy would clue in, she really didn't get it.

"Fine, whatever."

We settled into a booth at the admittedly less than atmospheric greasy spoon and ordered eggs, bacon, and toast. The waitress was churlish, the coffee not too hot, and I'll admit the clientele was a little on this side of trucker, but how bad could the food be? After all, this weekend wasn't about gastronomy but about friendship.

Our steaming plates of eggs arrived, and Elenor and I dived right in. Missy sulked. Playing with her food like a five-year-old, she poked at the sunny-side up eggs with her fork, letting the yolks run over the plate and get soaked up by the bread. She pretended to take a bite of bacon, then tossed it down and made a frowny face. Great.

"Suddenly not hungry?" I couldn't help but become a bit bitchy. "Good thing that you didn't order the $15 eggs florentine at the hotel."

Missy shrugged.

Elenor, for her part, seemed oblivious to Missy's fuss and gulped her coffee. "Wonder if there are any good stores nearby."

I wanted to scream that she had no money to shop, but instead I took the bill from the snarky waitress and paid it. All of it. And Missy let me. I thought at least she'd say thank you, or better, apologize for behaving like a troll and cough up her share. But no, with her newfound riches there also seemed to come a matching set of entitlement and snobbery. For the rest of the weekend she was cool and distant, insisting on spending time in all the boutiques Elenor and I couldn't afford but making us watch her buy, buy, and buy. Now, I didn't begrudge her the money that came with her marriage, but I couldn't help thinking that she could be handling it with more grace.

While Elenor was broke, I was in debt. Since landing my job at the magazine I'd been on a bit of a shopping bender myself. I had maxed out my cards. And now the bills had begun to pile up on my doorstep. Funny how it is with credit cards. Shopping is easy, but it always seems to cost so much more when you see it all added up in print, with 18 percent per annum. But that's what money was for, right?

∽

◌◦ *Money* ◦◌

THE FABULOUS GIRL MAY not know everything there is to learn in life, but one thing she is clear on is that she doesn't want to end up like the Victorian Fab Girl Lily Bart: poor and friendless. Of course, thankfully, much has changed since Edith Wharton wrote *The House of Mirth*; a woman need not rely on marriage and "proper society" to keep herself cozy or, in the case of poor Lily, alive. The modern FG can earn her own keep, thank you very much. However, along with financial independence comes financial responsibility.

An important part of becoming a real grown-up is learning how to manage money. This is absolutely vital to the fully formed Fabulous Girl. Many women are not raised to be knowledgeable about, let alone assertive and creative with, money. Many, in fact, have inherited their mother's ambivalence about finances. Not only does this mean a girl can't be as fabulous as she could be, it can also mean she puts herself at actual risk.

The first hurdle to overcome may be the Fabulous Girl's fear of finance. Numbers can terrify her. All through school she may have received bad marks in math and so was convinced she was incapable of handling her money, a trait in her early twenties she thought was attractive in an "oh, how cute" kind of way—in the back of her mind she may have imagined some man would at least share the burden of all that icky financial stuff. Hah. All that happens to the finance-phobic FG is debt, maxed credit cards, and overdrawn bank accounts. Surefire symptoms of the money-scared FG is that upon withdrawing cash from an ATM she tosses away the receipt— too anxious to see the balance and learn the truth—and at home her bills pile up unopened. These are the bad habits that any FG must learn to break.

We all know a woman needs a room of her own, but let's add to that a portfolio as well, shall we? No matter how much or how little she makes, an FG should have her own financial plan. If she has very little there may seem to be no point in this. There is. You may have nothing at all to save, but just knowing where your money is being spent is a useful tool and a good habit to get into.

∽ *The Rich FG* ∽

YOU'RE SUDDENLY RICH

With all of her talents, there may come a day when the FG is re-munerated in a big way—whether through an inheritance, a major career-related deal, or vested stock options. This can manifest itself in many forms, from being able to buy a home for herself (and by herself) to quitting her job and becoming an integral part of the international jet set. How much money constitutes life-changing wealth varies with the individual Fabulous Girl. What doesn't vary from FG to FG is her gracious demeanor. Never a money flaunter, the Fabulous Girl may spoil her family, friends, and, naturally, herself, but she does so in a way that doesn't scream "filthy rich" but rather "generous." While a non-FG—known as the newly crowned Miss Rich Bitch—may turn to gaudy wardrobes, dripping gold jewelry, and name-dropping here, there, and everywhere, all the while snubbing her old friends, the FG acts as if little has changed—she just can afford nicer things.

Putting your money where your mouth is
It is terribly tiresome to be around a newly minted rich person who talks about nothing but money all the time. This is one of the reasons that the term *nouveau riche* is used with such derision by both

the old-money and the no-money crowds. If someone you've just met compliments you on your silver cargo pants, you need only say thank you. You don't need to add, "They're Balenciaga." Consider this the rule of thumb: when elaboration is unnecessary, don't do it. "I've been out of town" is the perfectly appropriate response to "Where have you been lately?" Unless you're asked for details, which you probably will be, don't start with "I've just come back from wintering in St. Barts aboard the Casiraghi yacht . . ."

Besides, the less you blather, the more intriguing you are. Everyone likes a good mystery, and you'll be a more desirable part of your new and old social settings if you appear well adjusted to your good fortune.

The accountant

Once you move into a new income bracket, you need an accountant to help you deal with your money. Depending on what field your success is in, try to find an accountant who is familiar with the issues and tax laws associated with it. Ask other people in your field for recommendations.

The bank

Banks are not the place to find good manners. Whatever they may profess in their advertisements, most banks have little interest in individual accounts. You must be very assertive to get what you want out of any exchange with banks. Refuse to be treated like a child. Sadly, charm and warmth—two very useful elements in an FG arsenal—make very little difference within the walls of finance. An FG will get further employing a businesslike tone.

Even when she does assert herself in a reasonable way, an FG may find herself receiving less than acceptable service. At this point she needs to get tough. Let the person you're dealing with know exactly what you want and by when. If it's been a month since you applied for a line of credit and you've left three unreturned calls to Bingo, the fourth should go like this: "Hello, this is Ms. Fab, your client. I came into your office on November 8 to apply for a line of credit. I have left three messages for you checking on the status of my application. I have not received a response from you. I need to hear back from you by the end of tomorrow before I assume that there is someone else I should be dealing with on this matter." And if you don't hear back, call his manager and ask her to take over your application.

Investment firms

If an FG suddenly—or not so suddenly—has a lot of money to play with, she needs to find people to help her with the rules of the game. It's a very good idea to get a financial adviser on your team as soon as possible. There may be significant tax breaks you're missing out on by not discussing your new situation promptly.

Don't be afraid to seem dumb in these meetings. Ask whatever questions you need to in order to be satisfied. Ask more than once if you still don't get it. Let your investor know how much you want to spend, what risk you're comfortable with, what your goals are. Listen to the advice offered, but don't forget to stand up for yourself. You may choose to sink all your savings into a house or other real estate—even if your consultant advises against it. These people make money by keeping your money in the markets, not by your taking out a mortgage.

Saving

Do think about the future. Indeed, it is easier to be frugal now that you have a little cash. Somehow having even a little extra money allows you to look at your financial state more closely, more comfortably. Take advantage of this feeling of freedom and start putting money away. And not just in your checking account either. Educate yourself on higher-earning places to put your money.

Philanthropy

There is an unfair and unkind perception of a certain kind of wealthy woman who gives to charity. The word *socialite* is often tossed around instead of *philanthropist*. Whether she makes her own fortune, married it, or was born into it, a rich FG does not allow this perceived slight to hinder her generosity. When she makes money, she likes to give her friends gifts, treat them to dinners, and so on. But she should also consider donating time and money to charity. While this may seem corny, there were no doubt many people who helped the FG on her way to the top, and supporting a cause is one way to give back. The Fabulous Girl is not afraid to make time to volunteer or to write a check. And there are numerous charities that will appeal to her: children, animals, the environment, medical research, and art are all high on the FG's list of worthiness. On every level, giving money to charity is a good idea. It balances an FG's karma. It gives her a break at tax time. It establishes her in the web of society. The FG knows that one of the responsibilities and privileges of wealth is philanthropy. Altruism is definitely a part of the FG vocabulary, and she encourages others to do the same by becoming involved in fund-raising for charity.

YOU ARE THE WEALTHIEST PERSON IN YOUR SOCIAL CIRCLE

The Fabulous Girl who has more money must be aware that not all her friends are as wealthy as she is. That said, an FG shouldn't have to feel guilty about her successes. She should enjoy them. If your winning streak is a recent one, it may be hard for the people around you to cope with the new you. This doesn't mean you have to accept rude treatment, however. It's not appropriate for people to intimate that your life is trouble-free now that you've hit the big time, even if things have been a little sweeter lately. Remarks like "What do you care how much the bill is, you're rich" or "Must be nice not to have to worry about money like the rest of us" are rude and make you feel bad whether they are intended to or not. The best response to such comments is to laugh them off rather than engaging in a conversation about money, or worse, getting defensive. If it goes any further than this, you should draw the line. "Jokes" along the lines of "Can I borrow twenty bucks? No, really, can I borrow twenty bucks?" shouldn't be tolerated. Be direct with the fool. "Oh, I see, you're joking about the money that my last film made. Right. Actually, I only carry fifties now, so I guess I can't help you out."

The wealthy FG must also take into account different considerations in style and taste while socializing with her pals who have less. An FG on a budget may not be able to dine at the finer restaurants or shop in the ritzier boutiques with her more well-heeled sisters. But isn't a large part of being a good friend making adjustments to suit others?

You Make More Money than Your Mate

If you make a lot more than your mate, it can be stressful—for both of you. Although most modern couples don't expect the woman to be at home while the man is out hunting and gathering, there are still residual feelings that a man should make more than a woman. When this isn't true it can create tensions. Does he feel emasculated? Do you feel responsible for both of you in a way that you're not comfortable with? When couples have very different incomes it is important for them to decide at what level they are going to live. Do you live at the level of the lower earner so that he can be an equal contributor? Or do you decide to supplement his standard of living by paying the lion's share of the mortgage or rent? Be honest about how the disparity makes both of you feel. If you are paying more, are you going to feel that he should then pick up more of the housecleaning duties? If you're living down to meet his income, is he going to feel that you could be making things more comfortable if you weren't holding out? Likewise, the FG may find herself feeling resentful about not enjoying the finer things that she can well afford. Whatever you decide, neither of you should refer to your financial discrepancy when it comes to decision making. The person with the bigger paycheck does not have the final word on all issues of conflict. Even after establishing some safeguards against the possibility that inequality in your earning power will create inequalities in your relationship, things may still sour over your differences. It may be impossible for your low-earning man to admit that he's jealous or bitter over your paycheck. Some fat-cat FGs have been accused by their mates of being career obsessed or neglectful. Their men can't be honest about their discomfort so instead take their shots in other ways. If you suspect this to be the case you must try to address it directly. "Bob, I think you need to be honest with me. Do you feel uncomfortable earning less than me?" You should never feel bad about your success; you've probably worked hard for it and even if you didn't, it's still not your fault. Still, money—not sex or politics—is the final frontier in male-female relations and it's very hard going. You may have to admit that your man will never be comfortable with you as the moneymaker, and if it's affecting the rest of your relationship, it's time to consider liquidating.

You Marry into Money

You've fallen in love and so has he. In fact, he just proposed. He's funny, smart, sexy, and—hot damn!—he's rich. And so is his father and so was his father before him. It sounds like one of those movie endings . . . you kissed a lot of frogs and then, finally, your prince. In reality this can be a tricky union, particularly if you come from a significantly different tax bracket. People in your social circle (hopefully not your friends) may wonder at your true motivations, his family may be suspicious of your intentions, and his lawyer may wonder what's taking you so long with the prenup. You and Mr. Rich need to get things straight between the two of you. How are you going to handle the discrepancy in your bank accounts? An FG may want to insist on keeping her money separate so that there can never be a whiff of gold digger in her reputation. Another may be more comfortable with allowing his wealth to become her wealth. Whatever you decide, you'd do well to keep it between the two of you and your lawyers. Your united front will go a long way to silencing the rumor mill that may begin around you. If anyone is crass enough to ask you what it's like to have hit the jackpot, you must answer with a steely smile, "I certainly am lucky to have found a man as wonderful as Mr. Rich." Do not honor these rude remarks by getting defensive or going into details. As for his family, he must make it clear to them that you are his chosen one and that he will not brook any kind of snobbishness on their part.

YOUR BOYFRIEND WANTS A JOINT ACCOUNT

This decision, made by every soon-to-be live-in or married couple, can be fraught. It is, in some respects, a question of trust. And of course, an FG trusts her mate—she's about to move in with him, right? From her experience and from the stories of others, however, the FG knows that everything can change and often does. We've all heard tales of the FG whose husband ran off with the dog walker, only he decided he'd fund his escape by emptying out their joint account.

Every FG needs her privacy and a decent sum of her own money. In her grandmother's day it would have been called "mad money" or "rainy-day money." Now let's call it three months' rent and one great dress. The Fabulous Girl needs to be in control of her own finances and make her own educated decisions about what she can and cannot afford. If all you have is a joint account, you will end up having needless discussions and resentments over your choice to buy those Prada pumps instead of the new DVD player. In other words, he needs his own cash, too. Why not have both? Have your own accounts and share one checking account into which you each put money every month for rent, food, phone, and utilities. This will mean sitting down and creating a shared budget. If the love of your life gets pushy about having only a joint account, stand your ground.

It's your money and you need to be in charge. You will never regret sticking to this policy. Nor will you regret losing a lout if he's not willing to give you the freedom you need.

DEALING WITH MOOCHERS AND FREELOADERS

Moochers, spongers—you know the type. This isn't your friend who's down on her luck, this is the person who simply doesn't want to part company with her moolah. You're out for drinks or dinner with a group of friends. The bill comes and everyone reaches for her handbag. Everyone except Miss Mooch, that is. She forgot to go to the bank machine. She could have sworn she had a fifty in her wallet this afternoon. Sure. Whatever. When this happens three times or more, you are in the company of a moocher. Whether or not it's intentional, this person is a manipulator. Either she can't afford the same lifestyle as her friends but isn't willing to admit it, or she is just childish and exists in the delusion that somehow the world will always provide for her. You can still be friends with this person—although not close, let's-go-for-pedicures-together-on-Saturday-afternoon type friends—you just have to monitor what kinds of activities you invite her to.

It's sometimes helpful to exaggerate things to clarify them. Let's say you bump into Miss Mooch at a book launch. After an hour a group of pals decides to move on to dinner. Suggest a restaurant on the expensive side of what everyone is willing to spend. This will help the moocher to think about her financial situation and beg off. If she doesn't and she tries to worm out of the bill, you may have to politely point out, with a hint of sarcasm, "What a coincidence—there happens to be an ATM just on the corner." Or sweetly offer to lend the mooch the money and tell her she can pay you on the walk home by stopping at that very ATM. And do it.

∽ *The Poor FG* ∽

Rich is fun. Rich is good. Poor sucks. But most of us are more likely to be poor than we are to be rich. Poor, however, doesn't mean that one does without every fabulous necessity, or that one can't climb out of the rut that often befalls the indebted and the low-income earner.

YOUR FRIENDS ARE WEALTHIER THAN YOU

You may be poor because of your chosen profession. It's unfair that modern dancers make less than lawyers or that poets make less than accountants. It's also unfair of the world to treat you as if you are less valuable because you work in a profession that doesn't pay well. But just as it's not your fault that you don't make a lot of money, so it is not the fault of the high earner that she does. It is the height of bad manners to make cracks about people's worth based on their income—no matter if they're rich or poor. There exists a false logic that says that if a person makes a lot of money, he must have duped the world and is necessarily crass and shallow. This is as unfair an assumption as thinking that all modest earners are lazy slackers. If you have friendships with people who earn considerably more than you, socializing together may occasionally be awkward. While your rich pal shouldn't always make invitations that necessarily exclude you ("Hey, how about a weekend in St. Barts?"), it isn't her responsibility alone to smooth over the rough moments. If your friend invites you to join her at a new swanky restaurant and you can't afford it, be honest. "You know what, I'm dying to try that place but I'm pretty tight until my next paycheck. How about we have a cocktail there and then go to Cheap and Cheerful for dinner?" If your friend is a friend she will happily agree to your proposal. Don't assume that your friend will only want to spend time with you in fancy places. It's not a big deal if you don't make it a big deal. Conversely, don't allow your rich buddy to pay for you every single time. While it is generous of her to offer occasionally and it is perfectly appropriate for you to accept, after a certain point you must decline. An FG never wants to be considered a freeloader.

You're Broke—But You Still Crave the Finer Things

The Fabulous Girl likes eating out. She gets invited out a lot. But the number-one budget killer is a consistent diet of restaurant fare. If you are in a serious or not-so-serious financial crunch, the best thing you can do is stop dining out. You don't have to be obvious about it if you'd rather not make a public announcement about your situation. Instead, you can start inviting friends over to your place for dinners. Although it costs more than feeding only yourself, it is still much cheaper than a restaurant bill. Another tactic is to agree to meet for a cocktail, or any other activity, rather than a meal. People with active social lives tend to get lazy about how they hang out with friends. You'd have a good time going to a gallery with a friend and it's cheaper than the little French bistro you normally frequent and just as chic.

Fabulous Girl tip: the working lunch

By this we don't mean simply working at your desk while you throw back some sushi. The FG knows how to work her lunch to save some money. How? By bringing her lunch to work every day. Sure, brown-bagging it isn't glamorous, but the FG may save herself at least $50 per week on lunches alone. This means $200 a month is saved, and that's a lot of money. And let's face it, most takeout lunches suck and aren't worth the money anyway, so why not take the cash? Don't be deceived into thinking that $11.32 each lunch hour doesn't add up.

The other working lunch

The other way to keep your lunch expenses down is to time your appointments around noon. Of course, you must be meeting with someone who is obliged to pick up the tab—a client or anyone you are working for. It sounds crafty, but if you suggest meeting someone at noon they will almost always come back with "Let's make it a lunch."

SPLURGING IRRESPONSIBLY

One thing that the financially conscious FG should avoid is the splurge, especially the impulse splurge. When shopping, it is tempting to dive into designer boutiques; however, such trips can also be a painful reminder of your lack of funds. Some FGs are able to window-shop and browse without incident; others may fall prey to the splurge instinct. This occurs when the FG, say, tries on a pair of very pricey Italian-made pants. They fit like a glove—in fact, for all intents and purposes it appears they were made just for her. Satisfied, she removes them only to check the price tag: $625. A tidy sum for anyone, most of all the nonrich FG. But she wants them, she really wants them. Her heart begins to race. She gets dizzy as she concludes that her life won't be complete without them. She envisions herself striding into a chic party wearing the pants, cutting a figure of feminine independence and mystery, taking a meeting with a soon-to-be big client who sees her as capable and creative, landing that dream job because of her take-charge attitude—all contingent on these pants. She may as well quit her job and wear pajamas every day if she can't have those pants. Then she remembers she has room on her credit card—it's about all the room available on the card, but hey.

This is when the FG must do the impossible: she must put the pants back on the rack and march out of the store immediately. She can at the very most put them on hold until the next day, but she cannot buy them then and there. She needs the splurge fever to subside. Ninety-nine percent of the time it will. The FG will come to her senses and know in her heart that she can't afford them and that, really, her life is meaningful without them, albeit a little less perfect. If in the next twenty-four hours the feeling doesn't subside, she can go and visit the pants, but if the FG doesn't wait, she will have a big gulp of guilt as soon as she brings her impulse buy home. And an even worse anxiety attack when the bill arrives.

Your Credit Card Is Denied

Even rich girls can forget to pay their bills, resulting in some pretty sticky situations. You're trying to impress a new client. You've booked a table at a cool—but not intimidating—place. The night has gone well. You're pretty sure that Mr. Rich is going to go back to his office tomorrow and recommend that they go with your firm.

Your boss is going to be very pleased. By the end of the meal it seems all sewn up. You throw down your plastic for the waitress to scoop up. Only she comes back a minute later with a pitying look on her face: "I'm sorry, your card has been declined." Of course, you die inside. But you must act fast. Get up immediately, saying to your guest, "I'd better just go and sort this out. I'll just be a moment." Hopefully, you'll be dining in an establishment where the staff won't announce it at the table but rather will ask you to come with them to a more discreet spot.

If you can put the bill on another credit or debit card, obviously that's the simplest solution. If you don't have another credit card and they won't take a bank card, ask for the nearest bank machine. If it's close by, just run out, use it, and pay the waitress in cash at the register (hopefully out of view of your guest). Then you can go back to the table and just shrug: "All sorted out. Don't know what the trouble was." The worst thing to do is to get embarrassed and flustered.

Actually, the very worst thing to do is to ask your guest for money. If you don't have the cash in your account or there is no bank machine handy, you may be faced with this terrible prospect. Chances are, however, that you can call a friend, a very good friend, and ask her to pay the bill. Your friend should be able to use her credit card over the phone, but if not (or if she's also maxed out), arrange for her to come down to the bistro and pay the waitress directly with cash, again so that your client is unaware.

The very, very worst-case scenario may still happen: you can't get hold of a single flush friend. So you must explain the situation very plainly to your client, express your embarrassment, and let him pay. But send him the money the very next day along with a thank-you note and a promise to have dinner another time, on you!

You Lose It All

It can happen to any Fabulous Girl. You toiled away for years as a jazz singer, hoping for your big break. One glorious day a record label exec happened upon your show and signed you then and there. Of course, the fact that the record company doesn't produce jazz albums didn't seem to matter. You went along with the producer's vision and lo and behold, you cut a techno-pop CD. You really can't stand the sound, but it hit number one in a week. The album made you very, very rich.

This kind of sudden wealth can make you tempted to spend in an easy-come, easy-go way. This isn't uncommon. Many famous Fabulous Girls have gone broke by buying too much too fast (or by having bad managers). And you may discover that money isn't that easy to earn—your second album tanked. If you find yourself in the sad situation of having blown through five million dollars in two years, you have little choice but to pick yourself up and start all over again. What's done is done. Is it embarrassing? Yes, it is. Will you get over it? Hopefully. Will you get rich again? Maybe.

Once you've had money it's difficult to go back. You may feel as if you are the kind of person who should have money (and an FG does rich well!), and so it can be very difficult to accept your reversal of fortune. But you must. It is dangerous to keep living at your old, more affluent level because you are too prideful to acknowledge the change in your life. Rather than revealing your financial woes, just tell people that you need to keep it real right now and that you want to get back to your jazz roots. Hopefully the people in your life will understand when you start declining invitations to weekends in Gstaad or proposals of a shared villa in Tuscany for the month of July. Anyway, you have no choice but to make these sorts of changes whether or not your social circle accepts it. If they don't, you should absolutely make new friends. On top of dealing with the loss of standing in your field, you shouldn't have to cope with the unkind judgments of "friends." The hardest thing, however, may be adjusting to your own new sense of self. Who are you as a poor person? Who are you as a not-famous person? This may take some time for you to adjust to—a few good visits to a therapist may be in order.

There is little sympathy for the newly impoverished FG. She will learn the hard way that society tends to resent those with money. Some people are only too gleeful, despite surface pretensions, to watch a wealthy person fall to a lower level (all the more reason to handle your wealth with quiet grace when you do have it). Of course, this sets the stage for a great comeback, yet another fave story for the public to latch onto. The FG will ride the highs and lows with equal panache.

Selling your life

Unfortunately, going broke means that to make ends meet, you may have to part company with things you love. Your beloved Warhol silkscreen must go to Sotheby's. Selling off pieces of your life is an emotional ordeal. No matter how many times you tell yourself, "They're just material possessions," these articles represent your life and often have deep sentimental value. The best thing to do is to sell what you must and sell it to strangers. You don't want to walk into an acquaintance's home one evening to see your Warhol hanging on his tacky wood-paneled wall.

Your Friend Loses It All

Friends should take note: if someone in their lives is forced to purge her assets, then "Oh, I saw your Warhol sell at auction for three times what you got for it" is not welcome news. Neither does it help to remark, "At least you have a Warhol to sell."

Debt Overload

Face it. If you have a sudden shift in fortune, you may find yourself with a debt load that you cannot comfortably handle. Maybe you built up debt when you were making more money and now you're drowning in it, or you just finished grad school and now you have a master's degree and a huge bill. The worst thing you can do is go into denial. Terrifying as it is, you must look clearly at how much you owe. Have a friend over to help you through this. FGs have been known to sit with their debt-addled friends, a stack of bills, and a bottle of red wine, and help them face the music. Open the bills, make a list of the amounts, add it all up and make a plan. Call the people you owe money to. If you speak to creditors before they have to come after you, things will go much better.

Collection Agencies Are After You

People who work for collection agencies are the meanest people alive: those nasty phone callers employed by collection agencies to terrorize you. Once a debt has been handed over to a collection agency, you have little recourse but to deal with the agency over the outstanding bill. Although you are clearly in a position of weakness, try to keep up a professional manner with these people. Be firm about negotiating a reasonable payback schedule with them. Even if at the moment you can only offer to give them twenty dollars a month, make that offer. They may cancel your credit card, but if you are making an offer to them rather than refusing to pay, then generally they'll work with you.

You Have a Bad Credit Rating

If you suspect that you have a bad credit rating, you probably do. Again, it's better to face the music than to cower in the corner. You have a right to see your credit rating. You can apply through various agencies to see it. You will be assigned a number that rates you to potential lenders. You can also see who has ratted you out as a bad credit risk. Deal with these people first: clear your debt with them as soon as possible. Many creditors automatically report you to the credit bureau as soon as a single payment has been missed or is even late. Find out which credit cards or bills work this way. Even if you can only pay less than the minimum on these debts, do it. If you're worried about it, phone in and report your payment or the fact that you're going to be late so that you're not reported to the credit bureau.

You can improve your credit rating by—obviously—paying off your bills. But you can also improve it by taking out a small line of credit and making regular payments on it. It's difficult to get a line of credit, but it does wonders for your credit rating so it's worth the effort.

Bankruptcy

There may come a time that you are so seriously in the hole that you can't possibly dig yourself out. This is what bankruptcy laws are for.

If you declare bankruptcy, you won't be able to get a credit card or loan for an extended period of time. Again, hire professional help. An insolvency lawyer can help you file for bankruptcy, but there are also debt counselors who can see you through the process and help stop those harassing collection agency phone calls. You also do not have to announce to anyone in your circle that you are bankrupt.

◌ *Criminal Money Matters* ◌

YOU THINK YOUR BOYFRIEND MAY BE STEALING FROM YOU

You could have sworn that you left a fifty dollar bill on your nightstand. Trying to recall what happened to the missing bill, you run through the previous evening in your mind. You emptied your evening bag of cash, lip balm, and the business card of the cute restaurant you took your boyfriend to; you went to the bathroom to brush your teeth while your guy lay on your bed flipping through magazines; then you turned out the lights. This morning, you rolled over and the money was gone. And now you feel sick wondering if it's possible . . . that your boyfriend pocketed the money when he got up and headed out earlier. If you can hold this thought in your head for more than five minutes it's worth considering seriously. It's so unlikely that if you suspect your boyfriend of being not only a thief but your thief you are probably picking up on something very real. You can confront him if you like, but honestly there's little point. If he's a thief he's not going to come clean just because you ask him about your missing money. If this kind of thing happens more than once, end the relationship. You are involved with a real creep, someone who gets off on fooling the people he is close to. God knows what else he's up to.

The bills kept coming—credit cards from the bank and from my favorite department stores. I could not resist them; neither could I pay them. I had three months of bills creating a mountain on my kitchen counter, all unopened. Somewhere along the way I had neglected to make even the minimum monthly payment. I don't know what had come over me, but those gray number 10 envelopes terrified me. The trouble was I didn't know how to manage my monthly income. When I was freelancing I couldn't get credit, so it was never an issue. But as soon as I had a real job, I became legitimate in the eyes of all the stores and banks, and they were throwing cards at me like confetti. I became their prisoner. I tried to pay down chunks at a time, but between rent and restaurants, I just couldn't make a dent in my bills. Every time I withdrew cash from an ATM I would toss away the receipt, unable to look at the balance.

I was managing to exist in this state of extreme financial ignorance until one night, as I was sitting at home cuddled in Nice's arms, Kitty at my feet, the phone rang. It was a bill collector. In one of those nasty envelopes had been a letter warning me that if I didn't pay up, the bill would be sent to a collection agency. Of course, not having opened any of those letters, how would I know such a thing was possible?

I tried to whisper into the phone. Nice didn't know about my situation, and I was hoping to keep it that way.

The man on the other end of the phone, however, was mean and rude. He wouldn't listen to me. In answer to his threats, I promised to pay the bill the next day, knowing full well I didn't have the money. When I hung up, Nice was suspicious.

"Everything okay?"

"Just fine," I lied. "That was the production department at the magazine. They need my copy earlier than normal."

The calls kept coming, both at work and at home. It was awful. Still, I kept my worries to myself, living from paycheck to paycheck, making deals with the devilish collection agencies and not living up to them. I probably would have gone on like this indefinitely, or at least until someone sued me, if it hadn't been for the shower.

I was in the shower when one of those bastards called, and Nice answered my phone. He didn't usually answer my phone, but this time he did. And the collection guy left a rather detailed message. I tried to be angry with Nice, figuring I'd distract him with an argument about privacy, but he wouldn't listen.

"You should have told me about this, I could have helped you."

"I can handle it myself. I'm just a bit behind."

"A bit? Let me give you the money. We can consolidate your debt—"

"No."

I just couldn't stand the thought of being in debt to my boyfriend—it was a point of pride. It took awhile, but finally Nice did take "no" for my answer. It had been an exhausting fight and we had parted angrily. That, however, was the least of my worries. Nice was right—I needed to pay off the bills and have only one payment. I couldn't get a bank loan; the less-than-helpful manager had said I was too risky. Boy, did I hate banks. So I called Missy.

"How much do you need?"

I told her, waited for a lecture, a scream, or something. She was silent.

"I know I can pay you back."

I could hear her breathing at the end of the line. Perhaps I had pushed our friendship too far. I'm not sure how I would have reacted in her shoes; money does do strange things to people.

"Okay, I'll write you a check."

Missy had one condition to her loan: I had to learn to budget. She came over one night, wine bottle in hand, and we systematically opened up every bill I had accumulated, tallied it up, and then Missy gave me the money.

It was simple. I was freed from the evil creditors, and Missy seemed happy to help. As a thank-you I invited Missy out for breakfast—at a five-star hotel, of course. When the bill came I naturally reached for it. But Missy beat me to it.

"It's on me."

I resisted. After all, I wanted to thank her for the help. But she wouldn't hear of it. That was the last time Missy or I ever mentioned the loan. I simply paid her back an agreed-upon amount every month. She was much more gracious than any banker.

CHAPTER FOUR

Friendship

"What can I get you ladies to drink?"

Missy, Elenor, and I were in celebration mode and had met at our favorite haunt, Dominick's. It was a homey Italian place that still did the whole red-and-white-checked-tablecloth thing but somehow always attracted a youngish crowd. It's strange that the place where Missy and I had slaved as waitresses just a couple of years ago had now become our regular spot, but there you go. We were always model customers and tipped the waitresses generously.

"Champagne for the table," Missy ordered. She was obviously in a money's-no-object mood.

Exactly what we were celebrating wasn't clear. It had been about two months since the whole Bingo-Muffie-Dudley affair, and life had pretty much glided by without incident. Elenor had decided it was time to move forward with her life and had suggested a girls' night out.

"I'm ready for new challenges."

"And new men," I suggested hopefully, as Elenor had a long history of getting back together with Bingo no matter what the indiscretion on his part, though thankfully this last time seemed to be sticking.

The champagne arrived, an extravagance that only Missy could afford, but since she was paying I made sure the waiter filled my glass to the brim.

"Should we make a toast?" I thought it was the simplest of questions with a straightforward "Cheers" as the answer.

Elenor raised her glass: "I'm pregnant." She sipped just enough bubbly to wet her lips. "That's my last taste for the next seven months."

I looked at Missy. Had she known? Missy stared at me. Obviously, this was news to her too. The two of us sat dumbly with our flutes raised.

"Um, you going to drink that?" Elenor looked a bit annoyed.

"Congratulations," I spurted out.

"Holy shit," was Missy's well-thought-out response.

"I know, my doctor only confirmed it this morning."

"How do you feel?" I asked.

"Oh, forget her feelings! Are you going to keep it? And who's the father?" Missy demanded. "That's what we really want to know."

"Actually, yes, I am going to keep it."

"That's huge, Elenor."

"But the father will remain a secret, for now."

"You're choosing to be a single mom?" Missy had a knack for stating the most terrifying facts out loud.

"It won't be that bad. My mom can help. I have a good job with great benefits."

"I wouldn't raise a kid on my own, not in this city."

I wanted to quietly wring Missy's neck.

"Have you thought of adoption?"

"Missy!" I couldn't stay silent. "Elenor, this is very exciting, you know we're both here for you. Missy and I are just in a state of shock. Why didn't you say anything?"

"Denial."

We continued with our celebratory dinner, discussing the usual: men, books, work, and now, baby stuff. To tell the truth, in my quest for career I hadn't spent much time thinking about children. They were cute but messy, lovable but loud. Now there was going to be one in my closest circle of friends. But that wasn't the thing that got me. I still couldn't help but wonder if the stranger in the bathroom had knocked Elenor up. Or was it Bingo? I suspected that my scariest thought was somehow closer to reality: Elenor didn't know who the father was. There was only one way to find out for sure.

"Does Bingo know?"

"Haven't told him." Elenor evaded my attempt at sneakiness.

"Should he know?" Missy was on to my plan.

"Not from either of you." With that, Elenor continued cutting into her rare steak.

∞ *Friends* ∞

THE FABULOUS GIRL HAS many friends and acquaintances. They are, after all, a necessity for a thriving social life and provide a much-needed support network. The FG herself is a good friend. However, as in any intense relationship, there may be pitfalls. The Fabulous Girl recognizes that the people who matter most to her are sometimes the greatest disappointments. Conversely, they can also be the recipients of her poorest behavior. There will be occasions when the FG's friendships are tested or even ruined. To navigate these extremes of friendship, the Fabulous Girl must develop a very special skill set.

∞ *Meow* ∞

There are few relationships in life as complicated as best gal pals. Women are often heard to exclaim that their friendships with their girlfriends are much more secure, honest, trustworthy, and long lasting than relationships with the opposite sex. Is there any woman who hasn't wished her relationships with men were as solid as those with women? However, the flip side of intense female friendships can be less than ideal.

YOUR FRIENDS LIKE TO BITCH ABOUT EACH OTHER

Women, we're sorry to say, can be capable of treating their friends in an unfair and thoroughly rude manner. You know the scene. There you are with your two best friends. You gab, you drink, you eat, you share secrets, and then it happens: one of you gets up to use the washroom and the remaining pals launch into a bitchfest behind the absent one's back. "I just don't know why Esther can't get her life together . . . she can be so stupid sometimes." "Did you see what she's wearing today? She just doesn't have the legs for that mini . . ."

The Fabulous Girl will think carefully about what she says about her friends while they're out of the room. She is aware that no matter what her own code of conduct is, she can never prevent others from dissing her. Still, she can set an example of discretion.

The FG follows these steps toward thwarting cattiness:

1. Never say something critical about a friend that you would not have the nerve to say face-to-face under the right conditions.

2. An easy way to avoid the gossip habit is to not catch up on the details of Pal A's life while chatting with Pal B. Don't ask Alice how Mabel is doing, ask Mabel. It's a slippery slope from "Mabel's still having a hard time at her new job" to "Why doesn't she grow a backbone?"

3. If you've been hurt or angered by a friend's behavior, go ahead and ask a mutual friend his or her opinion about how best to approach the situation. But don't use the third friend merely as a sounding board for your rants. The person you really need to be speaking to is the friend who hurt your feelings.

4. If you're jealous of a friend, better to admit it than to say disparaging things about her to others in the hopes of diverting attention away from her and toward yourself.

5. Try loyalty instead. When others are getting nasty about your friend, nip it in the bud. Tell them what a great friend Mabel is and that you simply don't want to participate in catty behavior. It's best to let people know right away your connection to the per-

son they're dissing so they don't feel stupid when they realize it later.

6. If all else fails, change the subject. Or just walk away from the catty conversation.

YOU CATCH YOUR FRIENDS BITCHING ABOUT YOU

If you know that a friend has been talking about you behind your back, you may decide you need to confront her. As calmly as you can, ask your friend what's up. Give her a chance to explain herself—after all, you've probably only heard a piece of gossip and you know how unreliable that can be. You may be angry at and hurt by your friend, but by remaining calm you will be showing your friend that is better to come to you directly with a problem than to mouth off about it to someone else.

∞ *Competition Among FGs* ∞

Another real issue between women is competitiveness. Few women like to admit that they experience these feelings—we're raised to believe it's just not nice. However, this competitiveness does exist. There are many different types, and they can occur between the best of friends, total strangers, and mortal enemies.

COMPETING OVER LOOKS

One of the mildest forms of competition occurs in the world of socializing. Women are often competitive at parties and other social events, each trying to look her best while checking out the other females to see who's got the best dress, shoes, hair, and so on, each one calculating silently where she herself lands on the evening's sex-appeal scale. The theory that "women dress for each other" is not without truth. But that's the fun part of being female—and of being a Fabulous Girl. FGs don't shrink from this type of competition. How many women friends call each other before attending a "do" to find out what the other is wearing? It's all part of friendly, supportive camaraderie, in a "let's both wear our miniskirts" way. Of course, while FGs save each other from fashion emergencies, this is also a way of gearing the FG's own look for the night. She may think to herself, "Betty is wearing black again—I'll wear red and really stand out." This actually isn't ungracious but a natural reaction to wanting to be noticed. Sure, Betty may turn up and say, "Ooh, I should really wear color." But you know that each FG will sincerely tell the other, "You look great," and enter the party armed with the confidence that this type of female bonding brings.

CAREER COMPETITION

Best friends have many levels to their relationship. And it is natural, especially if they are in similar fields, for them to be competitive. Even if this is not explicit, there may a current running below the surface. Hopefully, that's where it stays. This kind of competition can be motivating. If you see that your close friend has just accomplished something great—started her own business, produced a play—it can drive you to work harder in your own life. But be careful if you and your friend are in the same line of work not to pay more attention to her career than yours. Spending too much time playing the comparison game can close you off to opportunities in your own life. Don't be so busy trying to accomplish what your friend has that you don't realize your own genuine goals.

If you find yourself in an actual competition with a good friend—say, you're up for the same job—you need to talk about it. Remind yourselves that although this is an awkward situation, the final decision does not belong to either of you—it's out of your hands. Obviously, you would only go forward in this kind of competition if the goal is something you truly want. Check that you don't want the job just because your friend wants it. This is especially true if you know your friend is applying for a job but you proceed to apply anyway. Unless it is the job opportunity of a lifetime, there is something underhanded about throwing in your own résumé after you know she's told you she really wants it.

WOLF IN FG CLOTHING

Friendships are so important to the FG—particularly her friend-ships with other women—that she puts a great deal of herself into them. If she is disappointed by a friendship, it can come as a terri-ble blow. The worst kind of letdown that can afflict an FG comes when a woman pretends to be a friendly, FG-style girlie-girl only to be revealed as a backstabber. It's one thing to cope with someone who makes no bones about being after your man or after your job—you can deal with this kind of wench because her agenda is out in the open.

Far more complicated and difficult to recognize is the faux friend. Perhaps she even fools herself into thinking she wants a friendship with you. Whatever. When you first make the acquain-tance of this woman it is probably in the company of other women, where she seems like an entirely likable person. She's so warm and winning that you start to think how lucky you are to have made a new friend. You'll start to notice, though, that she makes you uncomfortable in the presence of your man. She makes eyes at him, touches him too much, maybe even tries to make social contact with him that excludes you. At first the FG will try to rationalize her pal's behavior: she's being a good friend by getting to know Mr. Nice better. But then your boyfriend admits to you that he's getting uncomfortable with the way she's been calling him at his office. A teeny bit of research will likely uncover a history of poaching on the part of this woman.

The other variation on this theme is professional. When you met your new "friend" she asked you ever so many questions about your job and your company. Being the helpful type you are, you went ahead and offered all sorts of details of how things are run at your workplace. And then didn't you just hear the following week that Miss Friendly just landed a job with the competition. She was pumping you for dirt under the guise of girl talk.

The FG is a busy woman and has no time for this kind of faux friend. While a thorough snubbing is not necessarily in order, all friendly overtures on the FG's part can stop. If the faux friend asks why you're not available for afternoon tea the way you used to be, you can be honest. Otherwise, the simplest thing is to just stop calling, stop making plans, and keep conversations with her at parties to a minimum. In all likelihood, she'll barely notice—it was never you she was interested in anyway.

Your Friend Has a Faux Friend

Sometimes it's easier to spot a faux friend in someone else's life than your own. What to do if you spy one in the midst of one of your very true friends? This is a very tricky situation for an FG. She adores her pals and naturally does her best to get along with her friend's friends—usually an easy thing to do. First of all, make sure you're right. Be honest with yourself: are you a tiny bit jealous that Sally is spending a lot of time with her new friend Alice? If so, you may be more inclined to read Alice's ribald humor as vulgar or her affectionate nature as cloying. But if after such soul-searching you do really feel that Alice is bad news you can proceed with caution. It's likely that Sally will bring it up herself: "The weirdest thing happened. Bingo and I were making dinner at his place and Alice called there. But I could tell by his side of the conversation that she wasn't looking for me; in fact she obviously wasn't expecting me to be there at all. Of course he passed the phone to me because he barely knows her, but then I could have sworn that she made up a reason on the spot to need to talk to me." Ick. All your suspicions have been confirmed. Gently let dear Sally know that you're not exactly surprised, that you've noticed other similar behaviors from Alice in the past. Don't push it too hard; give Sally a chance to let it sink in that she's been duped. No doubt she'll bring it up again in some way and you can make your point again. And at this point it's safe to add: "I just don't think Alice is your friend. I know you really liked her when you first met her but she's starting to make you—and me—very uncomfortable."

ENEMY GIRL

It usually begins in friendship. Or at least in acquaintanceship. But then you have a falling out. She asks your man out on a date while you're out of town, she bad-mouths you to a potential employer and then applies for the job herself, she repeats the secret she has sworn to keep. Whatever it is, you realize that this girl wishes you ill. And now you, the FG, have a mortal enemy. Yet if you are in the same social circle you are bound to see her all the time. You know that at every cocktail party, barbecue, or dinner she will try to outdo you. Being an FG, you know her plan and are compelled to foil it. Every opportunity you have to look the part of the head turner you must jump on, even if you're not sure that she's going to be there. You can't let your guard down. The key to this situation is to remember that it is a war, and no amount of telling yourself or your friends "I don't care what she does, she's only making a fool of herself" will change that fact. So while you should dismiss her pettiness in public, you should also be wearing killer heels, sporting great hair, and smiling all the while.

It may seem antifabulous to endorse a course of steely competition, but really, we are talking about pride here. If an FG has to find a way to coexist with the enemy girl, being better—better dressed, better behaved, and so on—will give the FG the confidence to face these awkward situations.

The FG wins the competition because she is sophisticated and silent about her grudge against the enemy girl. The first sign of victory is when the enemy girl is caught dissing the FG, or worse, bragging loudly about herself (especially within earshot of the FG).

If, on a rare occasion, your enemy verbally attacks you, do as one FG did when her enemy girl called her trashy and slutty in front of mutual acquaintances: laugh in her face. This only makes the enemy look really, really bad.

When Other Friends Are Feuding

If you're stuck between two good friends who are fighting over something—man, job, whatever—you must be firm with them or else you'll wind up in the middle of the scuffle.

1. Don't take sides. Really. Tell each of them that you will not choose or form an opinion as to who is right or wrong.

2. Don't mediate. Listening to them rant about each other for too long may tempt you to try to make them see the light. You want them to see that they don't need to be feuding. But again, you're being forced into their fight, and often you are being used to fan the flames.

3. Don't discuss it. Pronounce that you will not tolerate their bad-mouthing each other in your presence. That you like them both and intend to remain friends with them both and that they'll have to work it out for themselves. This will ensure that when they do patch things up, you're not the one suddenly on the outs.

∽ *Friends' Fortunes and Misfortunes* ∽
YOUR GOOD FRIEND GETS IT ALL

If she's not doing so fabulously in her own life, when others become instantly famous or rich an FG can be taken aback. For some inexplicable reason, hanging out with friends or lovers who have always been successful doesn't have the same bite as a pal with newfound luck. It may be that the FG simply wasn't prepared, or perhaps there was some codependence going on in the relationship—a bit of that we'll-never-get-it-together type sentiment. So that when only one of you (and not the FG) actually does make it big, it stings.

There is no point in pretending that this doesn't hurt or that jealousy is all bad. In fact, the FG will rise to the occasion to celebrate with her friend, even hosting a small party or toasting at a celebratory dinner at the friend's favorite bistro. Then the FG will use the jealousy to examine her own goals and move forward with her own plans.

However, it is not appropriate to use that celebratory dinner as an opportunity to announce your plans to others. This will come across as a rather pathetic form of stealing someone else's thunder— never a fabulous move. And what FG would desire the pity of others, who will see right through this tactic? An FG must know when to step into the limelight and when to bow out. Of course, the gracious successful friend, if she is an FG, will recognize the difficulty of your feelings and at some point will shift the attention over to you.

Adversity can bring out either the best or the worst in the FG. Yes, it is true, an FG can make poor judgment calls or act in a less than fabulous manner toward even her friends. Despite the best of intentions some of her jealousy may make itself known. If she acts in a less than gracious manner she must apologize for her breach in manners. Sometimes in apologizing to her now-wounded friend she can open up in a more honest and appropriate way about her negative feelings.

Your Good Friend Becomes Famous

The lifestyle of the rich and famous is addictive, and being a celebrity addict is no different from any other type of obsession. So if your friend's success comes with fame as well, things can get particularly tricky. Not only are you confronted with the fact of her rise, because of your friendship, but now her face is plastered on billboards all across town as well! Okay, maybe it's not quite like that but still . . . maybe your friend was a talented, hardworking chef and now she has a cooking show that becomes a hit. Or her little jewelry line gets noticed by an A-list celebrity and now her name, and her connection to Miss Hollywood, is splashed all over the pages of

InStyle. The most sticky part of this scenario may be your friend's ability to get used to her new life of fame. When fame pays a visit to your friend she may find it so novel that it's all she can talk about. That's right, your pal is now famous and she is also a bore. Try to be patient as she acclimates herself to her new status. In all likelihood, she will stop talking about her triumphs at every occasion all on her own. Your other role may be that of protector. As soon as a person is famous she is also going to be judged by people who don't know her. That's how it goes. People have seen her cooking show on TV and have opinions about her skill, her charm, how she wears her hair. Even if your pal is getting on your nerves in the early days of her fame, you must absolutely come to her defense if you hear people taking shots at her socially.

This situation is also a natch for jealousy, as was discussed previously. Try to allow yourself to overcome it, and discuss it with her. Then enjoy the fun side of celebrity friendship. The one thing that the Fabulous Girl must never become is a groupie or hanger-on. Don't become so involved in your movie star pal's life that you no longer have one of your own. Keep pursuing your goals; your friend will be delighted to hear about stuff that doesn't pertain to her. Heck, you may even parlay some newfound contacts to help secure your ambition. Whatever. FGs must understand the difference between taking advantage of being in the right place at the right time and being a star-fucker.

YOUR GOOD FRIEND MARRIES RICH

This is easy. You'll know if your friend is marrying for love if what she goes on and on about is the way Mr. Rich is so sweet, so funny, so thoughtful, so smart, so-so-so, and almost never talks about how he is so rich. If this is the case you can happily support her as you would any friend who has found love. As in the above scenario you might need to give your friend a bit of a grace period while she gets used to her new status as a wealthy wife. She may either go to town with extravagance or be touchy about pointing out how all her money is her own. Either way, give her a chance to settle into things. The mode of your friendship should not change. If the way you and Mrs. Newly Rich used to spend time together was Mexican and half-priced margaritas every Tuesday night there's no need to suddenly start suggesting caviar at The Ritz. You must also be on guard for the snide remarks that may get made about her choice of husband. Don't stand for it.

On the other side of the wealth spectrum, the Fabulous Girl does not take advantage of her friend's newfound financial freedom. Rich people have a sixth sense about being used, and no doubt the new husband will need to find you trustworthy. The FG will do better to not pry or talk much about money. Do not ask your friend for loans, unless you are about to be on the street, and she is your closest friend. Do not expect her to pick up the tab, do not hint at extravagant gifts. "I'm turning twenty-eight and would just die to have a new Jag . . ." The FG maintains her friendship as usual and any benefits to her six degrees of wealth will happen naturally. Who knows? Maybe Mr. Rich has a single friend.

YOUR GOOD FRIEND GETS DUMPED

Your pal was dumped and it was a hard one. Being a good friend, you know you have to be there for her. You let her cry on your shoulder, you take her shoe shopping, you send her e-mail at work to check on her. But if you are in a relationship yourself, you might be tempted to do something else: demote her. That's right, often a dumped girl finds herself invited out to more brunches and matinees instead of the dinners and cocktail parties that she used to get asked to as half of a couple. Not fabulous. Part of the pain of a breakup is the way it shifts a social circle—she doesn't see his friends or family anymore, she doesn't have him as a buffer with her more boring old friends—so the worst thing you can do as a friend is add to these changes. Singleness is not a contagious disease, and your coupled friends will manage just fine in the presence of your newly single friend. Trust that she won't bring the party down with her sadness. If anything, her recent drama will add some fizz to your next party.

YOUR FRIEND IS MAKING BAD CHOICES

We've all heard them—those brilliant ideas that sometimes seize friends, the same ideas that you know immediately are a really big mistake. Are we powerless to sway our friends? The Fabulous Girl must learn to distinguish between life-altering decisions when an intervention is required and harmless whims when it's best to keep your glossed lips shut.

Extreme decisions

Okay, so your best friend, who was dumped by her fiancé last week, has decided to quit her job as a floral designer and join the military. What's an FG to say? In a case of such poor judgment, you really must be honest, but not in a sarcastic, desperate way ("Are you nuts?"). Instead, try "I think you should give this decision a few months—after all, in the twenty years I've known you, you've never mentioned the army as a career choice." You may even go so far as to suggest that her choice of life change may have more to do with being hurt than with national pride.

Whims

Every woman at some point in her life may get caught in a whimsical moment. Your friend spent ten days in the country and, boom, she sold her twentieth-floor loft downtown and bought a bungalow in the middle of Nowhereville? Hmmm. When things seem to be heading down a dangerous path, you may of course express your feelings, but you may do so only before the decision has been made. Once that loft is sold, back off and be supportive. She'll feel bad enough asking to sleep on your sofa when she's back searching for a place in the city next year.

WHEN YOU'RE THE LOSER

Every Fabulous Girl will at some time encounter crisis in her life. Things just aren't working out—your career as a pharmaceutical salesperson isn't as glamorous as you'd thought, you despise your colleagues but like your job, you just can't stand your mate, everything he does is wrong. The worst of it is you realize that you're stuck in neutral with this issue. All you can seem to do is fixate on your unhappiness. An FG must recognize that repeated whining about a particular problem will wear thin on the ears of even her best friends. How many times can you complain to friends before you either shut up or make some changes? For major life-altering decisions, it can take months or years to actually come to some conclusions. And rightly so if what you're deciding is, say, to get a divorce. But in order for friends to remain sympathetic and actually keep listening to you, you must make efforts to improve your lot. You'll know that you've reached the limit of a pal's patience when she stops asking you for updates on your job or marital conundrum, or if her comments become blunt: "Bill's never going to leave his wife for you, so why stick around?"

∽ *Health Issues* ∽

We do live in a world of luxury and excess, and therefore temptations are readily available to us all. Alcohol, drugs, and even food can get the better of even the most "together" friend. If someone you care for is actually in crisis, you should push her to seek help.

YOUR FRIEND HAS A SERIOUS ILLNESS

If you know someone with a chronic but serious illness you must try to be supportive without harping about it constantly. Your friend's diabetes is a big enough feature of her life without your going on about it all the time. But you can be thoughtful about the kinds of foods you offer her at dinner parties and making sure she feels comfortable about dealing with her insulin around you. If you notice your friend neglecting her health, ask her about it. She may be burned out by it and need to vent her frustrations with a good friend.

If what your friend has may be terminal, such as cancer, it will be a very trying time for her and those around her. While it is appropriate for you to ask how she is feeling, how the chemotherapy is going, she may not want to discuss the details. Gauge her reaction and act accordingly. If you know she is going through treatment, offer to bring her meals or help with housework, babysit her children, drive her to the hospital. These small daily tasks can remove a large burden from an ill person's life.

YOU HAVE A SERIOUS ILLNESS

After coping with the news that you are seriously ill, the last thing you may feel like dealing with is the feelings of those around you. Eventually, however, you're going to have to tell your closest friends. This is going to be hard but you owe it to yourself as well as them. Your best friend is going to feel betrayed if you are suffering in silence and not giving her the chance to see you through this difficult thing. Decide which of your friends will be most supportive and strong for you. Sit them down and tell them what's going on with your health. Give them time to catch up with you—they're going to be shocked and upset. But once the information has sunk in, they're going to be able to help. You might not want family to go to doctors' appointments with you whereas your friend can go and distract you with the latest gossip. And if you wish, she can pass on the information to anyone you don't feel up to talking to.

YOUR FRIEND HAS A DRINKING OR DRUG PROBLEM

If you have an acquaintance who drinks too much—and who doesn't?—then it's easy enough to keep your distance. Once you've had enough call it a night and don't agree to the five more that your alcoholic friend will encourage you to join her in. Part of what makes alcoholism so rampant in our culture is how easy it is to just keep going. If the big drinker (or big toker, big snorter) is a close friend you must get tougher. We're not talking about a great friend who gets a little silly after her third glass of pinot grigio, we're talking about a friend who has a real problem that's affecting her work and relationships. If she's your good friend you must have a frank conversation about how you see things. If she's your best friend of twenty years, you may have to shove her into a car and drive her to a detox center, risking the friendship but knowing it's the right thing to do anyway.

The Constantly Dieting Friend

She's your on-the-side friend. Dressing on the side, sauce on the side. She can never just order something straight off the menu. The FG is not against diets as a rule; every girl has those weeks when she lays off the bread to make sure she fits into the killer dress she has planned for a third date night on Saturday. But she is definitely not a woman who talks about her dietary regime incessantly. She simply decides what she's going to eat and then eats it and keeps the whole thing to herself. Friends who do not follow such rules need to either be teased out of the habit or, eventually, told more firmly to knock it off. Nothing is more tedious than the assumption that when women dine together there must be an obligatory period of calorie counting before ordering. Not only is it a retrograde approach to female socializing, it has a nasty undercurrent. The girl who is watching her weight and makes a big deal of it in front of her girlfriends is not so subtly suggesting the same regime to the rest of the table. So boring. It's enough to make an FG want to order a burger with fries and gravy. Not on the side, please.

If your friend is trying hard to lose weight and is doing so gradually, be supportive. Ask her if she wants to be shielded from your snacking (at work or at home). While you would normally offer up a slice of cake or a cookie if you were going to have one yourself, refrain from asking your pal if that is her wish.

If your pal's eating habits are stranger yet, you may want to talk to her about it more gently. The difference between someone who is merely diet obsessed and someone with an eating disorder is fear. A woman on the anorexic spectrum will have very real anxiety about food and it's usually palpable. The way she looks at food, the way she puts it on her fork in tiny amounts, the way she chews will all tell you that you're not just dining with a dieter. You must tread very carefully here; eating disorders are complicated and serious. Ask your friend, in private, if everything is okay. Let her know that you've noticed she seems uncomfortable around food. If she seems open to the conversation you might offer her your help in the way of research. Maybe she hasn't known where to get help and you could go online and look for a doctor in your area who deals with adults with eating disorders. You may also discover that she is well aware of her situation and all you'll be able to do is offer your support.

If your friend really is overweight to a health-threatening degree—and by that we don't mean she's now a size 12—that really does warrant a one-on-one conversation. Ask gently if everything is going well in her life, and explain that you're concerned that she doesn't appear to be taking care of herself anymore. She may be depressed and in need of some help.

∞ *Extreme Friends* ∞

TAKERS

The phrase "ask and you shall receive" is often true when a good friend needs a favor. Have to borrow twenty dollars? A ride to the airport? Cat sitting? That great dress of yours for her first date with him? FGs don't mind doing the odd favor for their friends. It's when the same person asks the same person for help time and again that it enters mooch territory. If you happen to be going through a needy stage in your life, parcel out the favor-asking. And keep in mind the size of the favor. There is a difference between "May I sleep on your sofa tonight?" and "Can I borrow your Land Rover for the weekend?"

While the Fabulous Girl prides herself on being a loyal friend, she doesn't have to be a pushover. Remember, decorum doesn't mean doormat. If you're not comfortable with what you're being asked, then say the little word that could: no.

It may seem high school to say that some people will befriend you only for what they can get out of you, but in the real world this happens all too often. The taker is fairly easy to spot on the social landscape. If someone seems to be your buddy only because you keep lending her stuff or introducing her to the right people or inviting her to the right parties, she needs to be cut off. If you're unsure, say no and observe. The Taker is never interested in a reciprocal friendship, in which you are welcome to borrow her brand-new boots that she's never worn. Oh no, that kind of request would be the sole right of the Taker. The Fabulous Girl is never afraid of losing the Taker as a friend.

PRIERS AND BUSYBODIES

The sixties gave the Western world a great deal: good music, great fashion, and the pill. Coupled with this freedom is the notion that everyone is entitled to an opinion. The old saw goes that politics and religion shouldn't be discussed in good company—but there are many more things that should never, ever be spoken of. All FGs will avoid the following questions, and if asked themselves will politely decline to answer:

"Are you straight?"

One FG was asked this during a phone query with a real estate agent. Put off her game by the off-putting question, she stammered out her answer. This let the agent feel free to rant about how there weren't many of "them" in the hood. Questions from mere acquaintances about sexual preference, paternity, income, or religion are wholly inappropriate. What to do when confronted with such rude inquiries? Simple. "Excuse me?" usually works. It forces the other person to explain why he or she is asking such a personal question and it is often enough to make the offender back off. If the questioner persists, you are free to say you feel that it is none of his or her business.

"Are you pregnant?"

Never, ever ask a woman if she's pregnant. A smiling "Nope, just fat" in response will shut people up and teach them to never make that mistake again.

"Are you tired?"

What this really means is "You look tired," and that's just not nice. Anyway, the answer is obviously yes—isn't everyone always tired?

"Are you two getting married?"

Have you ever known people who are engaged to keep the news to themselves? No, we thought not. When people decide to get married they tend to tell people. Or they tell someone who tells everyone. When people (and let's face it, they tend to be married people) ask whether you and your mate are getting married, what they really mean is "Why aren't you getting married?" Feel free to ask them, with a sweet smile on your face, whether they are still having sex.

"What were you thinking?"

Though it may seem customary for friends and relatives to mouth off with personal opinions on intimate life decisions, only when solicited are you free to give your opinion. Here's the standard rule: If your pal asks you what you think of her purple dye job, is she telling you she just did it, or that she is going to do it? If it's a done deal, keep your mouth shut.

"If you want my opinion . . ."

Quit with this little number. Making friends listen politely to your opinion is not what a well-mannered person does. So don't be offended if your friend says, "No, I've already made up my mind. Thank you." If you are on the receiving end of unwanted advice, end the conversation. Restate your choice or decision and leave it at that. Do not fall into the trap of asking your opinionated friend why she hates the name Maria.

"Are you losing weight?"

Even if the answer is yes, when asked in a group this can be very embarrassing, drawing unwanted attention to the person's body. If you want to say something positive, try "You're looking great."

Polite prying

If you really must know why your best friend named her child Chadwick, ask how she chose the name. Asking a question is always better than launching into a lengthy diatribe on the problem of raising kids downtown or buying a loft or SUV. Forcing your opinions may only make your friends, who are going to do what they want anyway, clam up.

THE WHINY FRIEND

It's not so much what she says, it's how she says it. When you're talking to the whiner you start to realize your shoulders are up near your ears because her whiny tone is so irritating. Honestly, she's a bit like a child the way she sees the world—it's just all one big cookie that she's not allowed to have. At first you may find this person amusing; her kvetching can be initially hilarious but it is also strangely infectious and no FG wants to be a whiner. Be careful not to get caught up with the whiny mode yourself. A bit of friendly teasing may jolt your pal out of her whiny ways. "My God, you had to wait ten minutes in line at the grocery store? It's like a war zone in your neighborhood! Really, how do you go on?"

THE DRAMA QUEEN

This friend can also be entertaining. Whatever she does, by the time she's replaying it over cocktails it's grown to operatic proportions. She didn't just get into a spat with her boyfriend, it is a full-on, take-no-prisoners war. Her boss didn't just ignore her in a meeting, she's about to get fired. This sort of friend isn't really a problem unless she expects you to concur with her view on things and take sides to the degree that a drama implies. If you know your friend to be a DQ you shouldn't agree that you will also hate and snub the girl who looked at her funny in spin class. That would be irresponsible. Try to defuse the drama. Let her tell her stories; after all, they are so much fun to hear, but don't agree to play a part in her theatrics.

THE DOWN-ON-HER-LUCK FRIEND

There will always be one friend who is forever in a state of ruin and despair. Sometimes it is a legitimate concern—a lost job or inability to find employment. If the phrases "It must be nice" or "I wish I had your problem" are uttered repeatedly, it is a sure sign that someone in your circle is down on her luck. These comments may sting you and make you defensive, but really, they say far more about the state of mind of the person who said them than about you.

If the person is making efforts to change her situation, she should be supported. Encourage her, ask her how she is doing when you see her. But if she is interested in what you're up to, you shouldn't edit your life for her sake either.

Some people, however, are just complainers. Don't get sucked into the drama suggested by their whining. For the complainer, these repeated refrains are like drawing breath. You may point out,

"Wow, you've been unhappy about your apartment for a while now." If she doesn't at least admit this is a chronic problem, in the future you need only acknowledge her crabbing and then change the subject.

∞ *Friends and Men* ∞

The little dears can often be a cause of tension between women. Accordingly, there are certain rules of decorum an FG must follow.

YOU AND A FRIEND ARE ATTRACTED TO THE SAME MAN

You and a friend are both attracted to the same man, but whoever spots him first has first dibs on seeking his attention. However, if his attention, once sought, is not on the seeker, then he is open territory. If you're unsure whether or not your friend is interested in the man, ask her. And if you know she is but hasn't been successful, let her know that you are also interested. You're not asking permission (no one owns him), but you are at least being out in the open. Although you can expect some friction to come out of this conversation, it is much better than going ahead without letting her know what your intentions are. It is very unfabulous to make a fool out of your friend because you're afraid of "destroying her" when she finds out the man she pined for is actually mad for you. If, however, your friend is still in pursuit and it is unclear how the object of her attentions feels, you absolutely may not make a move. Two friends battling it out over a man just gets silly. It can knock a solid friendship out of whack. And let's face it, no man is worth it.

Of course, if the man in question asks you out you do not have to decline because you're worried about your friend's feelings. You may wish to probe first: "I thought you and Fifi were getting close . . ." This will determine his interest (and ensure he's not playing you both), and you can then come clean with Fifi.

YOU AND A FRIEND ARE BEING TWO-TIMED

There are certain types of men who decide to pursue two women at the same time. If such a man is really into living dangerously, he may attempt this with two women who know each other (or he may do so unwittingly, but he's still a two-timer). If the Fabulous Girl finds herself in this situation with another gal, she cannot be angry with her. The bad behavior is solely on the male's part, and it is he who should feel her wrath. Actually, both their wraths. This is not a man who plays fair, and he really doesn't deserve any FG. In this case there is no need for competition, and if the other girl confronts the FG, the FG retorts, "You can have him."

YOUR FRIEND IS HAVING AN AFFAIR

As the innocent friend, it is up to you to decide how much of a moral high ground you want to take. In other situations, the Fabulous Girl knows how to confront the cheater, urging a confession of his or her crimes to the significant other (her friend) before the FG does. However, if it's the cheater who is your friend, you have a more difficult choice.

Fine if you don't want to spill the beans. But do you publicly acknowledge this "other" man or woman when you see him or her with your friend? Is your buddy hoping you'll offer your apartment for "lunch meetings"? Or that you'll include the lover in a dinner-party invitation? The FG will not snub the object of desire—just be polite and pretend it's your friend's friend. Like a colleague. You don't need to befriend the individual or spend hours with him or her at a country cottage on holidays, and you certainly shouldn't enable their affair by allowing them access to your spare room, but you shouldn't be rude to them either. After all, this is really your friend's business.

YOUR FRIEND'S BOYFRIEND HITS ON YOU

The Fabulous Girl enjoys visiting her friends, especially those that she doesn't see regularly. However, if her friend has a new boyfriend, the FG will naturally expect the dynamics to be altered. The three of them share dinner and a few bottles of Chablis, the FG thinks she's getting to know the new boyfriend, and he seems cool. Then her pal passes out, drunk and tired. Suddenly New Boyfriend decides that this is the best moment to show the FG his erection and to confess that he's crazy about her and really wants to have sex. Naturally appalled, the Fabulous Girl declines and makes a hasty exit. The next morning she ponders what to do. Should she tell her friend about her lecherous beau? Her thoughts are interrupted by her telephone—it's her hungover friend calling to tell the FG to stay away from her boyfriend. Yes, apparently the rejected wannabe boy toy beat the FG to the punch, only he reversed the facts, telling his girlfriend that the FG hit on him.

Unfortunately, when it comes to love, a girl may sometimes believe what she wants to and not the truth. The FG, of course, would tell the truth and remind her pal of their long friendship and how the FG has never lied before, compared to, say, the few months of the boyfriend's loyalty test. In most cases the friend will believe the FG.

If the FG is the girl with the loutish man, she should consider the status of her friendship—how long, how honest, how well does she know her friend?—contrasted with the knowledge of a recent boyfriend versus, say, a husband. And she should glean the truth.

You Have Feelings for Your Friend's Boyfriend

You've been dying to meet Sally's new man. She's over the moon with how lucky she's been to find someone as compatible with her as George. A bunch of you go out for drinks so her friends and his friends can begin the blending process that accompanies new romance. She's right, George is amazing. Unfortunately for you, that is. He's everything you've been looking for, too. This shouldn't come as such a surprise, really. You and Sally tend to agree on everything—movies, books, shoes—so why shouldn't it be true that you like the same guys, too? If you realize you have a bit of a crush on her new man as soon as you meet him, you can crush those feelings immediately. Keep your distance from him, literally, by avoiding social events that include him if possible. If that would be too rude, and it might be, then stay on the other side of the room if you need to. You may think that your friend will appreciate the attention you're giving her new beau, but she will definitely be able to sense the difference between your questions about his job and loud and unstoppable laughter over his smallest of jokes. And don't start talking about your feelings with other friends; this will only add fuel to the fire and his unavailability may make him more attractive to you.

If you're developing feelings for a friend's boyfriend whom you've known for a long time you can follow the same advice. This is harder, as you probably have a legitimate connection to this man by now and your feelings have simply grown naturally. Again, avoid being alone with him. Mostly though, you must avoid sending him even subtle signals about the nature of your affections. This is destructive behavior you will almost certainly regret.

SPECIAL LOVES

Many FGs have a man in their lives who plays an ambiguous role. Her attachment to this man was originally an erotic one but has since become a friendly one. Maybe she met him and began a passionate affair with him while she was studying in Berlin. Perhaps they met in a lineup for a film festival in London. For some reason their affair never developed into a committed relationship, usually because of distance. But the FG thinks very fondly of this man and keeps in touch with him. When they find themselves in the same city, they often find themselves in the same bed. He is her special love. Although the FG and her special love have no formal commitment (the vague status of this relationship also means that it often has no end), it is understood by her friends that he is off limits to them. It doesn't matter if an FG's friend is going to be spending three weeks in Berlin and the special love has offered to show her around, the friend may not sleep with this man.

HOW TO STAY FRIENDS WITH YOUR FRIEND'S EX

Chances are you've spent a good deal of time in the company of your best friend and her long-time beau. But if they split you may find yourself under pressure to cut him from your life. Your good pal may even ask you not to talk to her ex anymore. This is unreasonable, especially if you knew him prior to their relationship or if she was the one who left him. There is nothing wrong with the occasional drink or suchlike to stay in touch and to let him know that you're still his friend.

It is also rude to snub her ex at events or parties, even if the bastard broke your pal's heart. Only if he did something heinous to you personally or was abusive to your friend can you employ the FG snub tactic.

FG rule: Set limits on topics of conversation when in the ex's company—don't discuss your friend and their breakup in detail. He may need to vent if he's hurt, but he should not try to get you to diss your friend. Nor should he try to get you to give him advice on how to win her back or ask you to speak with her on his behalf. There is nothing more annoying for an FG than to have messages from her ex relayed through you: "You know Bingo is really still in love with you—that night with Ethel meant nothing . . ."

FG off limits: Of course, if you are engaging in lengthy phone chats or flirty e-mail exchanges with him, your pal will rightly feel uncomfortable. She may even wonder if you're in hot pursuit of her ex. Perhaps you are. If so, you should come clean if you hope to maintain the friendship. You should let some decent time pass before pursuing the ex. But no matter how long a grace period you allow before beginning a romance with her ex, this new dating arrangement will make your pal feel awkward and perhaps hurt. You must be prepared for the possibility that your friendship will be altered for good.

Your Boyfriend Is Jealous of Your Male Friends

An FG has male friends. She may even have very close friends who are men. This can be difficult for her boyfriend to accept. He may suspect that his FG is being at best naive, at worst disingenuous, in insisting that her friendship with Mr. Friendly is innocent. If it's at all possible, an FG should try to find a way of bringing her man and Mr. Friendly together. Can they bond over their interest in Rohmer movies? Collect bottle caps together? If the FG can't quite put her finger on why she is uncomfortable with her boyfriend and her boy friend spending time together, she needs to take a closer look at these relationships. Do her feelings for Mr. Friendly run a little deeper than she's confessing? Is she protecting Mr. Friendly because she knows he's secretly in love with her? In fact, an overuse of the very phrase "We're just friends" implies that you are worried about it being otherwise.

How to Keep a Friendship After Sex

You and Gerald have known each other forever. He's always been such a great friend. Then it happened. Too many glasses of wine, a bad breakup—any number of things could have led you down the garden path with a pal. At first it seemed like such a good idea. You like each other so much, why not just take the next step? But as the sun rises, things look a little different. You look at each other and one of you regrets it and there's no denying it. Either things didn't go as smoothly as they might have or you just know in the light of day that your relationship is never going to make the transition to romance.

The main thing is to not overreact. Get up, make breakfast—

or better yet, go out for breakfast. A change of scenery will make you both more comfortable. You've been in diners together before and it's always been just fine, right? Someone does have to say something about this eventually, so the FG should be the bigger person and step up to the plate. It may be that all you have to say is "I really hope that what happened last night isn't going to jeopardize our friendship. How are you feeling about it?" If you suspect that he would like this incident to bring a shift away from friendship toward romance, you are especially obliged to speak up right away. Don't make him squirm, wondering how you feel.

I don't always agree with Missy's tactics. She can be a bit brash, but every once in a while she has a point. It was this whole pregnancy of Elenor's. We loved Elenor, but we also thought that being a single mom wouldn't be as easy as she was making out. Missy had decided that we couldn't just sit by the watch our best friend's life spiral out of control. She convinced me to stick my nose in and talk to Bingo.

"Just find out how he feels about Elenor. You don't have to tell him about the baby."

"But what if he's not the father?"

"What does that matter as long as he's a good provider?" Missy could be very calculating. "If he still loves her, maybe that would be good."

Begrudgingly, I agreed to call Bingo. Missy never could stomach the man, and I knew that if she were to call him he'd be very suspicious. He didn't seem that surprised when I asked him to meet me for coffee. He suggested cocktails, and not wanting to make him wonder about our upcoming conversation, I agreed.

I waited for him for forty-five minutes, drinking a glass of champagne. I was glad that I had suggested my favorite hotel bar.

It was a large room, but it had many private nooks for intimate conversation. I figured that if our little talk went well—I pictured Bingo breaking down and admitting his faults, confessing his love for Elenor and his hope that she'd come back to him so that they could settle down—he would be glad not to have an obvious audience witnessing his tears. To that end, I had chosen a sofa for two in a dark corner.

I sat and sipped for another full fifteen minutes. Finally, the man of the hour showed up, in scruffy jeans and a corduroy blazer. What did Elenor see in him?

"This is a pleasant surprise." He tried to kiss me on the lips. I averted my head, and his lips landed somewhere between my earlobe and my collar.

The champagne had made me brave, hopefully brave enough, so I decided to dive right into the business at hand. "Actually, I have something to ask you."

Bingo leaned in. He reeked of rum. "Not before I get a drink. Hey, can I get some service here?"

With every passing second I was reminded of why I disliked Bingo. I began to silently wish that the stranger in the john was the baby's father.

"Bingo, how do you feel about Elenor?"

"I haven't felt Elenor in months!" He roared at his own pathetic humor.

I tried to stay on course. "Are you saying you don't care about her anymore? You're in love with Muffie?"

"She dumped me."

"Elenor?"

"Muffie. Nay, my Elenor rocks."

Hmm. This was a sign of sorts. Maybe he did love her. Maybe his bad clothes and foul breath were all because he was pining for Elenor.

"I've been doing this nineteen-year-old since Muffie," Bingo winked. "Much fresher."

That did it—I was totally repulsed. I didn't want Bingo to know about the baby, his or not. Of course Elenor knew what she was doing; she'd do just fine with the kind of support she'd have. Missy and I would be good aunts. It would be a piece of cake. I started to get up from the sofa. "Look at the time—I have a date with Nice."

Bingo grabbed my arm.

"Don't go, I've always liked the looks of you, kiddo." He pulled me down onto his lap and stuck his hand up my skirt, pawing at my thigh. Now, I'd never hit a person before, but suddenly my inner Bette Davis awakened and whammo! Well, if you want to silence a room, slapping a man across the face is a surefire conversation ender.

"Do not ever come near me or Elenor again." I raised my voice for added drama, since all eyes were on me anyway. At least people would know my violent outburst was justified.

Looking straight ahead, I marched out of the room, catching Dudley at the bar on my way out. Had he witnessed my little performance? Whom was I kidding—the bastard was taking notes. Once outside, I slumped against the wall. Why did I ever listen to Missy?

The next thing I did was to tell Elenor everything. Well, that was the second thing—my first call was to Missy. She needed to be on the other side of my rant and rage. I insisted we spill all to Elenor, before she read about it and thought I was sleeping with Bingo.

Naturally, Elenor was furious. For a brief second I think she did suspect that I had a thing for her ex. Luckily, Missy was added proof to the contrary. I couldn't blame Elenor for her anger—she was at least relieved that I hadn't mentioned the baby to him. Almost too relieved.

"Bingo is not the father."

Missy and I were silent.

"It was that guy. My baby was conceived in a toilet." Elenor was getting drunk on that lethal cocktail of hormones and bad memories. "I can't even remember what he looked like."

Trouble was, neither could I. I hadn't seen him before or since. Elenor was truly on her own.

CHAPTER FIVE

Sex and Courtship

Dudley had a field day with the Bingo incident.
Newspaper Frank was all over me to fight back, to fight back as Manners
Girl. Bradley still didn't care what I did as long as my *Spank!* work didn't
suffer. So I battled it out with Dudley for two weeks. I tried to convey
that while I did not condone violence in any way, there was a certain
appeal to the centuries-old reaction of striking someone with a proverbial
glove. That duels have a place, and that communicating one's displeasure
or defending one's honor is an integral part of keeping society on its best-
behaved toes. That we often let people get away with terrible acts out of
fear of being disliked or being politically incorrect. But I added a caution:
such extreme behavior should not be tried at home.

Readers wrote both in my defense and in denouncement, but the
controversy sold like hotcakes, so the newspaper was happy. The section
editor seemed to indicate that he wanted more regular stuff from me, but
he wouldn't commit. In fact, I was lucky on two counts: Bingo wasn't
going to charge me with assault. Apparently he had a criminal record for
drunk driving and didn't want to mess with the cops, so he decided to
take it like a man and refused to discuss it. In fact, it made him seem
more glamorous to that certain type of woman who worshipped "bad
boys," and he got lots of female attention.

Glowing in my minor notoriety, we all attended a party shortly after my
altercation with Bingo. Despite the hoopla, or perhaps because of it, our

group dynamic was out of whack. Nice was behaving oddly, Missy was still without Joe (in fact, it had been months since I'd seen him with her), and Elenor was adjusting to being a party girl without alcohol.

Nice had brought along Francis, a new colleague from the investment firm he worked for. Francis and Missy were chatting up a storm. I tried to flirt with Nice, but his face was serious, as if something were on his mind. Meanwhile, Elenor had picked up a handsome guy named Josh.

At the end of the evening she whispered in my ear, "I'm leaving with Josh. He's going to drive me home." They took off. I thought nothing of it since (a) Elenor wasn't drunk and (b) she was pregnant.

"Let's go to my place," I cooed to Nice.

"I think I may pass tonight."

"Not feeling well?" I offered. Who was this guy, and where was Nice?

"Yeah, I'm sick."

Sighing, I looked around for Missy, but she was nowhere to be seen.

"We should say good night to Missy and Francis."

"I don't think we should disturb them." Nice pointed toward a small collection of potted plants. Sandwiched between a palm and a fig tree were Missy and Francis, necking.

"What do I do now?"

"Go home. She's a grown-up, you know. You can't spend your whole life meddling."

Nice wasn't being very nice. I didn't see what he was getting at. In fact, all I did get was a good-night kiss in the cab and my empty loft. Kitty, at least, was happy to see me. I tossed and turned all night. It was lonely without Nice. Lonelier not knowing why he was being so not Nice. The next morning, around eight-thirty, my phone ran. I was barely awake—it was, after all, a Sunday. It had to be Nice.

It was Elenor. "I hate men."

"You're pregnant. Of course you do."

"That Josh, he's one of the worst."

"Why, what happened?"

"I need breakfast. Can I come over?"

I scrambled some eggs for the two of us, still wondering why Nice hadn't called.

Elenor sat down and shoveled the food in like she was never going to eat again. Between mouthfuls she told me about the events after the party. Josh had indeed driven her home, and she had invited him up. They really connected. One thing led to another, and they had sex. The sex was great. Afterward he was loving and cuddly, and wanted to stay over. Things were just fine until around seven, when she woke up with severe morning sickness.

"I spent ten minutes puking—it was awful. Josh was all concerned, asked me if I had a hangover. I told him, 'No, you big dummy, I'm pregnant.'"

"'Pregnant? I thought you were just voluptuous.'"

Apparently Josh hadn't taken the news very well. He'd flipped out and split from her place barely dressed.

"What a bastard," spat Elenor.

"But Elenor, why didn't you tell him? I mean, being pregnant is a pretty big deal."

"It was none of his business." She did have a point. Still, it would be quite a shock to discover that the stranger you'd just slept with was pregnant. Elenor never heard from Josh again.

∞ *Sex and Courtship* ∞

The Fabulous Girl's life wouldn't be fulfilled without great sex, being courted by handsome men, and the discovery of love with the one of her choice. Sigh. However, all three of these necessities have their ups and downs, and the FG must learn to tread lightly on egos, say no to bad situations, navigate love triangles, squares, and hexagons, and keep the fire in her relationship—occasionally all at the same time! While this may sound exhausting the Fabulous Girl is never too tired to pursue a fine romance.

∞ *Sex, Sex, Sex* ∞

BOOTY CALLS

It's late on a Thursday night, you're home alone, and you're feeling a certain, shall we say, restlessness? What's an FG to do? Rather than ordering pizza, you pick up the phone for another kind of delivery. That dial-a-date call that's really not about a date at all. In fact, you're not going to be leaving your apartment. There are FGs who have the booty call down to such a science they've coined a code phrase: "Are you free for Cosmopolitans tonight?" It's perfectly acceptable to invite someone over for sex, but the Fabulous Girl gets some graciously.

Whom do you love?

You can make a booty call only when you are single. No exceptions, ever. And you can make booty calls only to other single people. We don't want to hear about it otherwise. Top of the list are those casual lovers with whom you've become friendly but not relationshippy. You must be careful that your booty call is not toying with the affections of a vulnerable man. Some guy you kind of like, but who you know is in love with you, should not be on the receiving end—in other words, no platonic Chapsticks (those chaps who stick by you through thick and thin). The best bet for booty is an ex-lover or a one-night stand from the past—your fuck-buddy Chapstick. The ex-lover must not be a newly minted breakup boy, but after a year or two go ahead and dial him up. You cannot underestimate the comfort of a familiar boudoir partner.

Cosmos?

Be clear what it is you're after. Men often think they have to lay on the romance to get sex, but this will only confuse the matter if what you want is just to get physical. If you make your position clear from the beginning, you will save yourself the awkward "But what did it mean?" conversation the next day.

Setting the scene

FGs know that even a booty call requires some ambience. Lay on the candles, wine, music, and freshly fluffed pillows. Just because it's only sex, there's no reason not to do it right. And if the FG is heading out for booty, while she doesn't need to show up in a corset (unless she wants to), she does at the very least need to shower! Bringing a bottle of bubbly is also decorous.

Once there

Pour the vino, sit down, and let the flirtations begin. And do take the time to make some conversation.

Thanks for having me!

Even if the booty calls get to be a regular thing, or even if it's the first time, the Fabulous Girl always rings the next day to say thank you—particularly if she was the one who made the booty call.

BOY BENDERS

A Fabulous Girl knows that she can have sex as often and with as many boys as she wants. It may be that she's out of university and is stretching her wings in a new town, or maybe she's recently finished with a long-term relationship. Either way, when the FG wants it, she gets it. But sometimes it's a case of so many men, so little time, because choosing partners for a boy bender is much less fraught than looking for a mate. He needs to be cute, single, and really cute. And since there are so many cute ones out there, why choose only one?

There are, however, certain protocols for managing a boy bender, as it's only a boy bender if there's more than one involved.

First of all, the sex is casual. You may have amazing in-depth discussions about Shakespeare or the plight of the rain forest, but the sex is just sex. If you start to fantasize about his being your boyfriend or you get possessive when you see him flirting with another at a party, you are no longer on a boy bender.

Booty calls are appropriate during boy benders. All you need to do is ask and they will come. You need to say thank you the next day, but you owe nothing more.

If your boys overlap, it is a good idea to select them from different social groups. While the notion of a bad reputation may seem outdated, it is wiser to keep your lovers out of the same gossip loop. You don't want one of them to mention to the other the hot night he spent with this babe. An FG doesn't enjoy seeing two men fight over her. Okay, maybe just a little. It also helps if one boy is in your city and the other is a long-distance romance. That's right, boy benders can still be infused with romance, just not commitment.

There is no need to answer prying questions from the men. "Are you seeing anyone else?" should be dealt with by a swift "I see people." But leave it at that. He doesn't really want to hear about how sexy that Italian actor in Los Angeles is. And you probably don't want to learn of his bombshell from Boston either. But you should be clear about being on a bender so no one gets their feelings hurt.

You're Part of Someone Else's Bender

Boys go on their own benders, too. Hopefully, though, if you end up in bed with a boy on a bender he will have been clear about it beforehand. In the best-case scenario you bump into this guy when you are similarly minded and everybody's happy. However, many men think the only way to get a woman in bed is to come on in the romantic mode of dinners, cute phone messages, compliments, and so on. This is wrong and unkind. The system of dating only works if we all agree upon the same set of semiotics. If a man has taken you out to dinner, suggested a hand-holding walk afterward, plied you with descriptions of your charm, and smooched you in a pool of streetlight and then called you the moment he got home to thank you for a lovely night, you might reasonably imagine he is courting you. If this is an agreeable proposal to you and you are looking for a relationship, you might even have sex with such a man. You might then be quite cross when said man turns to you, in bed, and says, "Oh, I'm not looking for a girlfriend." Of course, if you're the type of girl who will only have sex within the borders of serious relationship territory, it is your responsibility to clarify things before you get there. But it's fair to be irritated if a guy's been acting like he wants to date you when what he really wants is sex and sex only. The upside is, the guy who acts like he has to trick a woman into bed lacks imagination and an evolved view of womanhood and is well left behind. Out of courtesy for the next FG that darkens his door you might give him a tip. "Listen, it's no big deal. I don't know whether or not this might have turned into something else. Just so you know, the way you handled this could have been hurtful. You should say something about what you're after before sleeping with someone." You'll probably receive a call from him in a couple of days wanting to really date, which will be a problem as you've already decided he was kind of a foolish person. Oh, well.

FRIENDS WANT YOU TO KISS AND TELL

Everyone knows that women talk to each other about sex more than men do. Men live in fear of this fact, and with good reason. Girlfriends have no compunction about sharing the intimate details of their current and past affairs. However, there are limits to how much you should shag and tell.

"Was he good?"

You can answer this only in the affirmative. The only man who may be dissed on skill is a lout, an out-of-towner, or someone no one in your social group will ever see again. It's very badly played to sleep with someone all your friends know and then spend a girls-only dinner party detailing the ways that he let you down in bed. The worst thing you can allow yourself to confess is "We didn't click."

Size matters

To men. So unless you're telling war stories from back in the day, refrain from getting into issues of length and girth. Some cheeky
friends may ask you outright if your new lover is a well-hung stud.
A polite FG should answer simply, "Everybody is very happy."

Disease

You never have the right to disclose details of someone else's health
issues.

"He does this thing"

It's perfectly acceptable to describe technique to other FGs without
disclosing names. This is simply doing your part for the sisterhood.
"I had a boyfriend once who could do the most amazing things with
his hips. Have you and Alfred tried it with your legs inside his?"

HE KISSES AND TELLS

This is extremely rare. Everyone knows that it is women who indulge in locker room talk, not guys. Very few men talk to their
friends about the gory details of sex. The most they may divulge is
that it happened with Miss So-and-So. If a man wants to get into
more details with his closest friends there's probably no harm to you.
But if you realize that the guy you're seeing is telling all his friends,
or worse, all of your friends about the sex you're having, you are dealing with a particularly strange guy. He's an exhibitionist and is using
you to shock people. And probably also using you to turn himself
on. Either way it is both juvenile and rude behavior. Naturally you
must tell him to desist immediately but you may also want to con-

sider the motivations behind his actions. Is he trying to embarrass you? And if he thinks of sex as something to shame a woman over, head for the hills, this guy is trouble.

SEX IN PUBLIC PLACES

Got to have it right now? No, not that great pair of Jimmy Choos, but S-E-X. You and your boyfriend have been getting way too hot and heavy walking around the gallery and it's far too long a cab ride back to your place. The Fabulous Girl knows that sex in public isn't necessarily proper, but sometimes she just can't help herself. The FG does, however, know a few good rules for sexy conduct away from the bedroom:

1. Don't assume that if you can't see them, they can't see you. Any couple canoodling in the backseat of a car may have an audience. People love being voyeurs, so know that you are taking the risk of being watched. But then that is no doubt part of the excitement, isn't it? And yes, the car will rock and the windows will fog, so they know what's happening even when they can't see you.

2. Don't choose places where the physical discomfort outweighs the thrill. Avoid rocky beaches (sans blanket), and despite the reputation, airplane washrooms are too tiny and smelly. However, as one Fabulous Girl discovered, the wacky theme hotels in Vegas often have many nooks, crannies, and fountains to help camouflage your little party (especially at night).

3. Don't involve people around you. If you are one of those people who make out at the movies, make it a matinee where the crowd will be sparse and you can plant yourselves well away from

others. Never start anything when people are close enough to you to be made uncomfortable or to have their movie viewing disturbed.

4. Don't take all day. If you are making it in a washroom where people have the expectation of a short wait, make it snappy.

5. Do keep the noise down. Loud moaning or shouting your lover's name will only draw attention to your activity, and could get you arrested.

6. Do know your lover's comfort level. If showing up at his office wearing only a trench coat will mortify him, don't force the issue.

7. Do leave nothing behind but footprints.

PHONE SEX

It's what those old long-distance commercials really meant about that long-distance feeling. If you are separated from your lover or just too lazy to get a cab over to his place late at night, phone sex is a surprisingly good substitute for the real thing. Those who are new to phone sex may feel a little silly at first. It is only sexy if both of you are into it. And it is quite rude to be talking dirty while ironing or watching a gardening show on television. If you are, then you are not having phone sex, you are a phone sex worker. If you're not in the mood for it, your partner will know and it just won't work.

The optimal time for phone sex is late at night before drifting off to sleep, not during your office lunch break (too many distractions). Your lover may ask you to describe in detail things that your mother would scream at if she heard. Do it anyway. Phone sex has to be totally reciprocal to be successful—this means expressing your fantasies as well as playing out his. One of the real benefits of phone sex is that inhibitions fall away when no one is watching. It makes for good practice for later when you are together. Once success has been reached you cannot hang up immediately or answer the call waiting—it is time for phone-line pillow talk.

THE MAN YOU REALLY LIKE IS TERRIBLE IN BED

It's one of the most painful yet prevalent myths that if you really like someone, you'll have great sex. Oh, would it were true. But as every FG knows, having conversational or intellectual chemistry with someone does not necessarily mean your click will be heard in the bedroom. Still, it is possible to get what you want out of sex.

The confident Fabulous Girl understands that a spoonful of sugar really does make the medicine go down. Try a little inventive encouragement before anything else. Telling a man he has great hands will induce him to use them, and from there the FG can do the guiding.

Of course, some men need less subtle hints. If the compliment route doesn't get you there, you'll have to be more direct. Don't be shy. Forget the idea that it's not sexy to ask for what you want in bed. It would be rude not to give your lover the chance to rock your world just because you didn't want to speak up.

Tit for tat

The FG fancies herself good in bed, and part of maintaining that is knowing what her lover wants. So even if you despise having your ear kissed, indulge him; it's likely a sign he'd like the maneuver re-ciprocated. Likewise, if you swoon when your ankles are stroked, make a play for his; a sensitive lover will get the message that you'd like some ankle action yourself. But it's not necessary that lovemaking be exactly reciprocal. Sex would be rather dull if it were simply a Ping-Pong game of I-do-it-to-you-and-then-you-do-it-to-me. There is, of course, a comfort-level issue too: if you really get squeamish about a specific thing, then you should just say so.

Conversation

Talk is not cheap in bed. Conventional wisdom says you shouldn't engage in potentially difficult conversations about sex while you're in bed. Pshaw. Where are you going to have those little chats, in aisle 4 of Home Depot? We're not recommending a talk that takes place during lovemaking, rather some other quiet time in bed, say, Sunday morning. However, if you are in the throes of passion, there is no better time to whisper seductive instructions to him. In this case, it may be wiser to show than to tell.

Being a great lover, the FG also understands that it is better to give. The flip side of all this advice is generosity. Going out of your way to please a lover is not only polite, it ups the likelihood that he'll do the same for you.

HE CAN'T GET IT UP

You think everything is going swimmingly, and then suddenly it's not and he rolls off you and stares up at the ceiling. He's lost his hard-on and in its place a black cloud is hovering over the bed. It happens. No man likes it, and few handle the situation well. The main thing is to keep things light—at least on your part. Ask him if he'd like you to . . . or maybe he'd like it if you gave him a little . . . or would he like to take a break for a couple of minutes? Whatever you do, don't prop up on one elbow, look searchingly in his eyes, and ask, "What's wrong?" The word *wrong* spoken in the vicinity of a flaccid penis has very bad juju for men. Don't do it. And though you may be frustrated that things have ground to a halt, it's better to change the subject and talk about something else, maybe mention that you're quite tired yourself. Although you may be thinking, "Well, it doesn't stop me from being able to have an orgasm!" it's probably best to just let that slide this time.

I Love You, You Love Me Not

A surefire passion killer is confessing your love for a new beau only to have him go cold or simply pretend he didn't hear you. How do you handle it when you say "I love you" first and he doesn't respond in kind? It's a nightmare, basically. A good guy will try to make you feel okay about this situation even if he's not ready to speak the words you were hoping for. He'll tell you how happy that makes him and how much you mean to him. If he freezes or looks terrified, you're with a man with little grace. A man with little grace who doesn't love you. Get out.

You Have VD

The time to discuss health issues with a new lover is before sex. It's a given that you're going to be using condoms when you start a new romance. But what if there's something particular for you to say? For example, "I have herpes." You cannot in good conscience start a romance without being honest about the state of your health. You must give the new lover the chance to make a choice, and you must tell him about it before you have sex. The information needn't be dispensed on your first introduction—wait until you know that sex is a given in every other way. Maybe there's been some snogging on the couch and he asks if you can move the action into the bedroom. That's your moment. While you're still comfortably wrapped up, calmly tell him there's something he needs to know.

That is, of course, if your sexually transmitted disease is a permanent one. If what you have is something such as chlamydia, which can be successfully treated, you don't have to tell him. Unfortunately, many people consider VD a dirty, despicable thing that only the sexually promiscuous can catch. They're wrong, but the stigma survives. But while you can protect your privacy, you can't have sex with him—not even with a condom. Just be patient until you get your negative test result and then you can have all the fun you want.

Breaking it to your mate that you have VD

There's no easy way to break the news to your boyfriend that you have a sexually transmitted disease. Especially since the implication is so obvious it glows in the dark—you cheated on him. In fact, it may be better to tell him first about your indiscretion, then admit that the story doesn't end with the affair. What happens to your relationship will be up to the two of you. You cannot mess with his health.

Telling an ex-lover you may have given him VD

If you only recently discovered your "problem" and you're single, you have a different set of dilemmas on your hands. You realize that it could have been one of five men who gave it to you, and that means you may have given it to any and all of the others. Ugh. You need to tell everyone what's going on. This needn't be a long call, but a simple "You should know . . . I'm sorry." In fact, some STD clinics will do this for you. You give them the list, they'll place the calls without giving your name. The seriousness of the disease may determine how you handle the situation.

DISCUSSING HIS SEXUAL HEALTH

A new lover should definitely share any problems he has with his sexual health—be they chronic or a one-time issue—before the two of you get down to it for the first time. It's reasonable to expect that he'll wait until there's been some making out. After all, why tell you if it doesn't look like it's going to end up there? But he must slow things down and tell you the truth. If he does handle it in this responsible way, it behooves you to receive the news with grace. You must be warm and nonjudgmental about it even if what you decide is to end the courtship. If you don't feel comfortable moving ahead with someone who has herpes then you must tell him that you need time to do a little of your own research about transmission and think it over. If you do decide to continue with this person—and really, there's no reason not to—then keep the information to yourself. This is not one of the things you can share with your girlfriends. If you have sex with a man and he tells you about his gonorrhea in the afterglow you have every right to be angry. He's a reckless and irresponsible person who must be done away with immediately. He's also the reason you must use condoms until you've had this kind of conversation.

HE GIVES YOU VD

If you are in a long-term relationship and you've recently found suspicious bumps down there, you will probably be shocked and angered by your discovery. But if your lover is denying any wrongdoing, he may just be innocent. Learn the facts. If it is something such as warts or herpes, then it could have been dormant and only just surfaced. However, you have the right to be upset for not having been warned about the risk involved in even a dormant virus. This is a vitally important trust issue. Of course, if it is something that recurs, you may have a cheater on your hands. Unlike with a new lover, there is no need to behave with stoicism. Feel free to be angry. Feel free to storm out of the room. Feel free to dump him.

THE CONDOM BREAKS

It happens. A too-small condom slips off without either of you noticing or it tears and you realize it after—either way, the condom has let you down. If you're also on the pill then all you're concerned about is STDs. A trip to the doctor in a couple of days can clear up any worries you have. If the condom was your form of birth control, however, you're in a different kind of mess. Most emergencies or walk-in clinics are stocked with the dreaded morning-after pill, which is simply a super dose of birth control. Lover boy should absolutely accompany you on this little trip and check in on you later to ask how you're feeling. The answer will be terrible, as those pills contain nasty quantities of hormones that will rock your body and your emotions for at least a day or so.

YOU GET PREGNANT

No matter how super-extra-strength the condom she employed along with her birth control pill was, sometimes a woman gets pregnant without planning on it. If this happens, she does need to tell the man involved. This should be done in person and in private. No beating around the bush either. Just say it like it is.

Unfortunately, there are men out there who will doubt that they are the father of the child. Some cads may deny responsibility until provided with proof. It is sad but true that you may have to get DNA evidence to confirm what you already know to be true.

A certain famous Fabulous Girl was publicly humiliated when her boyfriend denied his responsibility for her pregnancy. Of course, she handled it with her trademark sophistication and did not resort to hysterics or mudslinging. And in the end, her quiet confidence prevailed when it was proved that the lout was the father.

Now, FGs are sexually liberated, so if you've been on a boy bender and find yourself with child but without secure knowledge of the father's identity, you need to inform the boys that fatherhood is pending for one of them. This may seem unreasonable or unfair for the FG, but it is not only her life at stake; the child and man have to be thought of too.

In all of these cases, an FG needs to think carefully about how she will manage her future. And her baby's future. Although she may be able to extract financial assistance from the father, it is not possible to extract a partnership from a man who was made a parent against his will.

An FG who is quite clear that she doesn't want to keep the baby created through this accident may be ambivalent about sharing the news with a man she's not that close to. After all, what if he doesn't feel the same? What if he's got strong feeling against abortion or has been longing to become a parent? There's always a risk that your lover may lay any of these surprises on you, but you still must tell him. It's not right to keep this kind of information from a man. It would be very difficult indeed for him to stop you from doing what you feel is right, anyway. It might be very difficult and painful for you both if you disagree but at least you will have done the right thing in a difficult situation.

∞ *Courtship* ∞

Sex without love can be fine for the single FG. But if a relationship is what she's after, she must enter the dating minefield. The truth of the matter is that no one really enjoys dating. Dating is a horrid ritual designed to weed out the unwanted and the undesirable. Of course, it may take years of marriage to truly know whether one made the right choice, but often one or two dates (or one or two minutes) may suffice.

HOW TO ESCAPE A NIGHTMARE DATE

Date going badly? He's a total jerk? The Fabulous Girl knows the difference between a dull man—she simply declines dessert and coffee and goes home—and the asshole who spends dinner ranting about what bitches all his exes (and women in general) are. If it's the latter, the FG can make a guilt-free run for it. A sudden headache, a forgotten meeting, an unexpected business trip with an early morning flight—all are acceptable excuses. However, heading to the ladies' never to return is not okay. If the man is truly offensive, there is nothing wrong with the FG speaking her mind: "You know, Bob, I think you're just too angry toward brunettes and your language is too offensive for me to want to continue our date. Thanks for dinner." With this and a toss of her hair, the FG can leave. If you don't care for the notion of owing this lout anything, then toss a twenty on the table as you flounce out the door.

YOU'RE ON A CRUSH TO NOWHERE

He's handsome, smart, and witty and has a dynamic career. So now you have a crush. He's also single. Your crush just got worse. You want to date him, sleep with him, fall in love, and marry him. Trouble is, he doesn't seem to know you're alive. But what is even more mortifying is that despite your FG-ness, every time he comes your way to talk to you (he seems interested), you yammer like a fool. Your jokes aren't funny. You stutter. The best plan of action in this case is to shut up. Do less and don't try to impress until your nervousness wears off. Your reticence will draw him to you. At least this way you'll seem mysterious, not goofy.

While crushes can be crushing, there is no reason that an FG has to sit on the sidelines when he's around. If he still doesn't get how fab you are, then allow the FG in you to take over and ask him out. That's right, this is where those art gallery tickets you just happened to have will come in handy. And since you've traded in your nervous-Nelly-when-he's-around self for the cool air of aloofness, if he does turn you down, it won't show.

YOU'RE OUT WITH YOUR CRUSH AND HIS FRIEND STARTS HITTING ON YOU

When you're in crush mode you may think that it's obvious to the world who the object of your affection is. Not so. An FG with a boy on her mind may simply be radiating generalized crush energy, which, like high-pitched sounds that only dogs can hear, will be apparent to other men as well. You may find yourself out with a gang of friends just waiting until you can swap seats with Alice and be seated next to your crush, when his friend makes his way over to you. Who can blame him? You're looking cute, you're making charming and amusing cocktail banter. How is he to know that it's not meant for him? Trouble is, he's your crush's pal. You can't shut him down the way you might with a perfect stranger. You have to handle this with some delicacy. Go ahead and have a fun, even mildly flirtatious exchange with the pal. Obviously you must keep things light and breezy. Try to include other people in the conversation you're having, a sure sign that you're not really interested. Give the friend next to you a little pinch so she starts paying attention to what's going on at your end of the table. Excuse yourself to the ladies' room and come back and join a different conversational circle, hopefully one with your crush. If you think that your crush is noticing a nonexistent connection between you and his pal, clear things up. All you have to do is say, "You know, I have a friend that Paul would like. He's such a nice guy, he should meet this great girl I know . . ."

YOU CONFESS YOUR FEELINGS FOR A LONG-TIME PAL—AND THEY'RE NOT RECIPROCATED

There's usually wine involved. After one of those great four-hour dinners the two of you have when you make each other laugh and solve each other's career dilemmas, you and your perfect male friend are smiling across the table at each other. Before you can stop them, the words are flying out of your mouth. "Why aren't we together?" And he does the thing. He makes that pained "Oh no, I have to hurt my friend" face. And you feel that you may be ill. Of course it's devastating to have confessed your feelings only to have them rejected, even if it's in the sweetest, kindest way (isn't that just like him!). You may want to cut the evening short now and he should understand that you feel embarrassed and need to be alone. You may even need to take a little breather from spending so much time together. It's not right if you've been concealing the true nature of your feelings for him, he's been thinking you're great pals, and you've been secretly pining. Take some time to adjust to the reality that you're not going to be a couple. Of course, he'll probably call you to try and talk it over or make you feel better about it. Try not to be angry at him; if it's too uncomfortable for you say so, but don't get nasty because he doesn't feel the same way.

He Has a Crush on You—But You Have a Boyfriend

Perhaps it's a professional circumstance that has brought you and the Handsome Stranger into such close quarters. You exchange casual banter at first, not thinking much about the situation—you'll probably never see the guy again, right? Then your chat turns serious, you start riffing on art, literature, cinema, you're really hitting it off. This is fun. Until at the end it seems that your Handsome Stranger now has a crush on you. But your boyfriend never came up. Why would he, considering that the intention of the meeting was business—who could have predicted such a spontaneous connection? Besides, this innocent flirting is fun. Why ruin it with a bit of fact?

Trouble is, Handsome has now invited you out for lunch to

discuss things further. Ugh. The nagging question is this: Has he asked you out? Or is he just being friendly?

When does an FG cop to having a full-time boyfriend? No one should introduce themselves to a member of the opposite sex by saying, "Hi, I'm FG and I have a boyfriend." Likewise, if Handsome does invite you to his home for a dinner party with a select number of people, how can you be sure that he doesn't simply think you're a fascinating person (which as an FG you are)? If you say, "I'd love to come, but you have to know I have a boyfriend," it can only lead to the embarrassing response, "That's fine, I'm not really interested in you in that way." Mortifying.

If, dear FG, you find yourself asked on some sort of quasi-date, you should simply decline. But do not use your beau as the excuse. Rather, next time you speak to Handsome, let it drop: "My boyfriend and I are heading to Florida for the weekend, I so need a vacation . . ." Or if there's an event where Handsome will be, bring your beau along and introduce them. Another last resort in desperate times is to have a mutual friend let Handsome know the truth. This can actually spare both of you the awkwardness.

MATCHMAKING FGS

So your friend Sophie is fabulous and single, and your Chapstick Harrison is amazing and surprisingly single. What's an FG to do? She wants everyone to be happy and find love, or at least great sex, so she sets them up. Only Sophie is still reeling from a breakup and Harrison just wants to have fun, so their date is a disaster. Sophie talks endlessly about her doomed affair with Bingo, and Harrison can't stop flirting with the cute waitress. This type of incident could have been avoided if the FG had done her research. It is highly unfabulous to set up two people who are not in the same mental place, no matter how cute you think they'd be together or how much you think they have in common.

Sometimes someone will agree to be set up without actually being ready. They'll feel pressured to get back into the dating game when what they really need is time alone. Often friends don't understand this need and keep nagging their single friend to "get out there." Wherever "there" is exactly isn't clear. It is far better to tell your friend that you know of another singleton when she's ready to date.

If the Fabulous Girl is the one being forced into setups, she should remember she never has to cave to these pressures. A firm "I'm not ready, but thanks for thinking of me" is enough.

Let's face it, most setups don't work. There's something inherently unromantic about them. One Fabulous Girl went hopefully to a friend's potluck to be set up; unfortunately, the intended man sat opposite her eating potato salad with his hands. An FG always favors the fantasy of meeting that sexy stranger on her own, where the two of them just can't take their eyes off each other. But if she's game, at least she can discover for herself if being set up is for her.

BAD BLIND DATES

In some cultures, blind dates are the standard mode of meeting potential mates. In others, it's hell in a bread basket. If you decide to embark on a date with a man you've never met—or worse, have never even seen a photo of—then be prepared to run.

Agree to meet only in a public place. Arrange for afternoon coffee so that you can escape as soon as possible if necessary. In fact, if you see him and know immediately that the thought of his laying a hand on you is grounds for antacid, then order a cold beverage, such as iced tea, that you can down in a hurry.

Dress nicely for your meeting, but not too sexy, just in case you have the above-mentioned reaction. You are also never obliged to give out your home number or address, or to agree to another date if you don't want to. If the blind date came through a friend, you are probably less concerned about his being a mad killer, but if you got him through the personals, on- or off-line, be cautious. In the latter situation you can even drag a friend along to sit anonymously at another table and keep her eye on things.

Always bring your cell phone with you on dates. That way you can nip to the ladies' room and make a quick call to a friend to discuss how things are going or ask for advice. Or ask her and her boyfriend to meet you and your new friend at a bar in half an hour so you can have a change of scenery.

SAYING NO TO THE SECOND DATE

If you went out on a first date with a man, it's likely that he will want to go on a second date with you. But if things didn't really go well on the first, the FG will have a hard time gearing up for another try. Being an instinctive, passionate girl, this just isn't likely. You owe it to the guy to let him know the truth right away. Not that you never want to see him naked—although that's obviously true. That you're not going to go out again. Tell him you're not ready to date right now. Tell him you don't think the two of you made that kind of connection. Whatever you do, don't sound overly apologetic. This is and will be perceived as patronizing. Avoid the really bad clichés—I'd like to be friends, you're a great guy. You shouldn't imagine that he doesn't already know that.

HE DOESN'T CALL

It's hard to fathom how someone becomes an adult without learning a few key concepts, like when it's appropriate to call the person you're dating. Alas, it's either true that some men don't know when they should make the call or they do know and are using the absence of a call as a tool of torture. If a man doesn't call after a great date it's because it wasn't great for him. This may seem impossible to get your head around. You were there after all, having a good time. But when a man wants to see you again, he calls. If he doesn't, he's just not that interested. Of course, you can call; particularly if he asked you out the first time, you may feel that it's your turn to do the asking now. That's fine but you won't know if a man really likes you until you don't call and he does. It's how they work. It's the same with sex; if he doesn't call you the next day or the day after that at the most, he's not thinking of you in a romantic way. If a guy is into you he wants to make sure that no other man has access to you and will want to book your time. It's hurtful in the moment but it's better to figure out what he's all about as soon as possible. As for the man who takes you out several times and then evaporates like mist? He's met someone else.

YOU DISCOVER HE'S MARRIED

When he said he was separated you had the reasonable expectation that what he meant was that he had a different address from his ex-wife, not that they were on separate roads in life. Occasionally an FG will have the misfortune to cross paths with this kind of cowardly liar, the man who lies about his marital status. Exactly what stage you're in with Mr. Married will have considerable bearing on your course of action.

A passionate kiss: You've always found him sexy; finally you're alone and sipping cocktails and dining on oysters in a swanky hotel bar, when he leans in and plants a fabulous kiss on you. Then he blurts out the truth, or worse, you ask (hey, you probably already expected it didn't you?) if he's married. If the answer is yes you can express your disappointment, even stand up and march out of the scene and out of his life. Don't call him again; he owes you nothing more than a feeble explanation.

You've had sex: You asked all the people you thought knew him, yet strangely, none of them knew if he was married. Then the odd times he telephones you, the cell-number-as-only-number he gave you, and the way you have sex only at your place hits you. He's married. However you discover his lie—and these guys are always found out—you'll have every right to be furious. You'll also have every right to send a note to his wife letting her in on his secret as well. You should not, at any cost, indulge in thoughts of his leaving his wife for you. If he couldn't even be straight with you about it in the first place, he'll never come clean with her.

YOU'RE HAVING AN AFFAIR

Whether it's your illicit sex or your friend's, there are certain rules of decorum governing cheating hearts.

For one, you should not directly involve your friends in the romance. You may initially want to discuss your transgression in order to seek their advice, but if what you're really looking for is approval you may be disappointed. If a friend gives you a figurative slap upside of the head, you should respect that and, even if you do continue your affair, refrain from discussing it with this person.

Do not ask your friend to lie for you. As we've said, your moral compromise should not be foisted on another. Again, your FG friend may tell your husband you were with her once or twice, but she probably doesn't feel good about it.

This is also probably one of the only occasions in which no introductions are necessary. Of course, being in the throes of passion with New Guy, you may be desperate to show off, perhaps even thinking that if your friend only met your lover she'd understand why you're cheating. Again, this is fooling yourself. It is best to remain discreet.

∞ *The Men* ∞

As the Fabulous Girl gets older, the men who are available to court her may shift in demographic. The single ones may be single for a reason, divorced, or much younger than she. These men represent the extreme ends of the single-guy spectrum and come with their own warning labels.

THE DIVORCING MAN

This is a man in transition. He's both vulnerable and bitter. The first may appeal to the FG, but the second will drive her nuts. This period will include long, intimate, and tearful conversations with the estranged wife and perhaps their kids.

Danger Zone: He's going to be sad. He's going to be angry. He's going to use you as his rebound.

Early Warning Sign: He won't stop talking about the divorce, the legal fees, and how he wishes it had all worked out differently.

THE SECONDHAND MAN

Stage two of the above. However, he's probably had his rebound. In some ways these men make the best potential partners. They've been through a marriage, so chances are their expectations are more realistic. In this situation the Fabulous Girl will shine. But if he's paying alimony or child support, the FG needs to be aware that his financial—and in the case of kids, emotional—priorities may lie elsewhere.

Danger Zone: Bitterness may still linger, depending on the divorce.

Early Warning Sign: Every time you have an argument, he compares you to his ex-wife.

MR. DAD

The older you get—or the older your dates get—the more likely it is that each of you will be bringing more than psychological baggage to the new relationship. You may meet a man who not only has been married in the past but has kids.

If you're dating someone with kids, it's wise to put off meeting them until you and your man are very certain that this is going to be a long-term relationship. It's too hard on you and it's not fair to them otherwise. Make this clear to your new guy right from the start. Let him know that you appreciate how important his children are to him. In fact, that's exactly why you'd rather wait to meet them, because you recognize that their well-being should be treated seriously. And really, you owe it to yourself to see how serious you are about him before you wade into what will certainly be a difficult situation.

Danger Zone: You need to decide if you can play second banana to the kids, or at least feel noncompetitive.

Early Warning Sign: He constantly cancels plans with you to be with the kids.

THE OLDER MAN

Some FGs swear by older men: they tend to appreciate the FG's wit, passion, and—okay, let's say it—her youthful skin and body. It would be unrealistic to say that the older guy doesn't on some level relish the simple fact that the FG is younger, but that shouldn't be the sole reason to be together. The Fabulous Girl will appreciate the older guy who has already accomplished many of his professional goals, who is happy with who he is and where he is at this stage of his life. This type of solid man can be a great support to the FG who is still working on her career. Sex with the older guy can also be great; he probably knows a few things the FG doesn't, yet he's patient enough to take time with sex. But be aware that women of his generation will often resent you and give you dirty looks—even in the supermarket.

Danger Zone: The FG may be a mere trophy girl.

Early Warning Sign: Your intimate dinner dates are few. Instead, he always takes you to cocktail parties and business functions where he can show you off.

THE YOUNGER MAN

The main benefit to the Fabulous Girl here is sex, sex, and sex. The college-age frat boy may not appeal to the FG for long, but his admiration for his "older" lover and his libido are great distractions in between more serious relationships.

Danger Zone: In the majority of cases, he is a mere dalliance.

Early Warning Sign: His age.

THE DIFFERENT MAN

If the Fabulous Girl is trying to change her "type," she may find herself in unfamiliar waters. If the dark, brooding sculptor is the one who makes her melt but breaks her heart, the FG may wish to go in the opposite direction and date a highly rational lawyer or scientist. For this huge swing, the FG must be open-minded and patient, not just dismiss the guy on the first date because he doesn't mold clay with his bare hands. She needs to uncover what other types of chemistry may be brought out.

Danger Zone: You may have a type for a reason, and the different man will not be challenging and engaging in the ways that matter to the FG.

Early Warning Sign: You keep telling your friends that he's great, but you can't understand why you're not more attracted to him.

THE RICH MAN

Many women target a Mr. Rich. The Fabulous Girl cannot deny the pleasure of the finer things in life. If she gets involved with a rich man, however, she may find that he not only pays for everything, he makes all the decisions too. Where you eat, what play you see, where you holiday. It is up to the FG to decide her threshold for passivity.

Danger Zone: You get too used to the fine life but can't afford it without Mr. Rich.

Early Warning Sign: You stop even reaching for the check.

THE POOR MAN

Depending on the financial status of the FG, dating a man of little economic means will resonate differently. If both of you are poor, there may be no tension around money. But if the Fabulous Girl has some money and has fallen for a starving actor, she may end up supporting them in a lifestyle only she can afford.

Danger Zone: It is easy for this situation to turn from romance to resentment—on both sides.

Early Warning Sign: He says no to your invitations to dine out.

THE CHEAP MAN

This one is easy for the Fabulous Girl. Get rid of him. There is nothing less attractive than a cheap man. Every single thing you want to do as a couple will be fraught. He will nix your choice of clothing, cars, decor, art. He seems to be saving for a rainy day that never comes.

Danger Zone: You'll convince yourself that he's just good with money.

Early Warning Sign: He asks you out on a first date and all you order is a cranberry juice, but he doesn't offer to pay and instead splits the bill.

THE CONTROL FREAK

Everything you do has to be done his way. Right down to how you slice bread. It takes a very strong FG to put up with this crap. She's going to have tell him where to put his "advice" until he learns to back off.

Danger Zone: You may start to doubt yourself and lose confidence.

Early Warning Sign: He starts most sentences with a version of "Why are you doing it that way?"

THE USER

It takes some time for her to see it, but eventually the FG attached to a user starts to sense a pattern. He wants you to introduce him to all the people in your industry (the one he has just switched over to). He wants you to set up meetings for him with your boss and your boss's boss. Worse, he wants to show you off to his ex and insists on going places she'll be.

Danger Zone: You feel guilty not being helpful; you doubt your own instincts.

Early Warning Sign: All his conversations start with, "Could you . . . ?"

THE PLAYER

At first he seemed sexy; now you feel sick to your stomach every time the two of you go to a party. When you meet a player he seems so charming, but then you realize that his charms aren't only for you but for every woman he comes in contact with. When you bring it up, he calls you jealous. And hey, you are, but that's how you should feel when your boyfriend flirts too much.

Danger Zone: You become desperate for his attention.

Early Warning Zone: You can't relax at a party if he's out of your sight.

THE FIXER-UPPER

He's 75 percent the great guy. He's smart but can't keep a job. He's funny but dresses like a bum. He's sweet but he eats with his mouth open. You look upon him as a diamond in the rough, only he is really cubic zirconia. It's not fair to him to constantly be giving him little tips on how to improve. In fact, it's mean. You'll both end up miserable and you'll be keeping him from the woman who loves badly dressed, out-of-work men with bad table manners. But that's not an FG.

Danger Zone: You end up making excuses for him.

Early Warning Zone: You don't want to introduce him to your friends.

BAD IN BED

No matter how much encouragement an FG gives to a new lover, there are times when the sexual chemistry just isn't there. And the sad fact is, it never will be there. If the sex is still bad after five months, it won't get better. This is cause enough to end the relationship. Those who say sex isn't that important have never had great sex.

Danger Zone: You convince yourself that he's perfect in every other way.

Early Warning Sign: See Danger Zone.

Elenor seemed to be accepting that being pregnant was going to alter her dating habits until the baby was born. One friend's drama solved. And what about Nice? He was still behaving strangely. He was distant yet refused to discuss it. Then there was Missy. She invited me over for dinner, sent the car and driver for me and everything. Joe was away on business.

"I want to have an affair with Francis."

"I did notice you kissing him at that party." I was trying to be calm, but I was wondering if all my friends had lost their minds. "Did you sleep together?"

"Not yet."

Of course, I wanted to ask why she wanted to have an affair, but it was usually better to let Missy ask the questions.

"What do you think?"

"I think you're married, Missy."

She sighed. This clearly wasn't the response she wanted.

Then she talked and talked and talked. How Joe didn't seem to love her, how he was just an idiot who couldn't rake leaves properly, let alone have sex with any degree of passion. He was always working and just wasn't fun anymore. She wanted a divorce.

Missy had gotten married in a hurry, so if her marriage didn't work it wasn't exactly a shock to me. Joe was nice, but in a vacant sort of way.

None of us, Missy included, really seemed to know what he did. Still, I couldn't lie.

"But Missy, it's your marriage. Don't you owe it to Joe and yourself to try harder?"

"Ugh, what do you know?" she snapped at me.

"I know that fucking Francis isn't going to make your marriage better. And that if what you want is a divorce then you should leave Joe and forget about the affair thing. It's not you."

I could tell Missy wasn't pleased. She'd enjoyed that exciting first-kiss rush she'd had with Francis. The rush that married people obsess over losing and that gives single people no small amount of anxiety.

"If you have an affair you'll regret it. What if Francis is the right guy?" Missy was piqued.

"If Francis is the one, do you want to begin the relationship full of lies and deceit? He'd never trust you."

Another sigh. "You're right, but he's so cute."

"What about marriage counseling?"

"I don't believe in shrinks, you know that."

"It's not a shrink, really, it's someone to talk to."

She was becoming more irritated.

"Why don't you and Nice see a counselor? You two don't seem so happy nowadays."

She had struck a nerve with her very special brand of Missy-ness.

"We're not talking about me. Go ahead, sleep with Francis. I just hope the sex is worth it."

With that, I got up and left. Her car and driver took me home. I was upset and anxious and wanted to call Nice. If Missy had noticed our relationship troubles, then it was obvious something needed to be done. I needed to know what he was thinking. Maybe I was about to become a single girl again.

CHAPTER SIX

Coupledom

Nice had been avoiding me—headaches, work, whatever he could come up with. But when I got home from Missy's, I found Nice lying on my couch, watching TV with Kitty. Trouble was, we hadn't planned to spend the night together. Sure, it was nice that he'd surprised me by letting himself in with the keys I'd given him. Well, to be honest, I'd have preferred it if he'd called first, but I was always so happy to see him that it wasn't a big deal.

We smooched on the couch for a bit and then moved to the bedroom. We smooched on the bed and then got under the covers, when something happened. Or rather, it didn't happen. It un-happened. Which had never happened before. We were both quiet for a while, lying in the dark.

"Is something wrong?" I asked, turning on my side and propping myself up on one elbow.

"*Wrong* is really not a good word to use in these moments," said Nice.

"I take your point. Okay. Um, how are you?" I asked.

"I'm fine. We don't have to talk about it. I'm just tired." Nice sighed.

"You did seem a little, um, distant when I got home," I said.

"I was expecting you to be here. Not that you have to tell me what you're doing every night. It just felt a little weird, that's all. To be here and you weren't here. It made me realize that I'd like to be here when you're not here and have it not be weird."

"Well, the only way I can imagine that is if we were living together." I started laughing and then realized that Nice wasn't. "Oh. That's what you meant. You want to live together."

Now Nice propped himself up on one elbow and smiled. "Yes, I do. We've been together for more than a year now. We're together all the time. I'm tired of us both dragging all our stuff back and forth across the city. I want to have all our stuff in one place."

"It's not so much stuff to drag around. Contact lens stuff and the pill . . ."

Nice rolled onto his back again. He pulled the covers up.

"It's just that after my experience with Groovy . . . It was such a disaster living with him and then splitting up."

"I'm not Groovy," said Nice. His voice was getting hard.

"I know you're not. I guess I'm still not ready."

We lay there in silence. I felt lonely and didn't know what to do for myself, let alone how to make Nice feel better somehow. There were suddenly miles between us rather than the couple of inches that separated us in my bed. Eventually we fell asleep.

∽ Coupledom ∾

THE FABULOUS GIRL LOVES being in love, and often for her love can best be realized in a long-term relationship. She values the closeness that comes with relationships that last and she doesn't stop behaving with decorum as her romance ages. Coupledom creates a variety of challenges that can only be met with experience. Not to say that it gets easier with time and age, but time and age do help the FG take things in her high-heeled stride. As well as contending with her own beau, an FG must also interact with her friends' men—and her own list of ex-boyfriends.

∽ Relationship Woes ∾

YOUR FRIENDS DON'T LIKE YOUR BOYFRIEND

You love your boyfriend, Billy. You're so happy to have finally met someone who has all the qualities you find important: honesty, sense of humor, handsomeness, and so on. Then why is it that your inner circle, your Fabulous Girl posse, hates Billy? Or if they don't out and out despise him, they are at best indifferent. When you discuss a future with your beau, your best gal pal doesn't get excited with you, but simply says, "Don't you think it's a bit soon to be discussing living together?"

This situation can be vexing, but since we're talking about your friends there is only one approach. Ask them *why* they seem to dislike Billy. It may take some convincing that you really do want their opinion—after all, friendships can be strained by such criticism—but when they do come clean, remember you asked. Don't be angry and try not to get defensive (which will be hard since you love Billy). Calmly explain why you don't think he's a player or whatever the issue may be. See if you can come to some understanding with your friends about their behavior toward your boyfriend; explain to them how their attitude makes you feel. If they are your friends they will make the effort to accept Billy. Consider also that you may not have given your friends and Billy the right opportunities to bond. One bad experience may have made you keep them apart, only exacerbating your pals' distrust of Billy.

FG Caveat: If your friends really get a bad vibe about your boyfriend, based on their observations about how he treats you, the FG must take their concerns to heart. After all, maybe they see something you don't, say a controlling or condescending nature that will spell trouble in the future. The Fabulous Girl owes herself a long look at the relationship; her friends may have put doubts in her mind for a reason.

Your Family Doesn't Like Your Boyfriend

Sure, your family loves you and wants what's best for you, but remember that families, particularly parents, may have vastly different ideas from your own about what's best. They may not like Billy because he's a struggling actor and they see you married to a lawyer instead. Or they may not like that he's older, divorced, and so on. When your family is hostile to your boyfriend it can be the most uncomfortable circumstance to be in. Unlike friends, whom you can have it out with in the ladies' room, family is more fraught with years of hidden meanings, skeletons in closets, and the ilk. Try to get to the bottom of it. If your mom keeps complaining about how Billy doesn't have a real job, you need to assure her that you're happy and that you know what you want. If she gets to the point where Billy finds himself uninvited to family gatherings, you will have to put your foot down. "Mom, Billy is my boyfriend; either we're both staying for Thanksgiving or neither of us are." This may seem harsh and difficult, given it's your mother, but as an adult the FG must stand up for herself.

Again, as in the case of friends, if your family's dislike of your beau is very specific—"I don't like the way he orders you around"—you should consider their concerns. Maybe they are right.

YOUR SEX LIFE IS OFF

Sex is central to a happy relationship. But relationships do change and you may have to remind yourself of what you found sexy about your partner when you were first together. "Doing it" during the day can be a great way to keep sex vital in your relationship. It says, "We're not just doing it because we happen to be in bed together— either at night or first thing in the morning—we're doing it because we're spontaneously drawn to each other." Of course, it's inconvenient, but that's part of what makes it good. You might have to cancel a meeting to do it. Call him at work and ask him if he can meet you at home for lunch. Or if he works in an office with good soundproofing and a door (with a lock), you could pay him a surprise visit at work.

YOU'RE IN A DOWN CYCLE

A relationship is a living thing, and although most patterns emerge within the first few months—sometimes it seems like just weeks—

they are not set in stone. The balance of affection can alter over time. It's hard to pinpoint why, but it does. You can be looking at the man you thought you'd chew your own right arm off for and suddenly feel, "Whatever . . ." You still love him, still love having sex with him, but it just doesn't feel as desperate anymore. Then a scary thought occurs to you: what if he feels the same way?

The Fabulous Girl doesn't panic about this shift in her sex life. She can, however, do a few things to ascertain if this is a temporary lull or if the sizzle has fizzled beyond repair.

It is never easy to discuss sex with your partner, whether the issue is not enough or just a general blah, particularly if you're in the middle of sex, so save the heart-to-heart until later. First, do what you can to see if you can jazz it up between the sheets, say skip the sheets altogether and seduce him on the sofa, in the kitchen, or on the way home from dinner in the back of a cab. If you both get hot and heavy, chances are your lull was just that and a bit of spontaneity will do the trick. If it is just a normal lull you can calm down and enjoy other things more, like going to films or art gallerys together. Your sex life will improve and go back to the way it was or better. The worst thing to do in this situation is to overanalyze it. Try to enjoy the shift and remember that things can always change again. Which is pretty exciting when you think about it.

If, however, your little FG sex tricks don't do it for him or you, you will need to move to phase two, the discussion. Don't begin with "Our sex life sucks." Try "Are you feeling stressed out lately? You don't seem as attentive as you were." Or "Have you noticed that we both seem to be so stressed out that we aren't spending the same time with each other?" Either of these two statements will launch the discussion. Just be prepared to hear the truth. Maybe he doesn't feel as he once did and his decreased ardor is playing out in the bedroom. This is of course the worst-case scenario and will lead to a breakup. Or maybe it's you who have turned off and he thinks everything is fine. Then you need to think about how you really feel.

Once the discussion is over give it a few weeks to see if it has sunk in for both of you. But if you're still feeling blah about him you may need to reevaluate. Sex is very important to a healthy relationship; you can't just trick yourself into staying with the man because he may one day make a great father or whatever. Hot sex is vital to monogamy; if he can't rock your world your best bet is to find someone who does.

He Won't Apologize

Women need apologies. Men seem to be able to go about their business after a snarl and can wait for days to revisit the subject of the argument. An FG could more easily flap her arms and fly to Australia. She must have a resolution to an argument, and she must have it as soon after the argument as possible. Until she has it, she will be unable to do just about anything else. To achieve satisfaction, then, an FG may need to shift her sense of what goes into an apology. Of course, what you really want after a dispute is for your man to realize he was wrong, to appreciate why you were right, and to suffer over the pain the argument inflicted upon you. Alas, this is rarely how it goes. In fact, it almost never goes this way. You may never resolve the misunderstanding. It is far more productive to apologize for the fact of the fight than to struggle for perfect mutual understanding. And if you are on the receiving end of an apology that simply says, "Baby, I'm sorry we fought, I hate to upset you,"

you should accept this with grace and move on. Never make a man—or anyone, really—regret putting himself out to apologize to you. He won't do it again.

YOU'RE DOING LONG-DISTANCE

We've all heard the refrain that long-distance relationships never work. Yet for many FGs they are inevitable. Why? Because the FG loves to travel and so will often meet desirable men from other cities and countries. What's more, the type of men she gravitates toward tend to be worldly and thereby inclined to do some traveling themselves. No matter how she meets Juan, Jorge, Giuseppe, or Vladimir, the FG must never abandon the long-distance romance without dabbling a bit first. Distance is simply not a good enough reason to turn down a handsome man, not to mention a free place to stay in a foreign port. Besides, there are times in an FG's life when being "together" while "apart" is the most desirable relationship of all. This unconventional couple can have deeply intense and romantic time together. They will always be thrilled to see each other and will have time set aside just for the occasion. And better yet, when Juan goes home, the FG gets her much-loved space back to herself, which gives her more time to pursue other goals. And she can enjoy the phone sex and the pining a bit.

Of course, while the honeymoon phase for this couple lasts longer, if neither party is willing to move it will eventually end. You may begin to resent him for not being around. You may get sick of going to events alone. Or one of you may meet someone else who does live nearby. But, alas, these are the risks of long-distance. The benefit, however, is that it is one of the few romantic relationships in which you can dump someone over the phone. That's right, probably three-quarters of your intimate discussions have occurred over the telephone and "this isn't working any longer" is one of them. And that's all that needs to be said. As with any breakup, just saying those few words will begin the dialogue.

But what if he then asks you to pack it in and move to his city? The Fabulous Girl doesn't answer in haste; if she doesn't know she says so and takes her time to think. Any move requires deep reflection, not a whimsical gesture of passion. The FG evaluates not only this relationship, but also her career, her friends and family, the city she calls home. As for the relationship, you must consider what kind of commitment you are making to each other. Your attachment should be of a serious kind to even ponder the kinds of sacrifices a move involves. Although you may see only the adventure in making this kind of leap, you should remember that you'll be launching a new relationship with him. Your romance must be solid enough to withstand what could be a rocky adjustment period from holiday mode to dirty socks on the floor. Only after careful consideration do you say yes or no.

HE TRAVELS CONSTANTLY

The FG who loves a man who travels a lot for work may feel that she is living in a long-distance relationship even if they share a home. There are three stages of separation. First, you miss him. It's that yearning, heartachy feeling, those late-night calls from hotel rooms, and back again to that phone sex. Second, you get angry. Enough time has passed that you're bored with phone sex and want the real deal. You're fed up with doing everything at home by yourself. You wonder what the hell he is doing out there without you. Third is relief. Eventually you forget you live with someone and rearrange the furniture or the kitchen cupboards. Then when he's back and he tries to put the Cheerios away, you have to tell him, "We don't put that there anymore." This is the stage when you don't actually want him back—when you have The Fight. FGs understand that an argument with her lover can have positive consequences. A good fight relieves tension, releases pent-up emotion, and it allows you both to stir up the passion for a good make-up session. A good fight is what can happen when your beau returns. There is nothing wrong in admitting to him that you are angry about being left alone, even if you understand that is the nature of his job. In other words tell him you missed him. And yes, he had better tell you how much he missed you too!

Types of careers where this is an issue: touring musicians, authors, actors, salesmen, and, of course, those in high finance—if your boyfriend gets thrown in the slammer for insider trading.

When an FG is the one frequently on the road, she may find these separations a little less painful. It's just not as hard being the one who is jetting off (even if the destination is not always glamorous). She may still miss her mate like crazy, but she does have the distraction of change that travel brings with it.

The most gracious way to handle either separation is by maintaining some kind of schedule of contact. This is a good way of normalizing what can be a stressful arrangement. Make a deal that you'll always chat before bedtime (or whenever). Try to invite him along or go on trips with him when it makes sense. Remember to give yourselves a bit of time to adjust when you are back from a trip. The tension created by being reunited is romantic but also discombobulating.

You Want to Move to Another City—But He Won't Go

You've always wanted to be a talent agent in Los Angeles—problem is, you live in Chicago. So you've been slogging it out in the local scene. Then lo and behold, one Friday afternoon you get the call from Hollywood. ICM wants you, they really want you. You jump, you shout, you say yes. Then reality hits you—you'll have to move. But will your live-in man, Wilhelm, move too? He's doing great at his job, but is his career in demand in LA? Is your relationship over?

This type of major life decision requires true fabulous finessing. While you want to celebrate, buying Wilhelm dinner out at a five-star eatery is not the way to tell him your news. Tell him at home, when you're alone. Chances are you've been communicating your dream to Wilhelm for your entire relationship so the LA move shouldn't come as a shock. He'll probably be thrilled that your dreams are coming true, but then he will naturally think about where it all leaves him.

The FG needs to ask:

~ How significant is this relationship?
~ Is Wilhelm the man she sees herself being with for the rest of her life?
~ Would she sacrifice her career for him?
~ Would a long-distance relationship work?
~ Can she reasonably ask him to quit his career for hers?

Only when these questions are answered—and it will take more than a few conversations with her beau to do this—will she know what the future of the relationship holds.

HE'S MOVING

An FG loves adventure and therefore will love to be involved with a man whose career keeps him on the move. Be careful, however, not to jeopardize your own career to accommodate his. If he's landed a job that will take him to Venice for a year, you may decide that a year away from the intensity of your career will be an oasis. Just remember to take the long view. What if you break up in the middle of his three-year contract in Hong Kong? If the move is within your own country, you need only consider how such a change will affect your job, your friendships, and so on. If the move is bigger—to another country—you need to talk about a bigger commitment. Of course, marriage may be necessary for immigration reasons—to live and work in a foreign country you're going to need to take the proper legal avenues—but marriage also makes it very clear where you both think your relationship is going. Whether you get engaged or simply discuss what kind of commitment you're making to each other, you must know the score before moving. Don't leave home without it.

Caveat: This type of situation can result in the FG's becoming engaged to the wrong person. Make sure you don't say yes to a proposal merely because of a move. Ask yourself if you would have said yes if there were no such move on the horizon. Your answer to "Will you marry me" must be the same whether there is a relocation involved or not.

Moving In Together

He wants to—you don't

You like your boyfriend, you really like him. So how come when he asks you to shack up you recoil and suddenly need to wash your hair? Moving in with your boyfriend is only a great thing when both of you want to equally. If you're not sure, or you're sure you don't want to, come clean. Not being ready is a perfectly good reason and all that you need to say. But it will make both of you question where the relationship is headed. Is the deep truth that you don't think he's the guy? Or are you loving things as is? Be clear for your sake as well as his. It's a rare relationship that can flourish without some movement forward, and if he interprets your reluctance to move in as reluctance about him, then you're looking at some tense times ahead. If you are one of those people who can be passionately in love, totally committed, but simply cannot abide cohabitation, you're going to have to make a strong case for yourself. And if you don't find yourself reassuring him, it may be time to consider moving on (rather than moving in.)

You do—he doesn't

Your roommate has moved out. Your two-bedroom is seeming awfully lonely. Wouldn't it be great if your boyfriend would simply move in? He's there half the time anyway. Splitting the bills would be easier financially. And who wants another roommate? So you ask him to live with you. How do you handle it with grace if he says no?

The Fabulous Girl doesn't take offense or burst into tears—yet. Instead she says, "Oh, may I ask why?" And hears the brute out. He may not be a commitment-phobe, but simply needs time. Listen to what he says carefully though; if he's says, "I don't see us getting that serious," he means it. Don't interpret it as "I don't see us getting that serious right now, give me a week and ask me again." If he doesn't want to lose you but still isn't ready, he'll let you know, he'll reassure you of his feelings. If all you're getting is static, he doesn't think you're the one. Don't bother waiting for a change of heart. End it. A rejection is a blow to anyone's ego, and the FG is not immune; this type of situation can be the elephant in the room if you don't resolve it.

Your parents/his parents disapprove

The two of you are ecstatic about your decision to live together. The timing is perfect, you've found the cutest apartment, now you have to tell your folks. Perhaps your parents or his are religious or conservative; perhaps they think you're too young. There are many reasons why parents may disapprove of your "modern" arrangement. Both you and your beau need to form a united front and present the situation to them in the best light. Keep repeating out loud how excited and happy you are. Rave about the place. Rave about him (will work wonders on his mom).

If, however, your parents or his are truly upset, give them time to let it sink in. But be forewarned, it may take an engagement before some parents' frosty attitudes thaw. All an FG can be is gracious, polite, and of course, fabulous.

Everyone is doing it

You're the only one in your close circle of friends who isn't engaged, married, or cohabitating. Yet you're not single, you do have a boyfriend. There can be a certain amount of pressure placed on a couple to move in together and take the relationship to the next level, even if the couple themselves are perfectly happy. If it doesn't bother you that you and Bingo have been together for three years and you aren't married or living together, it shouldn't bother your friends. Make light of any social commentary you receive about the status of your relationship. Engaging in a debate over the merits of your arrangement only encourages this rude behavior.

WEATHERING A CRISIS IN YOUR PARTNER'S LIFE

We all dream of finding unconditional love. As we grow up, we think that we won't settle down until we find a person who can accept all our faults and shortcomings. But what's an FG to do if she finds she's not up to that task herself? You're with the guy who for years has seemed like Mr. Right. The two of you are compatible in every way. And then disaster strikes—him, not you. While your career is on the rise, his begins to plummet. Your financial future looks rock solid and his is disintegrating. You notice that he's started to look a little shabby when he heads out the door in the morning. Over dinner, when you ask him what he's got going on at work, he mumbles and changes the subject. He's withdrawn and doesn't seem interested in going out anymore.

Loyalty is a prized quality in an FG and she won't want to point out to her man that things are looking bleak. But some situations call for a cold, hard look rather than rose-tinted glasses. Sit down and have a frank but supportive conversation with your mate. He may be grateful to you for acknowledging what is obvious to you both: that he's in a bad situation. Ask him what he'd like to do about his predicament and whether there's anything you can do to help. Offer suggestions: Let him know you're happy to stop going out for dinner for a few months to save money. Tell him it's more romantic to you to stay at home anyway.

You may find, however, that your man just doesn't want to confront his problems, and he doesn't want you looking at them either. He doesn't have to share everything with you, but if he won't talk about how he lost his job and he's been out of work for more than a couple of months, it's time to reevaluate. His life doesn't have to match yours, but you do have to know what's going on.

When to get involved

Months have ticked by and still your man hasn't found a job. You know this is not his normal modus operandi, he's simply in a rut. But the rut has grown tiresome. You're bored with his whining, his inability to get off the couch, let alone get a job interview. And worse, you learn that he has a potential job offer but hasn't bothered to follow up. What happens next is up to you. Can you call his pal at that top-level legal firm and invite him for dinner, thereby putting your man in the path of opportunity? Of course you can, but know that your boyfriend will recognize why you've made the invitation and he may be riled. You're going too far if you tell the pal that your boyfriend is down on his luck and needs a break. That is humiliation and not a fabulous thing to do.

Surprise ending

If after much soul-searching your man decides what he really needs is a big change in career, you will naturally be delighted that he's finally found inspiration. Of course, the shift he's imagining may affect both of you. If he's decided he can't stomach another day at his law firm and what he's always secretly wanted to do is to raise llamas, it's going to be a change in lifestyle for both of you. It's not his bank account you fell in love with, but if one half of a relationship makes a radical life change, it's to be expected that the romance may be seriously tested. You may feel that you can support this shift in focus but only as a friend. You don't want to move to the country and must sadly end the relationship. However, who knows—maybe you *can* get your head around those early morning trips out to the barn.

∽ Break Up and Make Up ∽

He Dumps You

"I think we should stop seeing each other." A very simple yet brutal sentence. Breakups are always painful and everyone has been through a few and can cope with a little help with their friends and a case of red wine. Then there are the really savage breakups, the kinds of endings that you don't see coming. Even an FG is challenged to keep her grace through these doozies.

~ He's in love with someone else.
~ He thinks the sex sucks.
~ He thinks you're too stupid for him.
~ He wants to live on a commune and make babies with multiple women.

Any of the above and even others yet unimagined are ego killers. When a man who has been in your life for a certain period, a man whom you have loved (or began to love) suddenly turns on you and issues such unkind statements, there may be tears. Hey, isn't that why the creep asked you to a restaurant in the first place? Worse yet, a Starbucks. The FG's initial reaction will be hard to control, but then she will strategize.

The Sob

The FG can feel a crying jag coming on. If this is you and you are in public, don't make a scene. While some people may take pity on you and recognize the dumper for the jerk he is, it is best to head to the ladies'. Let it out in near-private and then leave. Don't go back to the table if you possibly can muster the strength to not look him in the eye. That's what the next day phone call is for, to start the inevitable demands of "Why?"

The Shock

Didn't remotely see this coming? Some FGs may be so stunned by the news that they are completely silent. Again, cutting the meeting short is best in this case. Here's where the cell phone is best employed. Immediately call your best friend and meet her for a nightcap, even if it's Sunday afternoon.

The Ice Queen

If this is you, then use it to your advantage and decide to think about it later. Tell the lout you quite agree and continue on as though nothing happened. If nothing else, the fact that you don't appear to give a damn will puzzle him greatly and take his ego down a notch. This is where the FG makes her brightest and best conversation.

The Scene

You know you shouldn't and yet you find yourself in the middle of a scene worthy of Bette Davis. Your voice is raised and it's all you can do to stop yourself from reaching across the table and slapping his face. (Really try to resist this, as an assault charge is a nasty chaser to a breakup). Once you're in the middle of a public scene you may as well get the Oscar for it. Get in one more great line—I wish

I'd never met you, never speak to me again, you miserable bastard, etc.—and walk off the stage. Don't look back even if the room breaks into applause.

Get over him

Painful as breakups are, the one thing the FG must do is recover. If it takes three days in bed and two weeks of constantly bending the ears of all your nearest and dearest, so be it. Beyond that, you must make a conscious decision to get over it. Repeat it over and over. Then avoid every place and everything that reminds you of him. Now is not the time to indulge in sentiment.

He Dumps You—Then Wants You Back

He dumped you and broke your heart. Then just as you feel you're getting back on your feet, the call comes. He can't believe the mistake he's made, he's sorry, and he wants to get back together. It is reasonable that an FG who has been dumped and then "won back" by the ex will have difficulties with trust during the early days of Round Two. The Fabulous Girl will need to vent her anger and have several rounds of reconciliation chatter prior to accepting the invitation to get back together. But then, once she's back with her boyfriend, she needs a parade. Yes, this may need to be explained to him, preferably during the discussion phase, but it is expected. The FG's ex-now-boyfriend needs to be mindful of his FG's pride. She may be worried that she's foolish to trust him or that he will leave her again. (Which often happens in these scenarios.)

So, he'll need to throw a parade. This can take many forms. The obvious daily parades of I love you's and You're wonderful's are a must. Small gifts are also good. We're not talking about flashy displays of money, but of thoughtfulness and effort. Flowers, cards, romantic dinners, and so on are the kinds of things that will be useful.

The back-together backlash

If you are going back, you need to think about whether you can let go of the anger you felt over being dumped. Can you really be in the new relationship if you'll just keep taking it out on your ex-now-boyfriend? Try to get all the serious talking done in the early days of negotiating. Why things are different now, what really happened during your breakup, and so on. Then put your concerns on the shelf and just see how it goes. Round Two can't work if you don't give it a chance to be fun and romantic. But be honest about your feelings. If things are unresolved, talk it over as calmly as possible rather than letting things bubble up. "Did you leave an inch of milk in the carton? That's just like when you broke up with me" isn't appropriate.

If the FG is the one asking her ex to come back, she must expect a certain amount of flack from him too. She's obliged to take angry sessions and negotiations, and she also needs to put on a parade for him.

Caveat: If despite your best intentions you can't get over your anger about being dumped (or why you were dumped), there isn't much point in continuing. If you are truly going to forgive and forget it will be done within two or three months. If you really can't get over it, recognize that your anger just may be a sign that what was done is irreparable. Trust your instincts; your emotions are probably telling you something even if it isn't the answer you want to hear.

You Want to Break Up

When you've got to go, you've got to go. Probably you should have left three months ago, but you thought it might work out. It didn't. You let your boyfriend know that you were tired of waiting for marriage and kids and he didn't bite. You realized that crush on the guy at work was getting out of control. Whatever the circumstances are, you need to make a move. No matter how bad things are (unless you walked in on him with another woman), you must have a breakup conversation. You may like the dramatic flair that a note on the kitchen table has, but it's just not fabulous. Breakups are hard, but you must be brave and do it in person. Even if the very next thing you do is call a cab to stay at a friend's place.

Fake Breakups

It may look like a breakup, sound like a breakup, and even smell like a breakup, but it's not—it's a fake break. If you speak with your ex more than once a week, see each other at least once a week, and sleep with each other once a month, you are involved in a fake break. This is, of course, painful if you are the one who was dumped, but if you were the one who did the dumping it is downright mean. You may think you are weaning your ex off you, and naturally if he is brokenhearted he will encourage this line of reasoning. But as the person who wanted the separation, you must be the stronger party. You may subconsciously be hoping that the two of you can remain friends, that you can keep the things you love about him in your life. But if he's still in love with you, it's just not fair. It's selfish.

HE THROWS YOU OUT

Live-in couples are obviously committed. This situation only makes breaking up more complicated. If the Fabulous Girl moved into her boyfriend's place, the place remains his after they split. Remember, it is always better to find a new place as a couple rather than move into someone else's abode.

So there you are, the FG in the midst of a huge fight with the boyfriend. It's ugly, he's wrong, you're right, he's not listening, he loses his temper, and out flies from his twisted mouth, "Get out." Mortified, the FG gathers a few things and, calling her best friend, spends the night elsewhere. It would be wrong to stay and fight it out. If tempers have flared this high, then reason is obviously out the window. Clearer heads will prevail in the cold dawn. Right?

Wrong. The FG did the right thing by leaving—after all, she did what he asked. But when she goes back to their shared place the following day, what does she do if she opens the door only to find every single thing she owns is packed and waiting.

The FG must know first and foremost: does she want to leave? Yes or no.

Yes: If the relationship is over she can take solace in knowing that she has a lot less work to do. Packing is such a bore, isn't it?

No: Ah, now things get complicated. Assess his state of mind. If he's calmer it's time to have the talk. A rage last night might turn into constructive discussion in which as a couple you can make real progress. Even if things turn sweet and you're suddenly having make-up sex, don't move back in immediately. This has been a most extreme fight, and even if he was just acting out of anger you both need more than one day to cool down. Often when people have acted very badly—and packing up your things is up there—they overcompensate by trying to normalize a situation. But if you were both mad enough for you to sleep somewhere else you shouldn't just skip back even if you're both very sorry. Take a few days and be honest about how things could have spiraled out of control in that way. If the two of you decide you are going to stay together, let him unpack your things.

RECOVERING WHAT'S YOURS

You're single again. But that ex of yours still has a few of your most cherished possessions. Your Nina Simone CD collection, the salad spinner, or worse, the cat. How do you get back what's yours? Especially if he's being a jerk and won't return your calls, hangs up, or denies he has anything of yours (tough to claim with a cat). If there's nothing you need immediately you can wait for him to get over his childish stance. If you're honest with yourself you are probably insisting on having these administrative conversations to keep up the contact with him. Let it go for a month and he'll probably be a lot more reasonable about it. But if you have given him a grace period, or if he has something you really need, you can turn up at the door and demand your stuff. You can call the police. What works best however is the personal Repo Man. Know when your ex is home and show up with someone—a girlfriend, male friend, your parents. When confronted with third parties people, even assholes, usually are shamed into better behavior and tend to give in and give back what doesn't belong to them.

CHEATING BASTARD

Despite the Fabulous Girl's many charms, she may still one day end up with a cheating bastard boyfriend or husband. Unfortunately, it is true that the FG's beauty and grace are not protection against such a man. What does the FG do if she comes home early from work or that weekend with the girls only to discover Bingo in bed with another woman?

The FG, as difficult as it may be, does not lose it. She doesn't scream or throw anything. She is the perfect picture of calm and good deportment. Remember, girls, they're scum, so let them writhe. The FG will instead grab a chair or lean against the wall, arms crossed, and stare. Wait for him to utter the first words. And don't think you should leave the room so she can get dressed with dignity. No way. No matter how much it kills you, it's killing them more. In fact, your stoic silence is gut-wrenchingly loud to the cheaters. What will happen is he will blurt out explanations or apologies and she will try to hide. If he asks you to leave, refuse. A simple, calm "No, I don't think I will" should suffice. If she gets hysterical, let her. In fact, don't bother to look her in the face at all. It's as though she's not there—after all, this is between you and him. Once she's gone, walk out of the room, sit in the living room, and wait for him to come to you to talk. The rest will unfold as you see fit. But this way the FG will maintain control of the situation.

How you handle this domestic issue in public is as vital as how you cope in private. A certain movie-star Fabulous Girl is a stellar example of grace under pressure. Her equally famous boyfriend was arrested one night on Sunset Boulevard, having engaged in sexual acts with a hooker. His mug shot found its way onto every newsstand and current affairs show. Yet our FG remained silent, choosing to keep the incident between her and the boyfriend. She issued a simple public statement, but that was that. And showed up on his arm at a film premiere soon after.

HE CHEATS ON YOU—WITH A FRIEND

Even in the worst-case scenario—when you know the woman in question—staying in control still works like a charm. You'll just need to have two conversations instead of one. Each one separately, please. The female betrayal being worse somehow, this conversation requires its own time and place.

Time: Wait as long as you can before contacting her. Even if she's been ringing you repeatedly do not return her calls. Let her stew. When you're ready, in a week, two weeks, or two days, then you call and tell her you need to talk and you tell her where and when.

Place: Despite the dramatic flourish, a cocktail party with other friends watching is actually not the best moment for the confrontation. Better to meet her in a noisy-enough bar or café so that you can speak unself-consciously. In the calmest manner you can muster tell her that as far as you're concerned she's made her choice and that she's out of your life forever. If you run into the she-bitch unexpectedly in a social setting and you decide to let her have it, be a tough guy and ask her outside to have your talk. Then let loose. Swearing does have its place and can feel amazingly cathartic in this situation. Never talk to her again. Snub her and try to forget her.

What if, after all the dust settles, you opt to forgive if not forget your friend? Often an FG can do without a certain kind of man, but a best friend is more difficult to replace. Of course, we're assuming the friend is repentant and misses the FG too. If the two women decide to remain friends, they will have to endure the whispers of others. This will be particularly hard on the FG since she is the wounded party, and she will find that strangers will have an opinion on her situation. Even other friends will not fathom how you could still be friends with the she-bitch. The FG must ignore these people. She simply refuses to discuss it. If the FG is willing to socialize and be friends with this woman, the rest of the FG's social circle must also accept her. It is the gracious thing to do.

His Friend Makes a Pass at You

Perhaps you suspected that your boyfriend's buddy Blair had a secret crush, perhaps you didn't. Either way it was a bit of a shock when he cornered you in the kitchen and tried to shove his tongue down your throat. Saying no to unwanted advances of this ilk is not that difficult. Push him away and give him a firm "Knock it off!" and whether or not he's drunk (he probably is) it should be enough to shake him out of his ridiculous behavior.

Hopefully, buddy will realize his error and apologize; he may even confess his deep affection for you. This would be the time to be sympathetic and tell him you don't feel the same way. Otherwise you're heading down affair alley.

Do you tell your boyfriend that his best buddy is a betrayer? This is tricky, and depends entirely on buddy's reaction to your rejection.

Ashamed and apologetic
If his inappropriate advance was made once and you feel he won't do it again, you can keep it between the two of you.

Arrogant Asshole

He gets defensive and tries to tell you how you've been leading him along and he's only following your signals. Run to the nearest phone and call your boyfriend. This is war. Be assured if you don't make the call buddy will, only the story will go like this: "I hate to break it to you, man, but your girlfriend just hit on me . . ."

YOU CHEAT ON HIM

You swear it will only happen that one time. You and your boyfriend have not been as close lately, and you know the sexy architect you've been working with is attracted to you. You've had after-work cocktails, taken a few unnecessary, romantic walks, end up talking on the phone when an e-mail would do. You get the picture.

If you have taken one misstep (a snog in the bar or a quickie at his place) and are sure you'd never do it again, it is best kept to yourself. If you value your relationship, hurting your boyfriend this deeply will forever alter it.

If it's a full-blown affair and you have never been caught—yet—you obviously need to reevaluate your so-called relationship. Cheating is never fabulous, and if you're not married—and thereby don't have the complication of a divorce—there is no excuse. If you want sex with someone else, leave your boyfriend. It is that simple.

If you end the affair and are convinced that you still love your boyfriend, you probably should fess up. An affair is a much deeper issue than just sex—it involves emotions with someone other than your partner and is a symptom of a major problem.

"I love you, but I've been having an affair. I won't see him again, it's over now" is the icebreaker. What happens after that will depend on him, and how well you can persuade him that you're going to be trustworthy in the future.

Guilt

Cheaters do feel guilt. What is worse, however, is a cheater who brags about her transgressions to all her circle. This is a sure sign of the cheater's wanting to get caught but not having the guts to be honest. In such an emotionally fraught time, the cheater should pick one friend and confess only to that person. Your best friend will likely not think you the evil bitch from hell when you admit, "I've done something terrible, I've been sleeping with Tom" (Dick, or Harry).

YOU'RE THE OTHER WOMAN

He's smart, fun, sexy, and, oh yeah, he's married. A single FG can often be attracted to married men, particularly as she gets a bit older and there seem to be fewer great guys out there. Perverse as it may sound, she can also find the fact that he's been able to make a commitment very attractive. So attractive that you want him to break it up now and be with you. If after a few drinks and months of flirting you end up in bed with a married man it's probably going to be great. The illicit nature of your tryst can make for very hot sex. Just don't get any ideas about having an affair with this man. We all know that married men almost never leave their wives for the women they have affairs with. If you are the other woman for a man who is basically happy in his marriage you can end up feeling quite melancholy. He's going to feel terribly guilty and want you to promise that you won't breathe a word of your mistake. The fact that he's so concerned about losing his wife now can make a nice girl feel like a ho. Just remember that although it was a bad move (and not fabulous to the wife, who is undoubtedly an FG herself), it wasn't you who made vows to keep her happy. Keep your distance from him and don't make the much worse mistake of angling to spend more time with him or try to lure him away from his marriage.

OTHER PEOPLE'S BREAKUPS

A breakup in your social circle is a stress for everyone, not just the couple that is splitting. Naturally, when people who seemed well suited can't keep it together, it makes you wonder what it takes to keep it together. Do you and your man have what it takes? And how is he feeling, exactly, about your relationship? As best as you can, try not to make this the moment you choose to have a big relationship talk. It will, of course, be the most tempting thing in the world. And you won't be able to avoid talking about the broken relationship. But try not to draw parallels.

Breakups never affect only the two people directly involved—there's a whole network of relationships rocked by the disintegration of one. And the longer a couple has been together, the more their separation will send ripples through their social circle. Of course, well-mannered couples try to end their relationships with as much grace as they can muster. But some etiquette pressure does fall on their peers, and there are rules of decorum to help ease the stress.

If you only ever really liked Fred and never could stand Ginger, you don't have a problem. You can just enjoy Fred's company and allow your connection with Ginger to fade away. But if you've always palled around with both of them, you have a few duties. First, you must immediately let both parties know you will continue to be their pal. The newly broken-up couple will have some anxiety over whose friends are whose. Make it easier and let them know you're not tak-ing sides.

And while you aren't obliged to keep the splitters away from each other, in the early days it's diplomatic to warn each of them if they're invited to the same event. Obviously, we're talking about large gatherings, not tiny dinner parties, where only a fool would in-vite both residents of Splitsville.

Which brings up the next issue: never interfere in someone else's breakup. Don't try to fix it because you really miss spending time with Bob and Bonnie. If they want to get back together, they will; your faking an invite to a party only to shove the two of them together in a closed room is the stuff of sitcoms not fabulousness. And don't fall into the trap of acting as a mediator on behalf of Bob or vice versa. Bob and Bonnie can talk to each other themselves.

If you are in the rare position of being equally close with each part of a relationship on the rocks, your diplomacy will be tested. You've known and adored both Bingo and Fifi for years and now they're in a trial separation. Fifi's been seeing someone and Bingo is brokenhearted. Of course, Fifi will be dying to talk about her new romance, and as a friend you will feel compelled to indulge her. While you needn't make the new man's name verboten, it's not a good idea to be a cheerleader for this affair either. If Fifi is on the rebound—and she likely is—she doesn't need any help getting car-ried away. And since Fifi and Bingo may still reunite, you may as well not invest too much emotional energy in the other man.

Finally, refrain from discussing the comings and goings of one half of the breakup with the other. You can listen (preferably neu-trally) to Ginger analyze all of Fred's shortcomings. But you may not, ever, add, "Well, he certainly looks cozy in his new romance, so I guess New Girl doesn't mind that he doesn't pick up his dirty socks."

∞ *Ex Marks the Spot* ∞

It doesn't matter if the Fabulous Girl has one ex or a list of exes that, if read, would have the music start to signal her exit stage left. These men can sometimes still figure prominently in her life. Feelings for them, be it anger or love, may lie dormant and bubble to the surface in unexpected moments. An FG must learn when it's time to bow out gracefully from maintaining a friendship with an ex, and when hanging out is just dandy, thank you.

ENCOUNTERS WITH YOUR EX

There are many occasions in life when we get caught off guard, but few will be as fraught as those accidental encounters with an ex. What makes these meetings worse is seeing him with his new gal. But be careful: how you react will say much about the state of your feelings.

1. If it's over, it's over. So why are you frequenting Bingo's fave bar? When you keep "running into" him, it will be obvious that you have unfinished business. If that is so, ask to see him alone and speak your piece. Then move on. After that, attempting to make your meetings seem coincidental is simply stalking. And if both of you refuse to give up your pasta joint, be prepared to have each other and the new dates in your lives.

2. He's unavoidable. You were both invited to the wedding/

cocktail party/birthday celebration long before you split up. It's not obvious which of you has more claim on the event and so you're both going to go. You must do your best to be civilized. But you must also do your best to look as good as you ever have. It's time to employ the Fuck-Him Dress, with a salon blowout for good measure. Have a plan for the night. Don't drink too much—three champagne cocktails and you may suddenly feel like it's the perfect time to rehash your breakup. And have an exit plan in case you decide you can't handle it. Discuss a subtle hand signal with a close friend. A tug on your ear and you're both heading for the door.

3. What if you are the dreaded ex? You know you broke his heart and he is pining, so guilt may induce you to avoid him at all costs. Not a bad decision—unless he spots you doing the avoiding, and then you are the boor. Once you've made eye contact, you must acknowledge him no matter how awkward it is. You should muster the courage to say hello and then move on as quickly as possible.

4. Can't stand the sight of Felix? The only good thing you got out of that relationship is that you got out? Then feel free to snub. Avoid meeting his eye and pretend not to see him. If he does approach, say hello and continue on your way. You are not obliged to engage in conversation, nor do you have to invite him to sit down with you.

BUMPING INTO HIM—WITH HER

It never fails that the one day you didn't shower, comb your hair, or look in the mirror before you left your home is the time you run into your ex and his new playmate. Other than dashing behind a parked truck to hide (always an option if done quickly enough), you must pretend that you are looking your best and act accordingly. Say hello politely to both of them and keep the chat to a minimum. Whatever you do, don't overcompensate by blabbering on about how great things are going for you. You'll only look foolish. Then make your excuses and walk on, not bothering to concern yourself with his new girlfriend's assessment of you.

Your Ex Is a Stalker

He seems to be everywhere you are these days. Is it a coincidence? After all, he used to go to these same spots when you were together. But he also keeps calling you, e-mailing you at the office, trying to get together for a "friendly dinner." Stalking is never good behavior to encourage, so it sounds as if you need another talk with your ex. If his stalker tendencies are making you uncomfortable, begin by not answering e-mails or returning phone calls. Tell him you're too busy to get together. If he gets whiny, insisting he's just trying to be friends, tell him you simply don't think it's a good idea to be spending all this time together as you both need to move on.

Of course if he becomes a real nutcase you should call the police and report him. Placing glue in your door lock and slashing your tires is well beyond maintaining your connection.

Your Ex Is Sabotaging You to Friends

Suddenly your mutual friends are giving you the cold shoulder. Or they are telling you how much your ex misses you, and how he never did anything wrong, thereby implying that you were somehow mistaken or to blame. In other words your ex has been bad-mouthing you to your friends. At a minimum he is trying to assert his version of things to the world. Try not overreacting to this tactic. After all, everyone is entitled to their take on things. And for the most part people will assume that the person who got dumped (in this case him) is going to have some bitter feelings. Your mutual friends will feel bad for him, and if he is really convincing that you were a cold-hearted bitch they may initially have a hard time keeping it from you. Try to let some time pass before doing your own damage control. But if your ex is putting it about that you were a liar, a cheat, a drowner of kittens, it must be checked before it gets out of hand and suddenly the new guy you like hears murmurs about how unreasonable and high maintenance you are.

Confront: He's your ex for a reason; tell him once again why you left him and give him another chance to vent to you (rather than to the world) about how hurt he is over your breakup. After he's let you have it he will probably calm down and you can let him know that you don't appreciate his tactics of spreading lies to mutual friends.

Damage Control: Explain to your friends that while it's kind of them to be supportive of their other friend (your ex), you need support too. Just because you were the dumper doesn't mean it's easy for you.

WHEN YOUR EX BECOMES THE STAR

When your relationship with Bingo ended, you thought you might never see him again. After all, there were times when it seemed as if he was never going to come down from his attic science lab. Then one day you're flipping around the TV and there he is, accepting the Nobel Prize for his work on particle theory. All the attention paid to your former lover can have personal ramifications—especially if you dumped him because he never seemed to get himself together. If he is a particularly wounded soul, he may even relish his new achievements and seek to rub them in your powdered nose. How you learn of his successes tells a lot about how he still feels about you and your breakup, and how you should handle the news.

1. You read about Bingo in the press. He's over it and is now enjoying the bikini-clad crowd in Cannes. Now is a good time to get over him.

2. You "accidentally" bump into one of his friends, who fills you in. This may not be idle gossip—your ex may or may not have encouraged his mate to spill the beans. Or his loyal friend just wants you to know what a mistake you made in dumping Bingo. Either way, it's a power play and he just wants you to be aware. Chances are he'll be getting a blow-by-blow account of your reaction to his success from the friend, so how you come across in this scenario is vital for ensuring that Bingo believes there are no sour grapes. Again, he's likely to hear about your reaction, so remain calm, poised, and express happiness for your ex—but don't overdo. A simple "That's really wonderful news. He deserves it" will send the right message.

3. Your mutual friends tell you all about it so that you don't have to read about it later. They may be trying to protect you. Time to reiterate that you're happy about the money, fame, and social life he now has and, oh, yeah, let's all remember that you dumped him.

4. Bingo calls you every time something great happens. He signs a recording contract. He's got a new producer who worked on the Stones' last album. He's touring with Bowie. Bingo wants you to feel really, really bad about dumping him. He wants you to have regrets. And yes, part of him is still in love with you. Try to be kind to

Bingo in this state, but know that he doesn't wish you well right now. When he does call don't only ask about his career; instead ask whom he's dating, tell him whom you're dating. Anything to encourage him to move on and let him know that you don't regret the termination of the relationship. It may be time to cut off the friendship with this ex for a while—don't communicate or see him. Get caller ID if you have to; just stop talking.

Your Ex Announces He's Getting Married Three Months After You Break Up

This is more common than you think. It is proof positive that all his discourses on "not wanting to get married" really meant "I don't want to marry *you*." There is little you can do in this scenario. It's his obligation to let you know himself. He should do this in person, and if that's not possible he should tell you over the phone (not via e-mail, as has happened to at least one FG). Even if you are over your own breakup with him you're still going to be hurt by his sudden change of heart, but you must be gracious and congratulate him. If you hear about the engagement through a third party, you needn't pass on your best wishes. This is a slight and very badly played on your ex's part. And obviously do not send a gift.

Your Ex Comes Out of the Closet

And you thought his erectile dysfunction was because he didn't find you attractive enough. Surprise! It turns out if you had a penis and an Adam's apple you would be more his type.

When your ex comes out it may come as a kind of relief and could resolve any lingering thoughts you might have about what really went wrong in your relationship. You may also doubt your own judgment—how could you not have seen that your own boyfriend was gay? Don't be too hard on yourself. If he didn't know, how could you? And at least now you can put aside the injuries to your femininity that this relationship caused. It's not that you weren't woman enough, you were woman enough to make him realize he needs someone who is man enough.

It is appropriate to have a heart-to-heart with him and you have every right to be upset. "When did you know you were gay?" and "Do you think that's why you kept saying that sex wasn't natural for you when we were in bed?" are both fair questions. You should also ask him to be honest about whether he slept with any men while the two of you were together (and follow up with your doctor about this). Just because he slept with a man and not a woman doesn't make the betrayal any less painful for you.

If you can, be positive about his discovery and wish him well.

YOUR FAMILY STILL LOVES YOUR EX—BUT YOU DON'T

You break up with your serious beau—and he was a charmer, charmed your whole family, particularly your mom. For years afterward you're hearing "Bill really was the one you let get away, dear," and "Oh, Bill always gave the most thoughtful gifts," and "Bill would have been a great father to your kids . . ."

What is an FG to do? You don't necessarily want to give your parents or siblings the gory details of your breakup. How he cheated on you, was cheap, and so on. But you will need to snappily come back at mom with "Mom, Bill is never going to be in my life again, can we just ban his name from future conversations?" Or if need be "You're right, Mom, Bill was great at everything; all the women he cheated on me with thought so too. In fact I think he has a few kids scattered around the city."

It's worse still if your parents maintain a relationship with your ex. He's fishing with your father on weekends or taking them out to brunch. When you ask why, your parents tell you that "just because you don't like him doesn't mean we can't be friends. It's not like he ever talks about you with us, dear, your name never even comes up."

This type of situation requires two conversations:

Parents: No matter how difficult it may be, sit them down and tell them that their behavior is hurtful to you and that you want them to discontinue the friendship.

Him: Tell him to bugger off and never contact your parents again.

He Keeps Resurfacing

There are some exes that never really go away—they fade and then resurface for a litany of reasons. These are exes that are never good booty call options as they want more than sex. How you tell them to take a hike depends on the resurface quest:

Needs Money: Your ex-boyfriend is between gigs again, or has gambled away all his savings. Either way he's broke and needs to borrow money/sleep on your sofa, and so on. It doesn't come as a total surprise to you, as these were his habits when you were together. He tries to be seductive when he gets in touch; this may work the first time he resurfaces, but then he hits you with demands. Squash this instinct of his before you see him; tell him that you're broke too or that you're now living with someone and it is inappropriate for him to crash at your place. Tell him to call his parents if he's down on his luck, or else you'll call them for him. Usually when a man like this realizes he can't get what he needs he backs off.

Favors: He wants to borrow your car, he wants you to introduce him to some influential people you now call friends, he wants to meet your coworker and ask her out. Whatever the situation, once a week he's on the phone asking for something. This guy is too "worky" for words. He doesn't so much see you as an ex than as an asset to his business and social life. This is where the FG employs the simple word no. "No you can't have my car," "Judy has a boyfriend so there's no point in meeting her," and so on. This does well to give him the hint to back off from asking you for stuff. Once he realizes he can't work you he'll find someone else, another ex perhaps, to prey upon.

Proposes Marriage: Your ex and you might have been married in another time. Suddenly he's at some strange crossroads in life and he's on your doorstep proposing. He's ready for that commitment you always wanted—only now you don't want it with him. If you still like this person and hope to maintain a freindship you must be kind. Tell him you need time to think (even if you don't), then let him down gently in person. Be as honest as you can as to why you don't see it working. "I don't feel that way about you anymore," is tough but gets the message across without being insulting, such as "You don't make enough money." If it's done correctly you two can still be friends when he resurfaces again.

❦ *Other Women* ❦

NEW FG IN TOWN

There are certain people who simply have no manners when it comes to meeting those who are new to their social set. It goes like this: Guy in an established clique brings a new date to a function. As the group reconfigures to make space for the new person, some people seem unable to make the transition with grace. Unfortunately, this lack of hospitality can come in the form of aggressive flirting: bitches behaving badly. A few rules need to be adhered to:

1. Back off. Whether the man on her arm was the love of your life or just a two-month fling, if he's at a gathering with his new girl, you have no business rubbing your shoulders up and down his (and knocking his girlfriend off her Jimmy Choos). And even if the man has only ever been a friend, you still must check your jealous instincts around this woman or you risk appearing (a) insensitive, (b) insecure, or (c) moronic. No trying to outwit and outcharm her during conversations (or whatever—don't make a fool of yourself because you feel threatened), dramatic displays such as blowing kisses, winking or hugs that end up dipping your old friend to the ground.

2. Zip your lip. One of the worst catty callings in life is gossip. Yes, we all love to do it and hear it, but it should always be done well away from its subject matter. A group of women huddled at a party discussing the new girl within earshot, and in an unflattering manner, is thoroughly tacky. Why not include her in your conversational circle instead of analyzing her outfit?

3. Don't judge. If your good pal Bingo has a younger woman on his arm, don't assume (a) he's her sugar daddy or (b) she needs a father figure. Perhaps this older man and younger woman are in

love. Be happy for your friend. If you swallow your surprise and engage her in conversation, maybe you'll discover the nature of their relationship.

4. Don't worry. If all the men suddenly seem to be flocking to this new woman in the circle you must maintain your fabulousness. Your male friends recognize and know this about you and aren't really ignoring you. And don't forget, like any new toy, her novelty will soon wear off.

5. Don't stoop. If you are a victim of such cattiness, there is little that can be done but ignore it. Don't stoop to making nasty retaliatory remarks. Of course, you can sweetly whisper about it into your date's ear and laugh out loud.

HIS EX

As a wise FG once noted, there is always one ex who broke his heart whom he just won't quite get over. That annoying one who got away, and if she hadn't, he'd still be with her instead of you. Suppose your beau is really close, even best friends, with his ex. That's right. She's the one he calls when he's fought with you, she's going to be advising him on how to deal with your insecurity over her or whatever else. What's an FG to do? Bite it. There's little you can do other than befriend her yourself. If you and she become close then she's likely to be less of an issue. But if you really can't get over their closeness (and many upstanding FGs can't) or she won't let you two alone, you may want to change boyfriends. Of course, if she's in another city, that helps!

I was halfway through an item on a new night-
club when the call from Missy came. It was in those moments that I
would curse the magazine for being too cheap to have caller ID phones
on every desk. You'd pick up the phone thinking it was going to be a
publicist you could blow off in less than three minutes, and instead it was
your best friend who needed to have a serious talk that would be better
suited to a bar. And Missy is not easily gotten off the phone once she's
on. Never mind my deadline—when she's got a crisis, everything else
must be dropped.

"I think Joe is going to leave me."

"Missy? Is that you? Let me just save this work. Okay. Hello. Now,
what are you talking about? What have you done?"

"Why do you assume it's my fault?"

"Um, because you were about to get it on with Francis last week,
maybe?"

At that moment, I swiveled in my chair to see that Cheryl was
standing at the edge of my cubicle, smiling and nodding as if she, too,
were amazed at Missy's recent behavior. I smiled weakly at her even
though it really drives me crazy when people do that. I mean, she could
see that I was on the phone. Clearly, she was listening in on the
conversation.

"Just a second, Missy." I covered the receiver with my hand.

"Hi, Cheryl."

"Just wondering when the entertainment listings are going to be finished? Everything else in that section is ready to go."

"I'm sorry, I thought it was going to be ready tomorrow—"

"But then you got busy doing another piece for the paper?" Cheryl raised an eyebrow.

"Within an hour, I swear. You know I'm never late with my copy."

Cheryl just nodded lazily and didn't move. "I know. Look, I'm not trying to give you a hard time. Just because he doesn't mention it, don't think Bradley hasn't noticed how much work you're doing for the paper. Don't give him any reason to think you're slacking here."

I nodded and held up the phone. "You're right. Thanks. I've had this person on hold for quite a while now, Cheryl, I'd better get back to it. Don't worry about the listings. End of the day for sure."

Finally, she left. I was worried about what she'd said about my work and Bradley noticing that my mind was elsewhere lately, but I had to put it aside to deal with Missy at that moment.

"Sorry, gotta love this open concept. Maybe we should just meet later to talk about all this?"

"Okay. Where shall we meet? The usual? Joe is playing hockey tonight, so we could meet for dinner."

"Great. Do you want to call Elenor and see if she's free, too? I'll see you at around 7:30."

I got to Dominick's a little late because I was finishing up that listing for Cheryl. The girls were already there. Once we'd ordered, we got down to business.

"Now, why do you think that Joe is going to leave you?" I asked.

"Because he can tell she's not in love with him anymore?" proposed Elenor. With pregnancy, she had become even more frank. Which for Elenor was saying something.

"I do love him! I know I've been a bit crazy lately. But I love him, and I do want my marriage to work. I've been so focused on his faults and the whole Francis issue that I hadn't noticed that Joe hasn't exactly been happy with me either. I've decided I don't want to lose him!" Missy's eyes were filling up with tears.

Elenor and I both reached across the table to hold Missy's hands. Of course, I was filled with sympathy for Missy's anguish, but I also got a lump in my throat thinking that maybe I was going to lose Nice by expecting things between us to be perfect before we moved in together.

"I'm sorry," said Elenor. "I was being stupid. It's my pregnancy mouth. I know you love Joe."

"Maybe you just need to create a little romance with Joe," I said.

"What do you mean?" asked Missy.

"Well, I mean don't wait for him to make a move. You can do a little seducing of your own."

"Exactly," said Elenor. "Turn up the heat a little, Missy."

"I don't know how. Joe has always been the one to do that stuff, you know? He pursued me." Missy looked miserable.

So we came up with a plan to rekindle the romance in Missy's marriage. By the end of the meal, we felt as if we'd solved the whole thing. I was glad that she seemed to be on the right track in her relationship. It seemed obvious to me that Missy's crush on Francis was simply her way of avoiding going deeper with Joe. She didn't really want to have an affair at all, she was just afraid of the real intimacy that she could have with her husband.

And I was feeling a little better about Nice as well. Surely the awkwardness between us was something that I could overcome with a little romance? Or could I? Maybe I was only good at giving at advice and not at taking it. Missy's driver took us home in the new Mercedes, and she came along for the ride. As Elenor got out of the car, she leaned over for good-night kisses.

"Whatever you do, Miss, don't lose this car, I mean marriage . . ."

Missy called me the next day to tell me that our plan was working well already. When Joe had got home that night, he'd found that Missy had poured him a hot bath and had a drink waiting, too. After sitting on the edge of the tub for a bit listening to how Joe had scored the winning goal, Missy had pulled off her dress, stepped into the bath with him, and told him she thought he just might score again that night.

CHAPTER SEVEN

Weddings and Divorces

I don't know why people think that weddings are romantic. Of course, I get how they're romantic for the couple getting married, but even they usually seem more stressed than smitten.

I wasn't looking forward to Helen's wedding, to be honest. I knew it would be beautiful. Helen and her fiancé, Sam, have excellent taste and the money to pull off a great-looking wedding. Which in my experience is no small thing. How many weddings have I been to where you can tell they spent a lot and it's still tacky as hell? Too many.

Nice and I were a little on edge. The conversation about moving in together still hung uncomfortably over us. I was trying hard to show Nice that just because I wasn't ready to shack up didn't mean that I wasn't in love with him. We walked through the entrance of the museum where Helen and Sam's wedding was about to take place, and I had to admit it was beautiful. The room was lit with a million candles and there were sprays of white flowers on every surface. As we found our seats I said, "Remember the last wedding we were at?"

Nice just frowned, suggesting that he didn't remember.

"Missy's wedding? Where we met?"

"Oh, yeah."

Okay, so much for that.

The ceremony was the kind I like, short and traditional. There's nothing worse than those couples who insist on writing their own vows and end up promising to make each other banana milkshakes and the like. Helen looked beautiful, and the way Sam looked at her during the ceremony was amazing. Did Nice and I look at each other like that? Did we feel the things you're supposed to feel? I just didn't know, and I didn't want to look over at him.

Helen and Sam were smart enough to hire a great band, and as soon as dinner was finished people were up on the dance floor. Things started to thaw a little between Nice and me while we glided across the room.

"This is how I started to fall for you, when we first danced," I said. And he did seem to remember that. We danced over to Missy and Joe, only to find them bickering.

"Well, I'm pretty sure I noticed you flirting with the waiter," Joe spat as we danced away.

Just then Elenor, now eight months pregnant, twirled by us with a gray-bearded gentleman at least a half foot shorter than her. She was gritting her teeth but still smiling as he whirled her around. As she turned I noticed one of the man's hands riding awfully low on her full hips.

❦ *The State of Matrimony* ❦ *and Acrimony*

THE VERY NOTION OF marriage is an extreme one. A lifetime commitment to another person is one of the biggest moves an FG (or anyone else) can make. What may surprise her most is the size of the gap between her assumptions about what getting married would be like and what reality delivers. The greatest myth that an FG may hold on to is that the wedding is an event that she and her man will share. Hopefully, it is that too, but mostly it is built around clannish impulses and therefore must accommodate many more people than just the couple getting married. And if history teaches us anything it is that the more people involved in any single enterprise, the more the possibility for drama. Lo, the drama of the wedding—whether it be the first or the third.

Of course, in the case of multiple marriages, there has to have been at least one divorce. Divorces also rarely live up to expectations and, like weddings, involve more people than simply the couple splitting up.

❦ *The Proposal* ❦

YOU WANT TO GET MARRIED BUT HE DOESN'T

An FG has to think hard about what she really wants from her life. Because she is so full of energy, she can sometimes trick herself into thinking that she'll get to everything she wants to do eventually. This is almost true. And if it's not, then it's still a great approach to life. But to get the most out of life, one does need goals. As an FG, you see this clearly in your career. It's a good idea to apply this same philosophy to your personal life. If you don't seem to care one way or the other about commitment, your man will likely not be compelled to make one. It's important to be honest with yourself and with him about what you really want.

Of course, being in a relationship means making room for someone else's perspective as well. If you always thought you'd be married by the time you were twenty-seven but you're almost there and the fantastic guy you've been with for two years hasn't asked yet, your life is not a failure. At the same time, FGs shouldn't fall into the trap of being afraid to bring up the subject of marriage for fear of seeming old-fashioned. If you know it's something you need in order to be fulfilled, you should be clear about it. For instance, as your relationship is solidifying, you should let him know in objective terms what your perfect situation would be: "I've always thought it would be ideal to be married sometime in my early thirties." And ask him how he sees his life unfolding. If he's still not making a move and you're into the second year of your relationship, you should bring it up. As neutrally as you can, ask him how he's feeling about the idea of marriage and how he imagines your relationship developing. And you've got to really listen to the answer. Marriage is hard, and you don't want to convince someone to do it against his will. If he's not making moving-in-together, you're-the-one noises during this conversation, you'll have to make a stronger statement yourself: "I love you and want to be with you. I'd like to move on to the next level of commitment. Let's talk about it again in six months and see if we're moving in the same direction." Present this bit of information calmly. And try to keep the conversation brief.

Do not resort to the age-old tactic of the ultimatum "Marry me or else we're through." No FG would want to enter into a marriage based on a threat. Likewise, be prepared for him to disappoint you. This is one of the toughest love moves to make because through your very desire for more commitment, you may be ending the relationship.

HE PROPOSES BUT YOU'RE NOT READY

If your boyfriend drops to one knee and you hope he's merely tripped, you're not ready to be engaged. This is fine for you, but right in the moment you have to say something sensitive, such as "I love you, I'm so flattered, but I'm just not ready . . ." There will be awkwardness and perhaps tears (from you both) as this is a highly emotional situation. If you do feel that one day he might be the one, now is definitely the best time to say so with conviction. You may also suddenly realize in that moment that he's never going to be the one you want waiting as you walk down the aisle. While blurting that out right then would be too cruel, you should share your newfound knowledge with him as soon as you're able to muster the courage. He deserves to find his future bride if it's not going to be you.

EVERYONE ELSE WANTS YOU TO GET MARRIED

Parents, pregnant friends, and smug married couples tend to lather on the pressure to the happily unmarried couple. If you're on the receiving end of a constant barrage of "So when is it your turn to get married?" just calmly explain that you're both very happy with how things are. If you are feeling particularly vexed by their annoying refrain you might add, "So is it true you married people never have sex?" Of course if the inquisitors are your folks, then a simple "Please don't keep harping on that . . ." will suffice. But let's face it, particularly with anxious parents, some people will never let it drop. The polite thing is to change the subject.

❧ *The Planning* ❧

PRENUPS

You have some money and some property, be it a home, jewelry, car, whatever. You either earned it yourself or inherited it from your family. Or perhaps you know you are going to inherit in the future. If you are an independent-minded FG, you have gone along for some time considering your assets to be your own. When you become engaged, it's time to reassess both your and your fiancé's feelings about cash. This means discussing the possible end to the relationship. While unpleasant and unromantic, bringing up the topic of a prenuptial agreement is a wise approach to modern marriage. Let's face it: more than 50 percent of first marriages end in divorce (monetary strife is a leading cause), so you will be saving yourself much grief and anxiety if you deal with your assets prior to marriage.

Asking your mate to sign a prenuptial agreement does not mean you intend to be unfair to him if and when your relationship breaks up. It does mean that the financial terms of a breakup are made clear in advance. Perhaps you'd like to insist that you would split only assets that are accrued during the course of your relationship and that money you had before would automatically go to your children rather than to him. Likewise, you can decide how to divide stocks, retirement plans, and other assets in the event of your (or his) death. If you are involved in a family business, without a prenup you may be forced (and therefore force your family) to liquidate the business or enter into a costly buyout of shares with your ex-husband.

There is no sense in mincing words. Take your fiancé out for dinner and inform him you want a prenuptial agreement. How he handles the situation may tell you a lot more about him than you knew before he popped the question. If he refuses, you may have to reconsider the marriage.

What if he asks you to sign a prenup? Again, it will feel like a hard-hearted move. It presumes a possible end to the relationship when you should be thinking of its success. Nevertheless, he's asking. You have to ask yourself what is really fair. How do you intend to live while you are married? Are you going to give up or take a break from your career? Doing so will put a serious dent in your future earning potential. If you divorce your wealthy spouse, is it going to seem fair that you then have to go out into the workforce as if it were an even playing field? Think of how your kids may feel shuttling from the home of a wealthy parent back to a poorer parent's place on a Sunday night. Once legal issues have been raised, it is not the time to get romantic and say that you don't care about his money. He's telling you he cares about his money—you may as well, too.

Legal eagle

If you do decide to go the prenup route, you must negotiate the contract with legal counsel. Better to spend on this than run up escalating costs between dueling divorce lawyers later. Be firm with your lawyer and encourage your partner to do the same. Lawyers should work toward a document that reflects your wishes as a couple. Lawyers are combative by training and have been known to create bad feelings in couples during the negotiation process. Don't be pushed around. Decide what you and your future husband want and stick to it.

Other prewedding negotiations

How money will be handled in your marriage is not the only conversation an FG insists on before she walks down the aisle. Don't assume that just because he wants to be your husband he wants to be the father of your children. Likewise, don't assume that he should know by your freewheeling ways that you have no intention of popping out a couple of kids. You should discuss what you both feel about children (if you want them, how many, when you're going to have them) as your relationship is solidifying. Don't wait until the honeymoon.

INFORMING YOUR EXES

They can't all live in Texas. Once you've made all the happy I'm-getting-married calls—to your mother, to your best friend, to the nice people at Vera Wang—you must make a few hard calls. You must contact (or be sure that someone in a good position to do it contacts) your most serious ex-boyfriends or ex-husbands (by serious we mean those you are on friendly terms with). It's not right to let an ex hear about your upcoming marriage through the grapevine. If you want to maintain some kind of relationship with this person, you should deal with it in a straightforward manner. Of course it's not easy, but you need to protect his pride. If you honestly think it would be better coming from someone else arrange it that way.

Your ex's family

If you aren't married in your early twenties you've probably had at least one other significant relationship—and let's face it, probably a lot more than that—before getting engaged. Which in most cases means that you were close not only to that person but also to his friends and maybe even to his family. They may have become as important to you as he was. It's one of the most difficult parts of ending long-term relationships: the corollary breakups with the people in his life. People who never even made you cry. You may try to maintain some of these relationships after your split. Should they, however, be invited to your wedding? This is a tough decision to be made by you and your fiancé. Maybe it's been a long enough period that you have new associations with your ex's mother and you can all be comfortable with her at your wedding. Maybe it's going to quietly bug your man all day and not be worth the hassle. But what other people think should not come into it: what it looks like to the other guests means nothing next to your own comfort and the comfort of your fiancé.

Nightmare Guest Lists

The longer an FG puts off getting married, the more complicated her invitation list is going to be. Do you invite his ex-wife and her new husband? Probably not. Do you invite your ex-boyfriend from high school who is now married himself and with whom you have remained close? Maybe. You and your betrothed should sit down and have a frank discussion about whom you feel comfortable including in your celebration. You need to be generous with each other. And we don't mean you have to let your husband-to-be invite his ex-girlfriend. We mean that if he feels squeamish about someone on your list, you need to heed his feelings and strike out the offender. That way your mixed feelings can be honored as well.

His Exes

This is a simple rule. No exes. Probably there is one ex of his you are fine with, but chances are there is going to be one that really irritates you. He probably feels the same way. So, no exes. Let's face it, unless one of you is really good buddies with an ex, former lovers don't really have a place at your wedding, do they? People who invite exes just for sake of showing them that they've moved on, or to illustrate to their betrothed how fabulous they are to have such good-looking exes or the like, aren't, well, fabulous.

Workmates

Without a doubt, the Fabulous Girl gets along with nearly everyone in her workplace. However, she does not have to invite them all to her wedding. Collect the home mailing addresses of those you wish to invite and leave it at that. While no one has a right to ask you why they weren't invited (how poorly mannered if they do!), if you are asked, a simple "It's a very small wedding" should suffice.

If you are the lucky workmate to be invited to the wedding, do not broadcast it around the office or tell the bride-to-be how excited you are about the invitation in the presence of other colleagues in case the others were not invited. This may prove uncomfortable for the bride-to-be.

Children

If you choose not to have little ones at your wedding, be sure when you send out invites you specify "Mr. and Mrs. Thomas" and not "Mr. and Mrs. Thomas and family." Please take note that if you receive an invitation that does not say "and family" your kids are not invited. This can prove tough to communicate, as it seems more and more modern parents find even one day's separation from their little bundles of joy excruciating and may think you improper. However, a formal wedding is no place for toddlers and definitely no place for babies.

If your wishes are ignored and you do have wailing babies in the church, you must not let it get to you. Now is not the time to ask your cousin Ruthie to find a babysitter.

Parents' friends

It has been known to happen that an engaged couple are unable to invite their own friends because their parents have insisted on inviting all of their business colleagues, neighbors, and so on. What is a Fabulous Girl bride-to-be to do? If Mom and Dad are footing the bill they will feel very entitled to ask whomever they want. All you can do is insist on some balance. It is your wedding and you want to be surrounded by people who actually care that you're being married—not Gary from the parts department at your dad's favorite garage. You may need to insist that you financially contribute if that is what it takes. Give your parents and his a number of invitations to do with as they please (minus Gary of course!) and ask them to include only people whom you have had some kind of relationship with. Just because the Goldfarbs invited them to *their* daughter's wedding doesn't mean they have to be at yours.

If you are paying for your own wedding or making a considerable contribution to the budget you have more negotiating power. Still, parents can be bullies, and an FG has to stand up for herself and simply take charge of the invitations and learn the word *no*.

RELATIVES ARE TRYING TO CONTROL THE WEDDING

Your mother has probably spent more time even than you in imagining what your wedding day will look like. And so has your future mother-in-law been dreaming about the wedding day of her son. Sadly, this can lead to these two women trying to hijack your day. They'll insist on their caterer, their fave music, their type of cake, what dress you should wear, the color of the bridesmaid dresses, and so forth. It can go on forever if you don't put your foot down. *No* is the most useful word in the dictionary, yet is one that a lot of young women have difficulty using. "Thanks for your suggestion, but I really prefer taupe bridesmaid gowns to lime green" is a soft way of saying no. Whatever you do, don't storm off in a tantrum; a reasonable tone will get you taken more seriously and not dismissed as a jittery bride.

OUT-OF-TOWN WEDDINGS

Your oldest friend in the world is getting married in Guam. It's what she's always wanted. You can remember her dreamily describing her future Guam wedding when you were small kids. You were so thrilled for her when she announced her engagement to her long-time boyfriend. And then out of the blue comes the wedding invitation. Sure enough, she has decided to have her big day in Guam—in one month. *Eek.* Your work schedule is punishing. Your bank account is at a low. What to do? Are you obliged to move heaven and earth to be with your old friend?

Yes and no. Deciding that your wedding is going to be held far from home automatically means that many of your desired guests won't be able to make it. You're asking them to spend considerable money and effort for the trip. And the best way to make that a possibility is to give them lots of notice. Even if you're not ready to send out the actual invitations, you should let people know what your plans are as soon as you can. If that's not possible you have to live with the results. Let your friends and family know that although you'd love to have them with you, you will understand if they can't make it. And really mean it.

This means that if close friends RSVP no, because of finances or timing or whatever, you cannot ignore them and remain angry and sulky over it. After all, you decided to do it overseas.

If you're the friend who has to say no do it promptly. Don't put it off because it's a tough call to make. A letter or phone call is fine. "I really am sorry, but I am unable to come to the wedding but I'll be thinking of you on the day . . ." Feel free to be honest about timing or finances. It's a particularly nice touch to send a telegram to the wedding party wishing them the best.

THE SURPRISE WEDDING

The perfect compromise for a bride who can't stand all the fuss involved in preparing for a wedding but who couldn't get married without her friends and family present is the surprise wedding. Invite your friends and family to a chic cocktail party—make up some good reason so that they'll really get there and look good—and when they arrive, they find you ready to get hitched (or for some tardy guests, already hitched). This saves you from the endless conversations that plague brides (often with their blessing), detailing every little doily and hors d'oeuvre in the months that precede a wedding. You also remove yourself from the wrangling with relatives over the guest list because you have to do it all yourself. Your immediate family may be cross with you for not allowing them to help you or to have more control over the proceedings, but they will quickly get over it when they have cocktails in their hands and they realize they haven't had to kill themselves helping you organize it all.

You Elope

You and the love of your life have decided to take a two-week getaway to Bermuda. It's hot, the sea is frothy, and he's never looked better to you. The sex is great, and finally the two of you decide that a life together will be exactly like this every day. So you track down some sort of official, get the local legalities out of the way, and there you stand, barefoot on a beach. Ten minutes later you're married! Congrats. You've just saved yourself (and friends and family) a ton of angst and money. However, recognize that some people will be disappointed about not being there. Particularly your mother. How upset you think people will be should determine if you call them immediately afterward to let them in on your secret or if you wait until you're home and can do it in person.

Either way, you cannot expect the same fuss or deluge of gifts as a traditional wedding would bring. However, if people do choose to bring or send you a gift, you must follow traditional protocol and send a thank-you note.

If you do think people feel cheated, or if you just want to celebrate, throw a party when you return. People will then feel part of the process even without having bore witness to your vows.

∽ *Fractured Families and Your Wedding* ∽

For many a Fabulous Girl the nuclear family was just not a part of her upbringing. On her wedding day she may have to delicately balance the various factions of what is her very modern-day family—parents who are divorced, remarried, and the like.

FEUDING PARENTS

(The FG may want to photocopy this for her parents.) So he left her for another woman? Sure it hurt, and it probably still stings a bit, but wasn't it also five or ten years ago? Parents need to be aware that the wedding day of their child is just that, and not another opportunity to put their kid in the middle. Even if Mom can't stand the sight of her ex-spouse, she's hurting her daughter by refusing to attend the ceremony or reception. Mom must also go to both. Mom must smile and be pleasant. And Mom absolutely must say hello to her ex. She must stand in the receiving line. She does not, however, have to pose in the same photo unless you have worked that out in advance. Of course, you must include both your parents' new partners. And yes, you must ask the stepparents to be in the wedding photos.

WHO WALKS YOU DOWN THE AISLE?

Haven't seen your dad since your were six? You don't have to forgo being walked down the aisle just because you can't go the traditional father-daughter route. Feel free to be creative with who walks you down the aisle. Your mom? A favorite uncle? Even a best friend (who doesn't have to be male). Since the assumption is that the father walks his daughter down the aisle, even if you're not close but Dad is still invited, you do need to let him know that you feel more comfortable with an alternative arrangement. Of course, if he has been a completely absent parent you do not have to inform him of any plans.

TRICKY TOASTS

If this ritual is tense with both parents and stepparents in attendance, a slight maneuvering of the speech order can satisfy all parties. The father of the bride is traditionally the first to toast the new couple, and there is no reason to alter this. If you are also close to your stepfather, by all means include him in the toasting lineup. But in order to make a distinction for your biological father (if you wish to), have your stepdad speak one person away from your dad—your father, the maid of honor, then your stepfather. This is all dependent on family dynamics. Again, warn everyone in advance of how you intend to organize your toasts so that there are no surprises. And by all means, allow Mom to say a few words too, especially if you are father-free.

ABSENT PARENTS

If the FG has no contact with either parent or if contact is particularly strained, she is not obliged to invite that parent to her wedding. A very famous television star who married an even more famous movie star was criticized for not inviting her mother. The woman who raised her had written a tell-all book in order to cash in on her famous daughter's life. This TV-star FG was well within Fabulous Girl protocol in excluding this badly behaved parent. The wedding day is very tense—why add to it someone who was supposed to give you unconditional love but totally betrayed and abandoned you instead?

∽ *The Event* ∽

WHEN ONE OF YOUR BRIDESMAIDS GOES BAD

Perhaps all the attention you are getting has turned your friend and bridesmaid into a jealous monster. Whatever, it's your wedding day. Yet, somehow you sense that she's up to something. Maybe she's a "scene stealer" (more on that later) but halfway through the planning of your wedding she starts giving you the cold shoulder treatment. Rather than take up the task yourself, since you want to have fun and not deal with a bitch, ask one of your other attendants to speak with the bad bridesmaid. Often a good slap across the face (figuratively of course) will smarten up the most bitter girl. If she still doesn't snap out of it you can make the extreme, but sometimes necessary, move of un-bridesmaiding her. That's right, if girlfriend won't show up to dress fittings, complains constantly about how much attention you're getting, or won't help you out with the simplest wedding task, go ahead and take away her title. Part of signing on for bridesmaid duty is to be helpful to your friend while she plans a very large and stressful party. Tell the bad bridesmaid you'd love to have her come to your wedding as a guest but that you don't feel it's appropriate for her to stand up with the rest of the lovely, helpful friends. If she goes bad on your actual day ignore her as much as you can, and when you do talk to her, keep being sweet and happy and continue on with the evening.

INAPPROPRIATE SPEECHES

The idea of speeches is such a nice one: the people who love you get to express their feelings on this special day. You father welcomes your husband into the family. The best man makes some funny but warm jokes about how thankful he and his pals are that Bingo finally met a girl worth marrying. If only it were possible to guarantee that this was the tone of speeches given at weddings. Alack, alas. Far more common are long speeches without focus that end up insulting at least one person in the room—usually the bride or the groom. It is the responsibility of the wedding MC to read the riot act to speech givers prior to the wedding. Everyone (and really, it should never be more than five speeches, and even that is pushing it) should be given a two-minute time limit. They will, of course, exceed this, but you may get lucky and end up with five-minute speeches. A good idea is to schedule a speech between each course of dinner.

What makes a good speech?

1. A Story. But keep it romance related. Tell a brief story about the groom that illustrates what kind of husband he's going to be. Telling a story about what kind of surgeon he is can wait until his retirement dinner—wedding speeches should be about the couple.

2. A Joke. Gentle teasing is an important part of a speech. But the best jokes make fun of either the speech maker or the person he or she is related to. The maid of honor may joke about the bride's kooky fashion sense; the best man may not. The father of the groom may joke about his son's historical ineptitude with women; he may not joke about the hundreds that came before.

3. Heart. A toast must include good wishes for the couple.

You may know that you're a real cutup and therefore rely on humor to keep the crowd on your side, but you must end on a sentimental note.

4. Brevity. Do not speak for too long. Keep it short. Write this on the top of your notes: "Shut up already."

Damage control

If, despite all good efforts and preparations, someone does let loose with an unfunny, insulting, or crude speech, or else they are on a drunken rant complete with slurred words, you need to know how to handle it. Make a plan (even if you're convinced you don't need to) with your fiancé. Decide on a signal, say your digging your nails into his thigh under the table, that says, "Stop the speech now." The MC of the night should know the signal, stand up and applaud, and run to the microphone and essentially take over. Everyone in the room will be so grateful that they'll also break into applause to help the MC out. "That was great Uncle Dan, thanks so much. And now over to someone who really knows Miss Fabulous . . ." The speaker may be bewildered but he or she will also certainly be speechless.

BAD GUEST BEHAVIOR

It happens at most weddings—a terrible gaffe. Usually it is alcohol related. His Aunt Agatha makes a pass at your handsome gay cousin, Ronald. The women under forty realize about halfway through the evening that they've all been goosed by Fred, an old family friend.

All Fabulous Girls should endeavor not only to behave well at a wedding, but to discourage bad behavior in others. If, for example, you are a guest and you learn that your close friend Patsy is about to drunkenly admit to the bride that she once slept with the groom, you may find it necessary to haul Patsy's ass out of the hall and give her a good talking to.

If you are the bride you must not get too wrapped up in your guests' less than suave behavior. If something requires your attention, say a crazy uncle who will listen only to you about his drinking, deal with it as swiftly as possible. Better if you can to delegate crowd "control" to your faithful attendants.

SCENE STEALER

You know your friends are happy for you—they've been saying so for the months running up to the wedding, right? So you rightfully expect that on your wedding day they'll be happy for you to be the focus of the celebration. Well, it doesn't always go that way. Some women are so unsettled by the happiness of the bride that they cannot help but interfere with the event. The FG bride must do her best to be gracious, not start a fight or sulk. "That's so great you're pregnant; how lovely to share the news with all of us on such a special day." This says, "Your timing sucks, you bitch," without actually saying it.

If you find yourself a guest at a wedding and these evil feelings are welling up, you must leave the party. If you can't leave the party you must at least stop drinking. Too much liquor could convince you that it's okay to pull the bride into the corner and trap her there while you weep for your own disappointments. Or worse, as one "friend" of the bride was known to do, loudly announce her own engagement at her friend's wedding reception. Very badly played.

SEX AT THE WEDDING

Sex really should wait until after the wedding reception is over. However, there are a few randy couples out there who just can't hold back. This is especially true for out-of-town weddings where guests and the wedding party are holed up in some quaint inn or cottages. This type of setup with the romance of true love in the air can inspire French-farce naughtiness. Receptions held at a banquet hall or outdoor garden pose more difficulties, yet it still happens that both guests and the new couple need to sneak off for a bit of cheek.

The bride and groom should opt for a hotel room. But clearly that will work only if their reception is being held in a hotel or inn. Otherwise, you're stuck in the washroom, and quite frankly, while it may seem indicative of your intense feelings for one another, none of your guests want to happen upon you going at it in a public space. Some level of dignity should be maintained at a wedding.

As a bridesmaid, again, no matter how cute the usher or that tall brute at Table 6 is, you should keep your attention on the job at hand, which is ensuring that the bride is happy. Get the man's number, but don't take this time to go outside for a snog in the back of his Chevy pickup.

However, if you're a guest the rules are a little different. So if you happen to notice that the Table 6 tall brute is looking you over, feel free to make tonight your special night too. Of course, keep propriety in mind and head for someplace out of the way. Again, the public washroom seems like the perfect place, but it is at that precise moment that you will encounter the bride or groom and then it will run through the wedding hall like wildfire and the bride will be furious. See "Scene Stealer" above.

If you happen to walk in on a couple going at it—especially the bride and groom—mind your own business. Even if that does mean peeing in the next stall with the bride's train covering your feet. Keep it to yourself. Unless, of course, you walk back into the reception only to discover that the groom is in the room! Then you may need to get the bride alone to ask her if she has lost her mind.

CALLING OFF A WEDDING AT THE LAST MINUTE

You and your parents and he and his parents have all spent a lot of money. The church is booked. Your dress has been altered for the final time. You finally found a photographer who won't make your pictures look like the portraits from Sears. And it happens. You wake up in the middle of the night with the clear, no-denying-it knowledge that there's no way you can go through with it. He is simply not going to be the last man you sleep with. And when you're really honest with yourself about it, you've had doubts about him since the beginning. You see other couples together and you just know that you don't feel what they do. So. The worst conversation of your life has to happen. You have to tell him. And none of this "Maybe we can just be together and not get married" stuff. This is the end. If you've been engaged to someone and you call it off, the relationship is over. And you have to be prepared that any kind of relationship, even a friendship, will probably be impossible after this. And then you have to make the next-worst phone call: to your mother. Both she and your father may flip out at you, they've spent tons of money, told everyone they know about your upcoming wedding, yada yada yada, but this is your life. If you explain how unhappy he made you or that in your heart it wasn't right, most parents will come around. After all, they love you and do want your happiness. You may want to have the conversation with your parents with a buddy. Maybe it's your would-have-been maid of honor, maybe it's your older brother—but having someone with you can help. You're going to be upset and your parents may interpret your tears as prewedding nerves and push you to go ahead with the plan. Having someone to back you up will help them to see that you mean business.

All that needs to happen once these two conversations have taken place is to have your mother and maid of honor call around to inform people of your decision. It is best for you, the bride, to remain out of sight for the next few days while you recover. All gifts should be returned to the senders.

∞ *Fabulous Girl as Friend of the Bride* ∞
She's Making a Mistake

A friend wants to meet for after-work drinks to tell you some news. Seated at your favorite bar she reveals her surprise: she's getting married! Before you can think through the ramifications, you ask, "Why?" Uh-oh. What you really meant was "Congratulations! You're going to be so happy!" No, actually, what you meant was "Why?" Your friend and her boyfriend can't make it for a week without fighting, and wasn't she just telling you about a crush she had on a guy at work? Whatever the circumstances are, your negative reply now hangs between you. You have two choices and very little time to make a move. You can plead surprise yourself and backpedal like mad. Explain that you were so shocked at her news that you blurted out a ridiculous question. Apologize and congratulate her with as much enthusiasm as you can muster. Or you can make the risky move of plunging in and discussing your concerns. This is difficult for obvious reasons. She's clearly decided to overlook the problems in her relationship and she's hoping everyone else will too. But if you are worried about her future happiness, you can give this a try. Explain that what you want above everything is for her to be happy and that you're just concerned that she hasn't always seemed content in this relationship. Acknowledge that what you're saying is upsetting and that you realize you are risking her friendship in making these statements. And tell her that you hope you're wrong.

Fabulous Girl exception: While the above is the standard FG modus operandi for sticky situations, there are a few notable occasions when you may need to really stick your neck out. If your friend decides during her engagement to have an affair, get pregnant, and then pass it off as her fiancé's baby you should have a more straightforward heart-to-heart. In other words "Do you really want to begin a life together on a lie?" Even if she goes ahead and somehow talks herself into being "mad for her fiancé," you will at least be satisfied knowing that you tried to shake her into sanity. However, she may turn against you and not want to maintain your friendship. But this type of dishonesty is hardly appealing for the FG, so what's the loss?

ENVY

Naturally, an invitation to a wedding can make even the most poised and happy FG wonder where her life is headed. It can also make her turn into a raving bitch on the day of the wedding. Her perfectly lovely and devoted boyfriend may find himself on the business end of a meltdown. "You were flirting with that bridesmaid at the engagement party!" "Where is this going?" You know how it goes. Since this kind of fit is one that you won't see coming, there's little you can do to avoid it. If you feel the undeniable call of the fit coming on, go ahead and get it over with, preferably before you leave for the church. The best plan of all is to avoid any contact with your boyfriend on the day of the wedding. If it's too late—you've already lost it and you haven't even made your morning coffee—then make sure you get some time on your own to chill out before calling a cab to go to the ceremony. If tension with your man does flare up during the reception, you must make an excuse related to your health and leave before actually having a fight.

Perhaps more important still is to be sure that your jealousy doesn't rear its ugly head in front of your pal the bride. If you're feeling resentful or bitter that you're not the one in the meringue dress keep your distance. It shouldn't be too hard; she has so many people to get face time with it won't seem at all odd if you leave her to it. Put on a big smile and congratulate the couple and then steer clear. Tone down the drinking, as alcohol makes everyone more "honest" and the type of confessions you'll be needing to make won't be welcome ones.

"When Are *You* Getting Married?"

Being at a wedding makes people think of other weddings. Often it makes people think of weddings that have not even happened yet. Like yours. "When are you getting married?" "So, who's next?" "What about you and Bingo?" As though if you knew the answer to that question you wouldn't have sent out the invitations by now. Or maybe the answer is "We're not getting married," but you really don't feel that someone else's wedding is the place to explain why you don't believe in marriage. The best tactic in this supremely uncomfortable situation is evasion: "Gosh, I just don't know. How are you doing these days?" This last bit should be delivered with intense care expressed through the eyes, hinting that maybe you feel things are not quite okay with your inquisitor. Resist the impulse, which may bubble up, to say, "I don't know, why don't you ask Bingo?" Remember that people are probably harassing Bingo in the same manner and that you are in this rude situation together.

THE BANKRUPT BRIDESMAID

Being in the bridal party of your close friend or relative is an honor. It is, however, one that is fraught with duty, both financial and emotional. The bridesmaid is usually expected to pay for her bridesmaid gown and accessories. Even though the bride chooses the gown—style and color—it is the duty of her attendants to cough up the cash. The bride should take into account the various economic levels of her bridal party and ensure that the dress falls into the budget of the bridesmaid who earns the least.

There is no shame in admitting quietly to your friend that you cannot afford the Gucci gown. Some women are shockingly unrealistic and will somehow take offense. If this is the situation, you can offer to withdraw from the bridal party. If she is gracious, and therefore an FG, she will snap out of her unreasonable expectations and the two of you can select another, more affordable option. Or, if she cannot imagine her wedding pictures without all of her attendants in couture, then she may offer to help pay the cost.

THE BADLY BEHAVED BRIDESMAID

A bridesmaid must cheerfully show up at all her fittings. If she is the maid of honor, she must throw a shower for the bride-to-be. All bridesmaids should help in shower planning by sending out invitations, deciding on a theme for gifts, and so on. A bridesmaid must also attend the rehearsal and, of course, the wedding.

Inevitably, one of the bridesmaids in a bridal party will behave badly. She's thoughtless, she's jealous, whatever. She does not do her duty to the bride. Don't let this person be you. Based on true FG stories of BBs, here is a list of activities to avoid:

1. Being late for the rehearsal and/or the wedding. This will naturally drive the bride out of her mind.

2. Refusing to sit at the head table because you can't be separated from your boyfriend for two hours. Or insisting that your boyfriend, who is not in the bridal party, sit at the head table.

3. Not noticing that the bride needs you to go the washroom with her to help take her veil off for the second half of the evening. Particularly if you're not noticing because you're trying to shag one of the ushers.

4. Telling the bride that the hairdresser has made her look like a character from *Star Trek*. If you really think her hair or makeup looks terrible, you must let her know—but be gentle and supportive. "I think it will be perfect if you just switch the blue eyeshadow to taupe!"

5. Complaining. About the dress, the shoes, the hair, the cost. Keep it to yourself.

SHOWER OVERLOAD

If you are in the bridal party of a big wedding, you may find yourself in the unfortunate position of being invited to too many bridal showers. The maid of honor throws a shower and, of course, you go to that. And, of course, you bring a gift. Then the bride's mother throws a party. Of course, she invites all the bridesmaids and so you go to that one, too. And bring a gift. An old school friend throws a party. And so on. By now you have spent more than one month's rent on your dress, shoes to match, and a couple of gifts, and you haven't even bought a wedding gift yet. Being aware of how much financial strain is being put on her wedding party is the bride's responsibility. If she realizes that there are going to be multiple showers thrown for her, she needs to let the bridesmaids know that under no circumstances are they obliged to attend all of them and that they are certainly not expected to buy gifts for every shower they do attend.

If you suspect that the bride in question isn't this type, talk to the other bridesmaids and make a plan. There will only be those moments of awkwardness if two bridesmaids buy ten gifts and three buy only one gift. If you don't want to show up empty-handed, come with a lovely bouquet of flowers and act as if this is what she expected. "I know you already have my shower gift from last week but I thought you might like these . . ."

By no means should you be bullied into breaking the bank. If you are acting alone—that is, the others are going to buy, buy, buy—you may still follow the rule on your own. After all, the Fabulous Girl knows she is behaving in the proper and gracious manner, even if others are not.

GIFTS

Registries

Despite the gift registry's inherent vulgarity, it can be useful if you don't know the couple's taste or needs well. Using the registry is not a breach of etiquette since you are only trying to please the happy, greedy couple. However, if the only choices on the registry are super expensive, say seventy-five dollars for a dinner plate, you may re-think the gift and buy something else entirely. You might look at the sorts of things they have on their list and ask a salesperson to find something in your price range. No matter what you choose to give to your friends, the couple should be gracious and thank you for the gift regardless of its presence on the registry.

How much?

The conventional reasoning is that you should spend about as much as your hosts will be spending on your share of the food and drink. The Fabulous Girl, however, knows that she is free to spend as much or as little as she can afford. If you're a student, no one expects you to spend as much as the bride's doting and wealthy uncle. And don't fall into the trap of feeling you have to spend more on a gift if the wedding is going to be formal.

Timing

Although it's nice to have your gift all wrapped up and ready to go by the day of the wedding, you really have a full year to send a gift. If the gift you really want to give has to be delivered after the fes-tivities, send a card to the bride and groom with your best wishes, saying a gift will follow.

Money

Generally, money does not show the same thoughtfulness as a gift. However, you can give money as a wedding gift, particularly if the couple is young.

Group gifts

It's perfectly acceptable to go in on a gift with a group of friends. If, for example, you know that your friend and her fiancé won't be able to afford a honeymoon without some financial assistance, it's nice to round up some friends to contribute together.

Taste

Don't go out on a limb, particularly when it comes to decorative gifts. Better to give a boring but practical set of steel mixing bowls than a cute-if-you-like-that-kind-of-thing lawn ornament.

BRIDE OF FRANKENSTEIN

The bride has become a monster and you're the maid of honor. She's an überbitch who is demanding, condescending, and rude. This girl needs a good talking to. By this point you've probably already tried the gentle tactics. "Are you okay? Do you think you need a spa day to relax?" If none of this is working you'll need to step it up. If your friend has been throwing tantrums for a few weeks you'll be so angry that any fear of a catfight will be gone. Tell it like it is: "Lesley, you have become the biggest bitch and if you don't start treating me better, I'm not going to be part of your wedding." Storm away if you have to, but make the point. Someone like her won't take a gentle nudge; she's too self-involved for that. Instead shake her up and let her apologize.

SHE CHEATS ON HER FIANCÉ BEFORE THE WEDDING

This scenario is more common than you'd think, and sometimes the culprit is the most unlikely type of girl. However, no matter your disapproval, there is little you can do. You can voice your concerns. Take her out for a sober conversation. "Linda, are you sure you should be marrying Robert when you've been sleeping with Gary these past two months?" or "Susie, was sex with the male stripper a sign that you're not happy?" Listen to her answers, but know that you cannot tell her what to do. Just know that when you're standing at the ceremony and the priest, rabbi, or preacher says, "If there is anyone present who knows a reason why these people should not be joined . . ." all you can do is dig your nails into the pew. Then hope that the marriage is as good as she deserves it to be.

You're Secretly in Love with the Groom

You're not the bride but have been in love with her future husband for sometime? Perhaps you're even the ex, and somehow the bride no longer feels threatened by you. Fooled her? Think again. You are truly the fool if you think that a drunken profession of undying love for Bingo will make him abandon his new bride. If you aren't a couple now, you're not going to be. If you have lust for the man, spill your guts to him before the wedding day, please.

Backing Out of the Invitation

You have RSVP'd yes to your friend's wedding. But as the time grows near, some financial or business fiasco occurs and you realize you're going to have to cancel. This call should be made no later than one month before the wedding so the couple still has time to make adjustments—unless, of course, it is a dire emergency that cannot be helped. Either way, you must inform the couple as soon as you know you will not be able to attend. Just not showing up is inexcusable and there is very little you can do to make it up to your friends.

⟶ *Second Marriages* ⟵

You've been through it once. You spent the money, wore the big, stupid dress, had it all come unraveled. This time—hopefully—you're more focused on the partnership that you're entering and less on the pomp of the actual wedding. Besides, you've also got better things to do with your money now—mortgage payments, investments, private-school fees, and so on. Which means you can actually have a nicer wedding this time. Your mother can't force you into a terrible dress. You can't be bullied by his mother into having more guests than you want. You can now just throw a very chic, small affair—something like a very festive cocktail party—to celebrate your wedding.

And do not wear white. Keep your ensemble to other hues. Think pewter, sand, even off-white if you must—but truly, anything too virginal becomes laughable.

YOUR FIANCÉ HAS CHILDREN

You've gone and fallen in love with a man who has children, either from a previous marriage or a one-night stand; it doesn't matter. He's committed for life, and if you say yes to his proposal, so are you. It doesn't really matter if his kids are brats or little angels, you have to decide if you can truly handle being a stepmother.

Top ten things to consider before saying "I do":

1. Age. How old are the kids? If they are quite young, you will have some influence over their upbringing. If they are teens, most of

the raising has been done and you will have to cope with whatever kind of behavior is already established in them.

2. Money. You may not think his child-support checks and his financing of his kids' college educations will bother you. Just wait until you can't go on vacation because he has to cough up cash for a French tutor.

3. Time. Will they be living with you? Will it be only every other weekend? Really think about how much of a life change this will be.

4. Phones, Internet, and television. As the kids grow, your access to your own electronics may be hampered. You may need to think about a separate phone line and about having to adjust your television watching to include horror films, sci-fi, and cartoons.

5. Mess. Kids are messy. Maybe you are too. How do you feel about picking up after them? How do you feel about not purchasing that very chic Bauhaus loveseat for fear of crayon marks and grape juice spills?

6. Delinquency. You think Billy's trouble with the law is a one-time offense? Wasn't there a twenty in your wallet this morning? And how do you feel about having the police come to your door at 3 a.m.?

7. Sex. Yours and theirs. Kids will cramp your sex life when they're in your home. If they're older, will you be able to cope with those "unofficial sleepovers"? Will your husband? Are you going to be running interference?

8. The Posse. If you live close to the kids' mom's house, chances are your place may also become a drop-in center for the kids and their friends. Add this point to the mess factor.

9. Her. What is the relationship between your future husband

and his ex-wife? Will she be calling you or criticizing you on how you coraise her kids? Can you handle this?

    10. Him. How is your future husband with his kids? Does he have control over them, or are they left to run wild? Do you and he have similar outlooks on how kids should be raised? And will he let you have a say in how his kids are raised?

All of the above

If you choose to have kids of your own at some point, you will probably wave aside all of these points as being just the way kids are. But when someone else's children are suddenly thrust upon you, you may find that the resentment and frustration are not what you bargained for.

I Do, Again

Second marriages can be fraught with tension if stepchildren are involved. Witness a certain knighted 1960s pop idol whose daughter refused to attend his second wedding. If you are entering marriage for the second time, you must invite your children even if you know they'll refuse—just think of the extra dollars you're saving at mealtime. Always make sure that the kids of a combining family are given equal billing in terms of their seating, both at the ceremony and at the reception. You can't put your kids at the head table and banish your new hubby's kids to Outer Siberia. There is also a balancing act in terms of attendants, and it is wise to invite kids from both sides to step into the bridesmaid/usher role, even if they decline.

The FG Stepmom

So despite all of the issues mentioned earlier about raising someone else's kids, or because of them, you're going through with the marriage anyway. And you know what that makes you? That's right: stepmom. If you think that the relationship with his kids will immediately get better once you're married, think again. If the kiddies are little tykes this transition will be smoother. After all, what the hell does a two-year-old know? But if you're marrying an older gent who has preteens and teens, look out. Just like those pop quizzes you had in high school, you will be tested. Fortunately, if your husband doesn't have full custody, chances are you'll only have the little dears every other weekend or on holidays.

As the new stepmom you are inheriting whatever type of relationship they have with their father. If they're quiet and sullen with him, don't expect it to be any different with you unless you are prepared to really work at it. However, unlike simply dating their dad, as a stepmother you now have more say in how they behave in your home. If they seem to consider weekends at Dad's a vacation where the adults cook, clean, and basically entertain them, you may have to make them understand that they are part of a family. And that means they have to do their part.

Contending with the First Wife

The first wife can be gracious and kind and not a problem at all. Or else she can be a living hell. It may be that she keeps calling day and night, keeps dropping by even when the kids aren't there. Or worse, she poisons the little dears' minds against you. First and foremost you must communicate your concerns to your new husband. Really, he should be the one to make the first few attempts at settling her down. If his talks don't help or result in a huge battle (after which she steps up her obnoxious behavior), you must step in. Arrange to meet for coffee, preferably on your turf so that she's at a disadvantage. Then as politely and kindly as possible ask her what is upsetting her. Does she disapprove of the way you're treating the children? The way your husband (this reminds her that he is no longer *her* husband) treats the kids? Of course you may end up with an uncontrolled tirade against the man you love, but listen. Then explain all the reasons she doesn't have to worry, and how very committed you are to making this blended family a success. Ask her to stop her irrational behavior. Depending on how reasonable she is, this may work. If you refuse to be her enemy by reaching out to her, her anger may dissolve. Or else it will wind her up more. If it is the latter you and your husband are going to have to form a brick wall around yourselves and lessen the communication as much as possible. Then talk to the kids and explain that adults will say things that aren't true when they're upset. Also really impress upon them that they are loved and shouldn't be caught up in any of it. This is a very difficult situation for everyone and cannot be taken lightly.

FG as New Stepkid

Even if you hate your future stepparent, you should behave like a grown-up and be at the wedding to support your parent in his or her new marriage. You don't have to have Sunday dinner every week, but you can show up this one day. You may grow to close to your step, and then you will be glad you didn't behave foolishly on the wedding day.

∞ *Divorce* ∞

LEAVING YOUR HUSBAND

If, as a married FG, you've finally decided that your marriage is over, the most difficult part may be having to say it out loud. Tell your closest friends first, before even telling your parents, for if Mom and Dad are still married they may not take it well, or if they too are divorced they may gloat or quip, "You're just like me." None of which you want to hear. Girlfriends, however, will provide the necessary comfort zone. Many people will say that you should tell your husband first, but women need to confide in their closest friends—that is part of the decision-making process. But beyond your closest pals, your husband has to be the first to know.

The Fabulous Girl needs a plan; she needs to have a place to go to immediately following the conversation, usually a best friend's. Select a time of day that gives you several hours to talk, not 11 p.m. Sit him down and say the words, "We need to talk. I don't think our marriage is working."

If you think that he'll react really badly, that is angrily, take the responsibility even if you don't mean it; your priority is leaving him without any danger that the confrontation will get nasty. "I'm sorry, it's my fault that things aren't working out, but I need space" will often do the trick. Talk about the situation as much as you can. You don't have to even utter the word *divorce* during this first conversation. Instead, use the discussion to transition into divorce-speak. Then leave and let him think and yourself think. You'll be fairly shaken up, which is why that friend's place is necessary.

As the Fabulous Girl friend, you will probably be aware if your best pal is going to sit down with hubby to tell him she's leaving. Stay by the phone. When she calls, offer to come over or invite her to your place. Either way, show up and be there if she needs you.

YOUR HUSBAND LEAVES YOU

If you're the one who is sat down and told, "I'm leaving you," it is an entirely different matter. In fact the whole separation process will be a shock. Whom do you tell and when? After the conversation you should call whomever you're closest to—a friend, your mother—it doesn't matter; you really shouldn't be alone. But you don't have to go around announcing it to everyone until you're ready. Some of us require time to heal and to adjust to the situation. Being abandoned is very hurtful and can take years to get over so there is no hurry to spread the word. When you are ready just say simply, "Bill and I have split up." People may react with shock and ask why, but you don't owe them the details. "I don't want to talk about it right now" is plenty to give them the hint to back off. And when you're ready you will.

Again, if you're the friend, be there immediately and let her cry and rant. Don't give too many opinions—"He's a rat who's never deserved you"—as your friend may turn her anger against you, for she may be blaming herself.

SUING FOR ALIMONY

There are laws that define how money and assets shall be divided once a couple separates and then divorces. But does that mean that an FG should take advantage of every chance she has to access her ex's bank account? If the two of you have children, their welfare should be the primary concern of you both. Any hesitation on his part to meet his financial obligations to your children should be dealt with seriously. But what if you didn't have children? Did you put your career on hold to support him while he went through med school? Did you alter your ambitions to follow him from one city to another for his career? Anything of this nature surely has had a financial effect on you, now and possibly into the future. You made these sacrifices thinking the two of you would be together forever and that whatever wealth came out of your mutual plans would be shared. It's fair then to expect some support from him after your split. If, however, the two of you were on an equal footing, you both worked during the time of your marriage, it's harder to rationalize his owing you money after the marriage ends.

What isn't polite is suing him just for revenge or to make him pay for whatever, say, an affair. These legal battles become bitter and lengthy and no one can move forward with revenge.

SIGNING THE DIVORCE PAPERS

This is the Fabulous Girl's Declaration of Independence—a sad ritual in which the FG must take pen in hand and sign the divorce papers. But sign them she must, and then it's all over but the crying, shouting, and perhaps cheering. An FG should not go through this day alone. Invite a friend along with you to the lawyer's office. Then go out for a cocktail.

Fabulous Girls must rally around their divorcing friends. Take them out for the night and don't talk about the divorce unless they want to. But be prepared for tears. Signing the papers may be the first time it hits your friend that her marriage is over. The second time will be when she receives her copy in the mail. Both of these occasions are yucky and will require you as the friend to offer up a shoulder and perhaps some scotch or martinis.

YOUR EX IS BAD-MOUTHING YOU IN FRONT OF THE KIDS

As tempting as it is, you and your ex should not under any circumstances vent your frustrations about each other in front of your offspring. No matter how tempting it is to say to little Timmy, "Your father is just too cheap to send you to private school—he's single-handedly denying you a proper education," don't say it!

If your ex is the one who's got the mean streak, confront him; you're divorced now so go for it. Tell him to back off with the negative comments. Then you may want to discuss it with your kids and explain how their father is still angry and doesn't actually mean what he says about you.

Once our dance was finished, I told Nice that I was going to the bar to get us some more champagne. Lucy, one of the bridesmaids, was also at the bar. I was asking her about her gorgeous unbridal-partylike dress when she suddenly let out a squeal.

We both turned and saw the gray-bearded man Elenor had been dancing with earlier, now standing beside Lucy. He had his hand on her butt and was giving it a mighty squeeze. Poor Lucy was mortified, but the gray-bearded groper just grinned and waltzed off.

"Who is that guy?" I whispered to Lucy.

"I don't know, but I feel like I need a shower now."

Instead, we went to the ladies' room, I carrying both glasses of champagne. There we found Missy, Elenor, and Helen, who was looking quite distraught.

"My Uncle Jack is going around grabbing women's asses!" cried Helen.

"Yes, he certainly is," said Lucy.

"Oh, God, I'm so sorry. I don't know what to do. He's always been a bit loopy but . . ."

Lucy put her arm around Helen and said, "Please don't worry; it's not your fault. It's a beautiful wedding, and one bad thing always has to happen, so now you can forget about worrying for the rest of the evening. Come on, let's go dance with our husbands."

And off they went.

I asked Missy why she and Joe were fighting, and she shrugged. "It's like he doesn't trust me anymore."

"What makes you think he doesn't trust you?" I asked.

"Um. Well, he read an e-mail I wrote to you guys about wanting to do it with Francis." Missy starting chewing on a fingernail but Elenor swatted her hand away.

"He read your e-mail! That is grounds for divorce. How dare he invade your privacy that way. How did he see it, anyway?" Elenor stood with her hands on her hips.

Missy explained that she'd left her laptop on and her e-mail program running one afternoon when she went to the gym. When she came home, she found Joe crying on the sofa.

"I couldn't even get mad at him for snooping. I mean, obviously I've been making him feel insecure or he wouldn't have been looking," said Missy.

Elenor still didn't look convinced by this argument.

"Come on, El, it's not like all of us haven't done a little snooping over the years," I said. Then I turned to Missy. "So what's going on now?"

"He's asked for a trial separation. Can I stay at your place for a bit? I don't want to be alone right now."

CHAPTER EIGHT

Home and Family

It's really not that Missy is impossible to live with. In many ways she is an ideal roommate. She's tidy, she's quiet, she bakes cookies. But very quickly it became obvious that my loft was not big enough for the two of us. I'd be trying to rush out the door to a waiting taxi when I'd realize that my keys were not in their normal home by the coatrack.

"Oh, keys don't go there anymore. They hang on this little rack here by the fridge." Missy smiled proudly.

Once the towels and sheets had moved, the kitchen had been entirely rearranged, and all the furniture in the living room had been spun around, I called a real estate agent. Although I was putting off telling Nice, I told Missy and Elenor over one of our dinners at Dominick's.

"You may as well do it on your own, that's how we all end up anyway," said Elenor darkly. As she neared the end of her pregnancy, Elenor was becoming more and more ominous. Missy and I had started to joke that we weren't going to make it through nine months.

"Missy, I know you were feeling like you weren't ready to be alone yet. I don't want you to think that I'm abandoning you. I could help you find a new roommate if you want."

"I'm fine. I don't want a roommate, actually. Can I just keep your loft?" asked Missy.

You see a lot of terrible places when you start looking. I went home crying after a couple of trips out. So many of the places I looked at were small and dark, and I began to panic that I'd never be able to afford something that felt like home. I'd go back to my loft and think, Why am I going to spend all the money I have to live in something that isn't nearly as cute as this? Then I'd trip across some new furniture project that Missy had dragged home with her and resolve again to find my own place. Betty, my real estate agent, kept telling me to relax, that eventually we'd find just the right thing for me. I loved her being about as far removed from a stereotypical real estate agent as you could imagine. She was cute and stylish, and we were always bumping into each other at vintage boutiques.

She called me at work on a Thursday about a place.

"I'm on deadline, I can't leave the office right now. Can we go and see it tomorrow?"

"Mmm. I think you need to find a way to see this place today. Like, right now. It's in *the* building. Oh, hang on a minute, I'm going through a tunnel. If I cut out, I'll call you back."

She did cut out. Which gave me a second to think of my favorite building in the city. It's a small place on a side street. Originally it was a college but it had been converted about five years earlier into condos. I had once gone to a party in one and had fallen in love with the place. I'd told Betty in our first meeting that it was where I really wanted to live. She'd laughed and said that things rarely came up there and to try to keep an open mind about what my future home might look like. I decided not to mention to anyone at work where I was slipping off to.

Betty called back to say that she was downstairs and to come on down. I ran.

· · ·

"It's my place. I feel like the guys who are in there just need to get out so I can move in. I can already see all my furniture there. I'm going to paint the big living-room wall lavender. And having the deck is going to feel like another room all summer." I gushed over dinner with Nice. He seemed to be taking it all in stride. He was nodding and smiling.

"It does sound great. But you'll need to see a lot of places before you know if this is really what you want to do."

"Um. Well, actually, I have been looking," I said. Nice started to frown. "I've seen about a dozen places and they've all been terrible. This just feels so right to me. It's what I want."

"This is what you want?" Nice was looking down into his drink. "I can't believe you didn't tell me you were looking."

"I guess I was worried about how it might make you feel. But it just feels like my home. I'm going to make an offer."

Now Nice was just nodding. "All right then."

I started to get worried. I mean, I'd thought that this was kind of a big step to take on my own, but I hadn't thought that other people would have a problem with it, even if one of those people was my boyfriend. I should have told him earlier, but every time I'd started to I'd gotten scared that he would take it badly. Sitting across from Nice, I realized I'd made a huge mistake and that all I could do was damage control.

"I can't wait for you to see it. I think you're really going to love it."

Nice shook his head. "I don't think so. This isn't going to work. You want to move ahead on your own. I'm ready for us to move forward together. We just don't want the same things."

"What are you saying? That if I won't get a place with you we're breaking up?" My voice was starting to crack. "I know I should have talked this over with you. That was really stupid. But you know there's room for someone to move in eventually . . ."

"Someone?"

"Well, I mean, you. There's room for you to move in if that's what we want to do."

Nice reached for his wallet and threw some money on the table. "It's obviously not what you want to do. Good luck with your new place."

❧ *Home Sweet Home* ❧

As an FG moves through life, with all the demands of career and relationships that usually go with it, she appreciates her nest more and more. It can be her sanctuary, her source of inspiration, or a reflection of her creativity. Her relationship to her home—be it a rental or her own—may also be complicated. Making a commitment to home and family is decidedly in the realm of grown-ups. And although the FG is a grown-up, she may occasionally have mixed feelings about her place in this world.

❧ *The Home Front* ❧

BUYING ON YOUR OWN

You've finally saved enough money to think about buying your own place. You phone the bank or a mortgage broker and lo and behold—they're going to give little old you a mortgage. You're elated! And so proud of yourself. You call to give friends and family the news, thinking they will be as thrilled as you are. Naturally, then, you're shocked when instead of hearing delight in their voices you hear—what's that?—sympathy? You've saved $45,000 for a down payment and they feel sorry for you. And you know why.

Going ahead and making this move on your own, particularly if you have a boyfriend, is like admitting defeat for some (okay, lots of) people. Instead of asking you what kind of place you're going to be looking for, your mother wants to know what the rush is. Your workmates want to know what his holdup is. And of course, if any of these feelings coincide with a bit of hesitation you might naturally be feeling yourself, these conversations can be devastating. Be tough. Be firm and repetitive, if necessary, about what a good thing this is that you're doing. Remind yourself that you can sell a house as easily as you can buy one (markets willing) if you ever decide you want to cohabitate. And then go out for drinks to celebrate with your more sensible friends.

Housewarming yourself

You've done it—you've saved up enough money for the down payment, you've jumped through enough hoops to make the bank happy, and you've bought a house all on your own. Naturally, you want to show off your new house or condo—and your accomplishment—to your friends and family. This is an enormous rite of passage for you. But FGs who make this move solo will often feel they are being left out of the gift loop. For traditional women there is a seemingly never-ending opportunity to be given gifts. Get engaged—there's an engagement party and lots of presents for you and your fiancé! Get married eight months later, the skies open and down come blenders, crystal wine decanters, 300-thread-count sheets, not to mention that check from Uncle Harold to help you out with your first house. First house? More presents of course. Have a baby? Get ready for more Snugglis and intellect-stimulating toys than you'll know what to do with. If you step off this road it can feel as if you become gift-invisible, which may strike an FG as unfair. Why isn't she being praised—and showered with presents—for looking after herself?

The thing about showers, and even weddings, is that ostensibly they are parties given by other people. Your maid of honor throws your wedding shower. A close friend throws a baby shower. You can, of course, give your own party when you buy a house. But it can't be a shower. You must invite people to see your place, but you must be offering them something: your hospitality. And isn't that one of the reasons you got your own place—to have a great space to entertain? Invite people over and proudly give them a tour of your new digs. Offer them cocktails and snacks like the grown-up that you are. Of course, when people aren't expected to shell out for gifts they often feel more generous than when they are.

High maintenance

Once you become a home or condo owner, you're going to need some new people in your life. An FG can't be good at everything. Owning a place is not going to endow you with sudden knowledge of electrical circuitry or the widths of copper pipes. Luckily, there are scores of those who do know these things, and you can employ them. The FG does not subscribe to the Zen of Motorcycle Maintenance. Many FGs believe their time is better spent making money or just making dinner reservations than it is learning how to rewire the living room. However, as unusual as it may seem, there may come a point when the FG-as-renovation-girl rears her head. Perhaps it's a desire for full-on independence, or simply that she loves the feel of that power tool vibrating in her hand. But just in case the do-it-herself project doesn't quite work, or the deadline for her cocktail party is looming, it is wise to have on hand the phone numbers for the following:

~ A plumber
~ An electrician
~ A handyman
~ A cleaning lady (Of course, if you can afford it, it's nice to have a standing appointment with a cleaning lady. But even if this isn't in your cards just yet, it's nice to know one you trust to call upon before a party or a visit from your parents.)

An FG can often find that she needs help making her life run. Having someone clean her house or apartment is one of the best time savers she can invest in. Having probably done nasty jobs herself at one time or another, she may feel a little uncomfortable employing such a person. Hiring an independent cleaning lady rather than one through an agency is a good idea. That way you know all the money you're paying goes to her rather than the agency's taking a cut. Many people who would never dream of being rude to a waiter—and there are plenty who would—for some reason feel that cleaning ladies do not warrant polite treatment. By hiring a cleaning person you are entering into quite an intimate relationship with someone. You should offer her a coffee if you're having one and discuss with her what is more comfortable for both of you—your leaving her alone while she works, or your hanging around.

IRKSOME, ANNOYING, AND TROUBLEMAKING NEIGHBORS

When you think of your home—be it house, condo, or apartment—you probably think of the space you actually own or inhabit. But the space that affects you is actually much larger than that. There is the street outside your home, the hallways of your building, the laundry room . . . and then there are the walls that separate you from them—them being the neighbors. Even if you have a cordial relationship with your neighbors, things can get sticky. As one FG discovered, the walls that separate your bedroom from your neighbor's may not stop any sounds from making the trip over. If your bedtime is now fraught with worry over whether tonight is going to be a lucky one for Sally next door because she and her boyfriend like to scream embarrassingly clichéd phrases, you need to politely let them know. No, not with a handwritten note, but with song. The next time you start to hear the sounds of love making their way through the walls, burst into song, just loud enough (and you should know roughly what decibel level) for Sally and Mr. You're-So-Hot to hear you.

Of course, sexually active neighbors are not the sole cause of noise pollution. The Fabulous Girl knows never to play music outdoors or to have an intimate chat at 2 a.m. on the front lawn (sound carries in the quiet night). But for the FG, especially if she works at home or needs to get some rest on the weekends, her neighbors' endless screaming or blaring radios can completely ruin her day. The Fabulous Girl gets tough in these situations. Yes, she might create some tension by doing so. But she's not trying to win a popularity contest, she's trying to enjoy her living space. Starting with her immediate neighbors, she goes over and introduces herself and lets them know that she works at home, or that she'd really appreciate it if they wouldn't start their chainsaw experiment until at least 10 a.m. on the weekends.

SCARY NEIGHBORS

Let's face it, you never know who might be living next door. Your neighbor's house is unkempt, there's trash everywhere, unsavory types are coming and going at all hours, or there is the perpetual stench of pot or garbage lingering in the hallways. What is a Fabulous Girl to do? Quite frankly if you're in a rental situation you may want to consider moving. But if that is not an option and your scary neighbor seems to be staying forever you should try to make peace. At a minimum, your creepy neighbors are unaware of how their lifestyle is affecting everyone else around them. It's awkward, but you're going to have to come out and describe what's bothering you, even though it seems painfully obvious.

But if their attitude is one of passive aggression you'll need another tactic. You're going to have to be willing to be the bitchy neighbor who won't stop complaining—politely, of course—until they pick up their garbage, turn down the stereo, or remedy whatever the situation is. If the central problem is messiness you may want to offer to help clean up his or her part of the common area. Or, you may try simply cleaning it on your own and often this is enough to guilt a slovenly person into tidying up. If not, unless there is a local law and government office to complain, there isn't much you can do. If the trouble is the unsavory strangers at 2 a.m. and they are disturbing your sleep, you will have to politely take it up with the neighbor. "I hate to complain but your visitors keep waking me up; is there any way to keep the noise down?" You have to be consistent, in fact relentless, all the while being as calm and polite as you can. You will not come off as a wimp; rather your neighbor will understand that you are standing your ground, and you'd be surprised how often assertive manners can work in your favor.

TROUBLE LANDLORDS

This is often a big hassle for renters. You almost never hear people talking about their fabulous, reliable landlord. Either the building is not maintained properly, or the landlord drags his feet in getting things done and you're the one left with the toilet that won't flush or a faucet that won't stop dripping. It behooves an FG to begin her relationship with her landlord, be it a person or a company, on a formal footing. If the person in charge is really a big management company and the man who fixes things works for the company, you have a way to complain. You must telephone the appropriate management person at the company, and write him or her a formal letter of complaint. It is vital to have official records with proper dates in order to get these management firms to listen. If the offending party is the owner of the property and your complaints are falling on deaf ears, you will have to take it up with your local government body that deals with these issues. Most cities and states have a landlord-tennant agreement in place to cope with these very problems.

Of course this is a great hassle, and again, you can try relocating.

UNWANTED GUESTS

When you have a place of your own you may find yourself on the list of free places to crash for certain types of "friends." There is nothing wrong with a friend who's had one too many martinis flaking out on the sofa once in a while. But out-of-town guests who want a weekend in the city and who perpetually turn up on your doorstep either unannounced or with one day's notice can be quite enough, thank you very much. You know the type: you don't hear from them for months at a time and then when they're with you they expect you to entertain them all day and night. Your home is not your buddy Billy Bob's holding pen. If this person is a repeat offender you will have to learn to say no. Even if no means making stuff up. "Sorry, Billy Bob, my cousin is in town so I don't have the room." But there's really nothing wrong with saying, "You know what, it's just not a good time for me. I'm so busy at work that I'm not up to it." Perhaps a suggestion that Billy Bob stay with another friend will be enough of a hint. Draw a line of comfort for yourself; how often do you want overnight guests? Of course this depends entirely on the person who wants to stay. But if there are people you can tolerate only once a year, stick to your guns and say no.

⧼ *Family* ⧽

YOU WANT A BABY

It can come over you unexpectedly, the desire to have a baby. Yesterday your biggest preoccupation was getting through all the work on your desk while still finding a moment to run out and get a glycolic. But today you can't keep your mind from turning to a more primal desire: you want to get pregnant. If you're in a relationship with someone who is as keen to procreate as you are, you're off to the races. You are probably going to tell a few close girlfriends, and maybe your mother, that you've made this decision. But you should consider not telling many people, or even those very close to you. You don't know how long it's going to take you to get pregnant or, sad to say, if you will at all. Many FGs put off the baby phase of their life as long as they can, hoping to achieve the career goals they're after before taking a break from the workplace. While this is a perfectly understandable impulse, it's one that can make getting pregnant that much tougher. The last thing you need is for every conversation to start with "So . . . ?" What you may not do is announce at cocktail parties that you and your man are "trying." (And you really, really musn't make the quote mark signs with your hands while saying "trying." Just never make the quote mark signs with your hands, ever.) Because when you say you are "trying," what you are really saying is that you are having sex, and why do you need to proclaim that in a party situation?

Sneak-a-Baby

An FG wants it all: great career, great apartment, great guy, great baby! Oops. Being the busy overachiever that she is, she will have to do some serious rearranging to make room for a child. Her sense of herself is going to have to undergo some renovations as well. She will no longer be the happy-go-lucky girl who can go out to a party on a moment's notice (unless she has a wonderful live-in nanny). She also has to convince the man in her life that this is the right moment for them to move from couple to parents.

And she must really do this—not present her pregnancy to him as a done deal. It's amazing how many women who did anything it took to not get pregnant throughout their twenties and early thirties are somehow caught off guard by birth-control issues in their mid- to late thirties. Women who have been on the pill for years suddenly find themselves conflicted over whether to keep with it as they get older. Maybe they have an unspoken pact with their men that this is the only way they're going to do it—by "accident." Maybe they're crazy. But it is both unethical and risky to try the Sneak-a-Baby route to motherhood. You may think he's a stand-up guy who will stick with you through this, but you don't know for sure. You also risk his resenting you, which could happen even if he falls deliriously in love with the baby.

Having a baby on your own, or Plan B

If you are ready for a child in every other way except being in a relationship, you may consider going it alone. Many FGs have what is known as a Plan B: a way to get pregnant that does not involve a romantic commitment from a man. This is tricky to pull off—tricky, but not impossible. Some Plan Bs involve gay friends. An FG may have a gay friend who is willing to knock her up (in some way or other). The FG may also have a male friend who is not a romantic possibility but who is willing to do the job. For reasons that are obvious, everyone involved in these scenarios must be very clear about what they are doing.

If you do decide to go ahead with a Plan B, you need a lawyer. You obviously should have a frank conversation with your potential donor, but you still need a lawyer. How involved is this man going to be in the future of your child? What are you going to do when your child wants to know who her daddy is? What if he goes on to have more children in the more traditional way? What if you do? Is money going to change hands?

You Don't Want a Baby

Choosing to remain child-free can be a difficult choice for some, or not a choice at all for others. We're not discussing women who for whatever biological reason cannot have a baby, but those who choose to not even try. This decision is often very threatening to other people in our society. They will say to your face that you are selfish and shallow. Well, maybe you are. You want a life that is free for travel and adventure. You may not want to put your body through the trauma. You want to work hard to pay for Prada pumps, not a pram. Instead of saving for a college tuition, you're saving for a winter house in St. Barts.

Be prepared that if you remark to a roomful of people that you don't plan on having kids, more often than not someone will ask why. Usually these people are parents. They may be resentful that you are not choosing the common path. They think that you are somehow being critical of them by not doing the normal thing. Take a deep breath and tell the truth: "I'm not interested; I like my freedom."

The phrase *child-free* was coined by people who chose to not have children but resented the incompleteness suggested by the term *childless*. Of course *child-free* is a source of much anger for parents, as they feel the term implies that they have lost their freedom by having kids, or that they are somehow imprisoned by their choice. Well, actually, by and large they are. Parents have lost the freedom to move about the world as they did when they were without the kids. But they obviously made the choice to have kids, and one would think they are happy to relinquish some of those freedoms. Nonetheless, it may be better to refrain from using *child-free* around newer parents of your own age group who are probably grappling with their decision or adjusting to their new way of life.

Of course, if you are around a new mom who can't stop talking about her spawn and bugging you to have one, then *child-free* becomes very, very useful and should be employed. Consider the term to be in the FG arsenal of conversational controls.

Pregnant Friends

When a colleague or someone you've simply been introduced to at a dinner party tells you she's pregnant, you know to express pleasure in her news. If you are of a baby-bearing age yourself, her confession may trip off other feelings as well, which are better kept to yourself. If you haven't yet had a child, or aren't sure if you are going to, try not to use this moment to air all your baby-related anxieties. You must be very close friends indeed to ask a woman how she and her man will deal with a declining sex drive in those first baby years. Do not ask her what the odds are that her baby may have congenital defects because of her age. Don't linger on the subject of the difficulties of blending the modes of motherhood and career. And don't go on and on about how you would never raise a child in the city as she plans to do. Rest assured that these are all issues that keep her up in the middle of the night. She does not need you to tell her how frightening having a baby can be.

When you wish it were you

As in the wedding scenario, a close friend who is pregnant can make an FG who wishes she were preggers jealous. Perhaps you always thought you would have a child first, or perhaps your friend never really wanted a child but is now in full eight-month glow. Either way this is not the time to air your envy. Pregnant women are rife with hormones and emotions. She doesn't need to hear your comments. Tell another friend your woes, but it isn't polite to whine to the mom-to-be. The most you could get away with and still be gracious would be a softly spoken "Oh, I really want a baby too."

BAD BABY NAMES

When chatting with parents-to-be, people commonly inquire after the list of potential names that are currently in play. Whatever names potential parents mention, your response should be the same: "Oh, that's nice." That is all that is required of you. No one is asking you what you would name your child or even what you think of their choice. Do not, as happens with shocking regularity, start a monologue about how you knew a Linda and, whoa, what a bitch! If they want your opinion they will ask for it. Learn to distinguish between what is being told to you—"I'm naming him Mark"—versus "What do you think of the name *Mark*?"

Of course, if your friend or relative is naming her child Dweedleduff or something truly crazy, you may casually ask the origins of the name and if perhaps he or she has thought through the culture in which the child will be raised and therefore whether it is an appropriate choice.

These rules must be applied even more stringently to babies who are already born and named. FGs have been known to be screamed at by horrified relatives after making the call from the hospital. Having just endured the emotional and physical trauma that is childbirth, the last thing an FG needs is to be criticized in any way. She certainly doesn't need Mom to ask, "What kind of name is Isabel? That's a terrible name! Why don't you give her a nice name like Mary, not an awful name like Isabel?" With the FG reduced to tears and the baby reduced to Mary, the only happy person is the FG's mother, although she will be slightly annoyed when the FG's three-year-old daughter can't stop calling the baby Mary-not-Isabel.

WHEN YOUR FRIENDS DON'T TEACH
THEIR CHILDREN MANNERS

One of the most important lessons we teach children is how to move through society with ease and grace. The child-rearing principles of the last few decades have been focused on fulfilling the child's creativity and self-confidence. Obviously these things are important, but if they are emphasized to the detriment of other, more cooperative values, the child is having a grave disservice done to it. Kids (and adults, for that matter) who cannot share, who do not know the value in thinking of other people's feelings, are not well liked and have trouble getting ahead in the world. Example is the best way to teach children the importance of manners. Particularly vital is how you treat them. Many people have a distinct set of rules for their own children, and it's often not nearly as decorous as it is for the rest of the world.

So what to do if your friends' kids are ill-mannered? Bratty? Rude to adults and mean to other kids? For one thing you can ask the parents to find a babysitter when you host your annual pool party. If you're not in control of the invitations and you are confronted with screaming spoiled rug rats, and the parents are too busy enjoying themselves confident in the knowledge that others will do the parenting for them, then do it. Take little Timmy aside when he swats the dog and say, "Timmy, do not hit the dog, it is mean," or "Timmy, you have to learn to share or else you won't have any friends when you grow up." Or if little Timmy is getting into things he shouldn't, say the fish tank or the Royal Doulton collection, then march up to the parents: "Excuse me, but Timmy needs your attention." Be ready for a shocked reaction. We live in a culture that, sadly, does not believe in the collective teaching of children. It used to take a village; now it takes an FG!

WHEN PEOPLE TELL YOU WHAT TO DO WITH YOUR KIDS

Everyone has a sense of what child-rearing should look like. Usually this is based on their own experience of childhood. Either they feel that their upbringing was correct and so everyone should raise their children in a similar fashion or they feel that they were raised wrongly and so everyone should do the opposite. In any case, no role in the world is as commented upon as that of the mother. Everyone's an expert. And many will not hesitate to tell a woman what she should be doing with her child.

This is both upsetting and annoying. The FG wants to do this job well, and she is susceptible to the hints that she is doing otherwise. We're not talking about the helpful, supportive conversations that can exist between parents—"Have you read this excellent book on getting them to sleep through the night?"—we're talking about people who jam a pacifier in your baby's mouth after you've told them you've decided not to use one. It's true that if you are firm and clear with people in these moments they may think you're a bit of a bitch—"I just said I don't' use pacifiers, please take it back and do not give it to her." But they will also stop sticking a pacifier in your baby's mouth.

WHEN THE BABY JUST WON'T STOP CRYING

You feel bad, the baby obviously feels bad, everyone who is staring at you in the mall feels bad. Your baby is crying. No, make that keening, and you know there's nothing you can do about it until you get to the car, washroom, or wherever. Meanwhile, people are staring at you as if they're ready to call Children's Aid. You do not need to give apologetic looks to anyone who is staring at you, and you may brush off any questions after your baby's health. There's very little you can do. Other than leave the situation.

The movies

Unless you are at one of those screenings reserved for parents and babies, you must leave if your little one fusses for more than a couple of minutes. Actually, even if you are at one of those screenings, you should get up if the baby screams for too long. No one in the cinema has paid to listen to your child express his teething pain.

Restaurants

If you are in a posh place, you probably should have already booked a babysitter. It's an excellent idea to introduce small children to the culture of restaurants. The more you do, the better behaved they will be. But some restaurants are better suited for children than others. You're not banished to fast food just because you're in the family way, but it is a good idea to go to laid-back places en famille. Even in a relaxed spot, you must get up and go outside if your baby takes a fit. A little whining or sniveling is fine, but you know very well when your child is about to go over to the other side. Step outside, walk around the block, see if you can shake it off, and then come back. Otherwise, it's just not fair to the other people in the restaurant.

The plane

This is one of the toughest situations for parents. There's just nowhere to go, and frankly, who can blame the kid for crying—commercial air travel sucks these days. The food, the seat size—you'd cry too if it were more acceptable. Talk to your pediatrician before your trip. If you're traveling with an infant, it's probably a good idea to nurse or give the baby a bottle during takeoff and landing to ease the pressure in his ears. Some doctors recommend giving babies or small children a dose of pain relief to make them sleepy for the duration of the flight. If all else fails and the baby cannot be comforted, there's nothing you can do. And you don't owe anyone an apology. Of course it's miserable for everyone, but what can you do?

A Death in the Family

Because an FG is such a responsible, caring person, it's likely that when someone in her family dies, many of the burdens of planning a funeral will fall on her. If she was close to the person who died, this may actually be a blessing in disguise. Having the tasks surrounding a funeral to look after can be distracting and even comforting. If she comes from a religious family, what needs to be done will be obvious to her. If her family is not associated with a church or synagogue, things are slightly harder to manage. The staff of a funeral home will help with many of the plans. She should organize some kind of get-together for family. An afternoon event makes sense if people with children will be attending.

How to help a friend during the grieving process
The Fabulous Girl should come to the aid of her closest friends during their time of need. The death of a parent or other loved one is always a shock no matter how prepared one is. If you receive the phone call from your friend, immediately offer your services:

1. Make telephone calls to mutual friends and let her employers know.
2. If she's single with little family, offer to escort her to the various funeral homes or dial them up and get quotes on packages.
3. Help arrange the service and any reception afterward.
4. Offer to have her stay with you, or you with her, for, at the very least, the night of the funeral.

SIBLING RIVALRY

Of course the Fabulous Girl would like to have outgrown her life-long case of sibling rivalry, but sometimes it's just the hardest habit to break. Unfortunately, a sister or brother is not as easy to escape interaction with as, say, a cousin or nasty aunt. How you cope with the rivalry will depend upon which of you is the sibling with the issue.

Their issue

So your sister cannot seem to get beyond her resentment of your successes as a star athlete. She hates the attention you get, the accolades, and so on. Yet growing up, you worked your ass off in the skating rink while she preferred hanging at the mall with her slacker pals. You may avoid her as much as possible but when forced to endure family gatherings you need to be as kind as can be. Your sister is insecure in her own achievements and this type of envy is not rational. And while it may actually bug the hell out of you that she thinks she has grounds for bitterness, there's no use in getting defensive. Your explanation of dedication and discipline (what it takes to be you) will fall on deaf ears and in fact may incite more vitriol.

Instead try taking an interest in her life. Ask her about her job, boyfriend, apartment, et cetera. This may seem as though you are compensating for your success but it will go a long way to bridging the gap. If, however, she is still hostile to you, you need a sister-to-sister confrontation. There will be tears and pent-up emotion, but you need to say, "Stella, you seem to resent my success. Can we talk about it and work it out?" You may be surprised how a good rant may alleviate years of tension.

Another type of situation that may develop over time is the "shadow." Your sister starts doing everything you do or a reasonable facsimile. Be it moving to a groovy neighborhood, or coaching girls' skating just to be successful in the sport, she may even trade on your name for advancement. There is, however, little you can do. If you complain about it to others or to her, then suddenly *you* are jealous or selfish. Instead, take the high road and allow her these rather sad attempts to copy you.

Your issue

When it is the FG who has an issue with, say, her starving artist brother whose upkeep her parents maintain while she earns her own keep, she navigates it with grace. Examine where the feelings of sibling rivalry originate. Is because you always felt your parents liked your brother more than you? Are you jealous that he is the creative one while you are merely a corporate lawyer? Does your brother put you down and make you feel inadequate in some way? Or are you simply unsatisfied with your own life? Once you determine where it comes from—your parents, your brother, or you—then you can deal.

Occasionally parents need to be made aware of their own behavior. Express to them how you feel about their less than democratic demonstrations of affection (wise to do, by the way, if you are the successful one). Tell them it hurts your feelings, and worse, hurts your relationship with your brother. Remember, being a parent isn't about cutting the pie equally every time. The fact that your parents help your brother out financially and not you is based on his inability to make ends meet. They know you can look after yourself. He's probably jealous of you for being the more self-reliant kid who gets a more mature relationship with your parents. But if your brother is constantly running down what you do and pumping himself up, he is merely insecure and can be ignored. Tell him you see what is going on and it doesn't bother you in the least (yes, lie).

If it is your issue deal with it on your own. Have a heart-to-heart with your brother or your parents and tell them how you feel. Find a way to spend time with your parents and your brother that's particular to you rather than constantly comparing yourself to him.

Sibling competitiveness

There is the other type of sibling rivalry, whereby both of you (or three or four of you) all have mutual resentment. As kids you always tried to outdo each other, and now it's the same in adulthood. Is it competing for parental attention? Probably. This can be unhealthy if the competitiveness is extreme—your sister is still stealing your boyfriends—and sometimes counseling is in order. You may find that you need to avoid contact with your sister or brother for a while and keep your own life private.

ENDING FAMILY FEUDS

The worst kind of family feud is the kind you inherit. You're not even sure why you don't like your cousins on your father's side, but you don't. The mere mention of them at family dinners spurs everyone to repeat the three irritating qualities they are known to embody. After a while it doesn't make sense to you. You've never met these people. You're not sure why they've been shut out. In fact, the feud likely has its origins in some generation before yours. It takes courage to break out of these family structures.

So when you receive a call from that "other" cousin who was—according to family lore—a no-good, you hesitate briefly before accepting his invitation to dinner. Sure, you've never had any firsthand experience with him, but such terrible stories couldn't be all conjecture. Off you go to dinner, anticipating much discomfort. Only it doesn't unfold that way. To your surprise, your cousin is gracious, kind, and open. It turned out that neither of you knows what started the family feud—which you rename the "family fuss." After some wine and laughs, you two cousins decide to remain close and ignore the crap you've inherited from both sets of parents. But you will definitely be upsetting people if you rock the boat by hanging out. You may need to warn those who may feel slighted by your actions.

If you're the one who wants to patch it up, start small. Send a letter to your long-lost cousin or whomever and introduce the idea of a reconciliation. This may send a ripple effect of disapproval throughout the family but you must stand up for yourself and tell them, "Cousin Jenny is my family too, and I have a right to know her."

Dealing with Family Fuck-Ups

Every family has one: the person who seems to channel the entire family's worth of trouble and project it out onto the world in spectacular ways. Your younger sister, who went from smoking joints at recess to getting pregnant by her drug dealer to engaging in petty crime herself. Your father's devastating problem with gambling and what it's done to your mother's future security. Your cousin's coke addiction, which she won't have treated, leaving her parents waiting for the phone calls that come randomly from around the country. When dealing with family fuck-ups, an FG needs to bring all her diplomatic abilities to the fore.

The problem with fuck-ups is that they tend to work in secrecy. If you are close to them, they will want to draw you into a web of secrecy as well. The FG should avoid this at all costs. Not only does it compromise her relationships with the rest of her family, it does not help the fuck-up either. Your knocked-up little sister may confide in you and then ask you to keep her secrets from your parents. Your father may rely on all his children to not call a spade a spade—a gambler a gambler—to keep up his dangerous habits. Be clear that you can't make any such promises and that you don't like being put in such a position. You can still be available to help this person, but not necessarily in the way he or she wants help. When the late-night call comes—it's always the late-night call, isn't it?—asking for money or for a place to stay, make an offer that you feel will really help. Your sister can stay with you for a month and the two of you will make it a project to find her an apartment of her own that she can afford. You'll phone around and look into treatment centers for your cousin. You'll be a help but not the solution to their problems.

WHEN TO CUT THINGS OFF WITH YOUR FAMILY

Sometimes there's just no way to resolve family disputes. You've tried to work it out with your parents. But your folks hate your common-law boyfriend and flatly refuse to include him in family functions or even to acknowledge him when you're together. You've told your brother you can't bail him out of debt again. It's time—at least for now—to take a break from being disappointed. If it's at all possible, you should tell the offending family member what your plans are. Let your brother know that until he at least starts making an effort to repay his debt to you, you won't be able to have any contact with him. You're looking forward to that changing, but until he stops gambling, there's just no other way. Try to make these announcements in as calm a way as possible. If you scream them out during one of your regular scraps with your stepmother, they will be lost in your usual fight-and-make-up pattern. To really cut people off you must be calm and firm in your communication. You have to let them know that this is an exceptional thing you're saying. You need them to hear that you've set a limit and you expect them to honor it. Of course, at first they won't. They will try to drag you back into the old dysfunctional way you always operated in.

MOVING BACK HOME

Despite the FG's best efforts, there may come a time, usually in her midtwenties (or after a divorce at any age), when she will need to bunk out at home—"home" not meaning that groovy loft you rented when you had that groovy job but the one you moved out of after high school or college. That's right, Mom and Dad's. This is a most difficult transition. For many young people, just when they've gained some respect from their parents and proved themselves as adults, disaster strikes and renders them teens again. Depending on the type of relationship you have with your folks, this can be a positive retreat to help regain composure or it can be hell in a bunk bed.

The conversation

It's humiliating to have to make the first phone call asking if you can come home. A few tears may elicit sympathy, but what you need to do is sit down with your folks and tell it like it is. Ask them what their expectations are while you're staying there. It's not a hotel, and you need to know what will make them comfortable. Remind them that you are not a teen any longer and will not adhere to curfews. You're not going to be updating them on the hour as to your whereabouts. Let them know you may sometimes opt to sleep at a friend's or your boyfriend's.

Meals

If your mom is in any way domestic, or if she isn't, she may see this as the time to be the perfect mom you never had. She may start doing your laundry, cooking meals for you, and cleaning up after you. For the first week or two this is fine—after all, some sort of drama must have forced you home, so a bit of TLC from Mom is just what you need. But after two weeks, it's time to pick up the slack and do your share around the house. Cook for your parents and help with the chores.

Calling

Because your folks do worry about you, if you're not coming home for a meal or don't plan to sleep at home, call them or leave a note before you go out.

Bills and board

If you really are financially strapped, paying board may be difficult, but you shouldn't take your folks for a free ride either. Two rent-free months or enough to save up for another apartment is plenty. More than that and you are a mooch. Discuss in advance what you all feel is fair. Even if your parents don't need your contribution, you may feel more comfortable about your stay if you make it anyway. Paying your share of the phone and utilities is the minimum gesture you should make.

A little loan

Things may be even tighter than that. You've been laid off unexpectedly and weren't ever making the so-called big bucks. You may need to borrow money from your parents as well as stay with them for a while. Again, be frank. Let them know that you intend to pay it back and propose a schedule for payments. You're going to have to live frugally if you decide to go this route. If you don't want them thinking you are just freeloading, you can't come home with designer shopping bags once a week.

The getaway plan

You may not know how long it will take to get back on your feet, but try to set a goal and tell it to your parents: "I only need three months." If it turns out you need longer, address it at that time. Don't let yourself fall into the trap of having time just pass you by.

Sex

If your parents let you do it in your room in high school, you may think it's all fine and dandy now. But really, there is something rather pathetic about boinking your boyfriend in your parents' house if you're over the age of nineteen.

A MEMBER OF YOUR FAMILY MOVES IN WITH YOU

You hope it's temporary. At least that's what your sister Joan says it is when she shows up out of work and evicted. But you know Joan. You grew up with Joan. Joan won't leave until she meets another man to mooch off. But for now, you're the one she turns to. You must lay down some ground rules. First and foremost is money. If she's staying longer than a month, she needs to contribute to the rent. If less than a month, she must ante up for groceries and long-distance calls. What do you do, however, if Joan just won't pay?

The FG may have to adopt the "it takes two" approach to life. As in "It takes two to keep two." So when you run out of toilet paper, don't replace it (keep a secret stash for yourself) and let Joan get the hint. Same for milk and other necessities. Insist she come shopping with you for foodstuffs, and inform her on the way that you'll be splitting the bill.

The second issue is guilt. Family members can really play the "but you're my sister" card. Or your parents may expect it of you—after all, you're the only family little Joanie has in the big city. Don't fall for it. It's one thing to help someone down on her luck, but it's quite another to become her doormat. You'll know which one you are. Try to establish how long he or she will be staying with you. As the date approaches, make some gentle inquiries as to how the evacuation plan is coming along.

When parents come to stay

This can be very difficult if the family member isn't sister Joan but your mother. Moms feel entitled to live with you—after all (and there is some truth to this), they raised you and kept a roof over your head. But moms who need a roof and have other siblings or offspring should do the family tour. Work this out with your family members. Caring for one's parent should never fall to one family member only.

Maintaining your life

Mom or Joan aside, you still have a thriving social calendar. Even if you have the grooviest parents alive, they can cramp your style. This is not to say that a dinner party or cocktail hour cannot include them, it is just a different affair. But you may conclude that even if they're under your roof, waking up with Bingo in your bed and Mom downstairs isn't the lifestyle you're after.

It is surprising how soon the parent-child roles return to their adolescent state when sex is involved. "Dear, do you really think that Bingo boy is right for you? I mean, he didn't even remove his shoes at the door . . ." Or if you do choose to spend the night elsewhere, "Is this how you conduct yourself? Sleeping around? You'll never get anywhere living like a harlot."

The FG will have to lay down her own law if family guests get too interested in her welfare. Firmly inform them that you are quite capable of making these decisions and you're happy they're interested, but that they needn't worry.

Of course, there is some benefit to the FG if she is close to her family—their presence will be soothing if Bingo proves to be a lout. Moms are great for late-night cups of cocoa and a shoulder to cry on.

Aging Parents

Caring for parents should never fall to one child, unless of course you are an only child then you have no choice. It may be that your brother Tony is the only sibling who still lives in your home town. Or Tony is the only kid who ever really got along with your father. Dad never understood your FG-ness. Nonetheless, Tony needs help. Offer to spend time with your parent on holidays so that the caretaker gets a break.

Be involved in big decisions. Does your mom or dad need to be cared for in a professional facility? Which one? Who will pay? These questions need to be decided by all parties—don't lay it on one person because he or she is in that part of the country. You may have to get on a plane and go look at seniors' residences with your sibling. It is the responsibility of all kids to take care of elderly parents. The FG gets proactive. And if you do all live in the same town, there is no excuse for one kid to do all the caring. If you find that you are in fact being saddled with *all* the responsibilities call a family meeting and plainly tell your sisters and brothers that they need to do their share. Make a regular meeting every month to ensure that everyone is holding up their end of the bargain.

Looking after an elderly parent isn't a chore. You may need to acquire new patience in coping with your new role—a reversal of parent and child. This may be an adjustment. But it does not have to be a negative one—it should be cherished.

However cherished, it can be stretch if you haven't spoken to your father in ten years or if your mother is an alcoholic. These difficult situations will make caring for your parent more emotionally fraught but it is wise to make the attempt. You never want to be a child whose parent died before a truckload of issues could be resolved. You may find that in their elderly and infirm state you can reconcile. If, despite all efforts, you still don't get along or the parent becomes abusive, you should seek a professional caregiver to ease the burden.

MONSTERS-IN-LAW

You love your husband. He loves you. Your parents love him. His parents hate you. God knows why—you're an FG. Parents usually eat from your hand. Some chromosomal defect on their part has created a glitch in their psyches and they've taken against you. They've probably hated every woman in his life. And you just had the nerve to marry him thinking that the solidity of this move would inspire them to rethink their reaction to you. Nope. They just don't like you. Moreover, they barely hide it. When you pick up the phone, they ask, "Who's that on the line?" When they come for dinner, they spend the evening asking after his work and his friends and ask you to pass the mashed potatoes. Things get worse when you have children. Of course, they adore their grandchildren, but they make no bones about the fact that you're doing a terrible job of being a mother. When the baby cries in their presence, they turn to you and ask, "Why is he crying?" As if they already know the answer: you're his mother.

Your husband absolutely must take a stand in this situation. Of course, you can handle yourself. But if he doesn't acknowledge how rude they are being to you, your hands are tied. It's more than a bit difficult for you to let them know how their behavior makes you feel if he's carrying on as if it's normal. But remember, the way they treat you is not just a reflection of their poor opinion of you, it's a reflection of their poor opinion of him. He needs to face this. And he needs to tell them in no uncertain terms that if they want to have contact with you, him, and your children, they'll play nicely. You're probably never going to be close with them, but they must treat you like an adult member of the family.

Any family dynamic (you don't care for your in-laws, your parents aren't crazy about your husband) that pits husband against wife must be dealt with together. Decide that regardless of the demands put on you as individuals, you'll face it as a couple. Eventually, your cranky family members will see that they're getting nowhere with their behavior and give it up.

If your husband fails to stand up to his mother or father, this situation will only get worse. You will have constant fights on your hands as a couple, and his parents will drive you apart. Really, he has no excuse; otherwise you won't be sharing family gatherings with him.

How to Avoid Family Gatherings

If you happen to live in another city, getting out of family events is a cakewalk. But if your relatives inhabit your neighborhood or are within commuting distance, wangling out of Thanksgiving or birthdays may be more tricky. If you're a known career FG, work is usually enough to let you off the hook. But really, you will need to be present for at least one family gathering per year. Call these command performances. Every FG will know which dinner or party is the one that she will attend lest she be disowned.

How to avoid his family gatherings

Many couples find it necessary to be democratic about holiday time, and to alternate which family gets the happy couple each year. Unfortunately, the FG just doesn't always enjoy her boyfriend's/husband's family. Perhaps his parents fight the entire time, or perhaps they pick on her beau constantly. Whatever the reason, the FG finds herself daydreaming about what her own family is doing that very moment and she makes a silent pact to never spend the holiday with these people again.

Now she has to put her plan into action. For one thing, she can be honest and tell her man that his relatives make her uncomfortable and ruin the holidays for her. Chances are, he too is confounded by his parents' and siblings' behavior and so won't argue this point. You'll have to make a compromise. Suggest that next year you do a cocktail hour with his kin and then move along to yours.

Here's where it is tricky and the FG needs to be fair. He may agree to your being there only for cocktails, but when you want to move along to your folks' he may insist that he stay put. You shouldn't be angry with him. He's entitled to stay with his parents, as you are to go be with yours. Even if you think his family total boors, he may enjoy them. There is no law that says couples must have Christmas or Thanksgiving dinner together. Another FG compromise is to host the holiday meal at her place. Invite both sets of parents and grandparents. Or if the FG has her own children or steps, she can tell her parents and his that she's doing her own family dinner. Keeping it small.

If you know when you are dating that you don't want to trade your family gatherings for his, make a deal prior to engagement and marriage. Simply tell him that you don't want the traditional arrangement and that you will be spending such-and-such-a-holiday with your family and you have no problem with his being with his. Then you can set up a romantic late-night meal or drinks for the holiday for when you both return home.

How to Survive Family Gatherings

The key to surviving family get-togethers is to remind yourself as you walk in the door that you are an adult. Family events tend to go badly when the whole family regresses to the last point in time when they all cohabited. You start acting like a seventeen-year-old and your father starts treating you like one, too. And since there are some nice features to this arrangement—there's some comfort in being babied—lots of people let it slide. The downside to family time-traveling will soon become apparent and you will remember why you left in a huff after Easter dinner. You happened to forget the broccoli, so your sister somehow used that as an opportunity to chastise you for forgetting her birthday. Then Mom chimed in, agreeing that you've always been a bit too self-absorbed . . . and so on. To avert total disaster and desertion, bring up work as soon as you can fit it into the conversation. Talk about the repair you just had done to your car. Obviously, this is not the most riveting chat you can produce, but it does set a tone. Don't take the bait.

YOUR NEW STEPFAMILY

If an FG falls in love with a man who was previously married, she may find herself in a new and unexpected role: stepmom. If she has no children of her own, this will be particularly challenging, as her first experience at parenting is going to be tougher than the more traditional one. Once you've made a serious commitment to a man with kids, the two of you need to decide how involved you're all going to be. If you marry, will the kids live with you or with their mother? These are conversations that must happen before marriage.

Biting your tongue

Fabulous Girls in general were raised in homes where manners were instilled. Obviously, if her stepkids are not raised to have manners, and "please" and "thank you" are nary in sight, an FG will cringe every time they lumber across her threshold. But now that you're the official parent, feel free to do what you couldn't when you were only the girlfriend. Correct them! Go right ahead and say, "You meant, 'Please pass the salt.'" This will drive them crazy, but just because they're rude to your husband does not mean you have to be treated thus. And quite frankly, you're only doing them a favor, as rude adults are not very well received.

The stepmother FG is also free to call the kids on their behavior. If your precious stepkids' idea for Father's Day is for you and their dad to cook them a meal while they loll on the sofa and they don't bother with a gift either, promising that it will come next time they see their dad, it is perfectly acceptable for the FG to "innocently" ask the very next time she sees them, "So what did you end up getting your dad for Father's Day?"

However, the father may resent the FG's honesty. Divorces involving kids can cause parents to be consumed by guilt. So correcting or criticizing the kids will seem evil to the father. He's essentially afraid of them. Perhaps they'll like their mom better. Who knows. Chances are, he'll deny these feelings, but you as the FG will know they exist and you have to be sensitive to them.

In other words, while you're dying to exclaim the next time they visit and they're ensconced on the sofa fiddling with their Playstation, "Hey, I see you're spending some real quality time with Dad," you may not want to risk upsetting your husband. Even though you're quite right and his kids treat him abominably, even disrespectfully, he may end up turning his frustration on you, and then you have a fight on your hands. You may have to bite your tongue to be supportive of the man you love, even if it kills you. But you don't have to indulge the kids in their slothful behavior. If it is clear that (a) they will never help around the house and (b) your husband won't let you make them help, then as an FG you are absolutely absolved from having to join in with your husband and cook and clean for them. Just point out to your mate that you don't feel you should do everything for kids of their age—after all, they are quite capable. He should not force you or be angry—he has no right to be. Being a slave to his kids is his choice. You may find that he will begin to see the light when he sees his kids through your eyes.

Poor babies

No matter how difficult it may be to become a stepmother, and no matter how difficult your stepkids are, you must remember that they are children. The combining of families is simply harder for children than it is for adults. They are necessarily in this against their will. Even kids who get along with their stepmom would prefer it if Mommy and Daddy had stayed together—no matter what they may say. The best course of action for the newly minted stepmom is a casual one. Friendly, yes; buddy-buddy, no. Don't think that you and your new stepdaughter are going to be instant best friends and that she will pour her little heart out to you. You are, after all, part of the problem in her eyes (at least in the beginning).

If the style in which you want to run your home is wildly different from what the kids are used to, let them know what kinds of changes you're going to be expecting: "We're all going to clean up these dishes together before watching TV, actually." You may be dying to also say, "I'm not a maid like your mother!" But don't, unless you want to earn the title of stepmonster.

Other people's money, other people's kids

Money can be a source of tension for any couple. Children—those that aren't yours—only exacerbate this. Even if you actually have a great relationship with your stepkids, money spent on them and not on you may irritate you. The truth is, if you don't have your own kids and don't want your own, you probably made that decision because you want to live a life that is freer and includes more disposable income to spend on, well, yourself. Forget about being called shallow—this is a perfectly natural feeling. While you are not expected to contribute financially to the rearing of your husband's progeny, you are expected to accept that he does. This can mean that your hopes for a two-week trip to Italy will be dashed as you watch him send his son on some European excursion. Or that you can't put the down payment on your dream house because he has to keep a wad of dough in safekeeping for his kid's tuition.

While the FG will applaud her husband's commitment to his offspring, she will have to make some tough decisions. If she is making good money, perhaps she may have to top off the down payment, or pay for her husband's airline ticket to Italy. Or choose to vacation with friends in lieu of a couple holiday.

I sat alone at the table for a bit trying to catch my breath. I was half expecting the waitress to come by and bring Nice back to the table, like the last course in the meal. But she didn't. It was just me. And it looked like it would be just me for a while. Then my cell phone rang. I couldn't tell who it was at first, it just sounded like a wounded animal moaning. I was about to hang up when the voice became clear.

"It's me. I'm having a baby. Can you meet me in the hospital?" panted Elenor.

"Oh, my God, Elenor! I can be there in ten minutes. Are you okay?"

"I'm having a baby. It hadn't quite occurred to me until about half an hour ago. See you at the hospital."

Missy picked me up in a taxi outside the restaurant and we rushed to Elenor's side. Things were progressing quickly, and Elenor looked scared. Even though we were in one of those birthing rooms that are meant to calm everyone down, things were pretty intense. Contractions came over Elenor like waves and she would yell as if possessed. Missy and I each held a hand and fed her ice chips between contractions, but we felt as if we weren't doing nearly enough for her. Twenty-one hours of labor later and still no baby, the doctor announced that he was worried about the baby's progress and decided El would need a cesarean. He was very matter-of-fact, and El took the news well, but I could tell she was scared. While they set things up for the C-section, I remembered a story I'd heard from a couple in a similar situation. The husband read stories to his wife during the operation to distract her from what was going on south of the white sheet. I excused myself, ran out to the waiting room, and picked up a few magazines from the limited selection.

"Okay, Elenor, do you want to hear about a religious conversion or shark attacks?" I held up two magazines.

"Shark attacks, definitely. I want to hear about people in worse situations than me." I began reading, and after about twenty minutes there was a loud *squack* as Elenor's baby girl took in her first breath. When they brought her over to Elenor, I think we all felt a bit shocked that it was a real, live baby. Her head was absolutely round and her skin was pink and perfect.

"Hello, Olivia, welcome to the world."

CHAPTER NINE

Entertaining

I called it a housewarming party, but I'd been living in my place for nearly two months before I felt I was really ready for the unveiling. I'd painted—lavender on the living-room wall looked fab!—planted a little garden on the deck, and tried a few different furniture arrangements until it felt perfect for Kitty and me. And that night, with votive candles on practically every surface, my little home really shone. Elenor and Missy came over early to help me set everything up.

I had invited Nice to the party even though we'd broken up. I'd become so used to having him in my life for the important moments that it just seemed wrong not to ask him. He sent me an e-mail saying he didn't think he'd feel comfortable.

"Well, can you blame him?" asked Elenor. She was polishing my wineglasses and lining them up on the kitchen island. It was her first evening away from Olivia, and so far she seemed to be holding up pretty well. She had phoned the babysitter only twice in the half hour she'd been at my place.

"No, I understand. It just feels weird that he's not here. Maybe I shouldn't have bought this place and brought things to a head. Then we'd still be together."

Missy shook her head. "This place is so great. You guys would have realized that you wanted different things sooner or later. Like me and Joe."

That didn't ring true to me, but the doorbell did, so I didn't need to get into a conversation with Missy about how our relationships had nothing in common.

Soon my place was full of friends. The music was just right, everyone seemed to be laughing and mingling—and, I must say, complimenting me on my decor. Even Kitty was having a good time, weaving through everyone's legs and receiving praise for her beauty, as she always does. I'd invited everyone from my office to come, even though I wasn't feeling that close to them. I knew I had to make more of an effort with coworkers. After all, I really needed my job now that I had a mortgage. Cheryl and Marshall showed up, but I was not surprised that Bradley took a pass. Frank, the newspaper section editor I'd been writing for, did make an appearance, though. Every time the door opened I couldn't help but hope it might be Nice. Maybe he'd changed his mind. But it never was. I went over to the bar to make sure there was still enough ice, and I came upon the thing that strikes the most fear in a hostess's heart: a gossip columnist.

There was Dudley, standing in my kitchen. How dare he show up here! He must have ducked through the door after some guests were buzzed into the building. He was as ridiculous as ever in a suit that looked as if it had come from the children's department, blue velvet with five buttons all done up and a blue satin tie knotted thickly at his throat. His nearly white hair was slicked back with grease.

I was calm. "Dudley. I'm at a loss. How does one express displeasure at your company since you're someone who so obviously doesn't care about the feelings of others?"

"Come on, Manners Girl, what are you going to do, throw me out of your party? You'll only be forcing me to reveal you as a less-than-gracious host, now, won't you? I mean, what am I doing to deserve to be kicked out? I'm just standing here."

"You little weasel," I hissed.

"Ooh, that's not polite at all!"

Okay, so I wasn't keeping my cool so well. What I really wanted to do was remove him bodily. Which would not have been so hard. I'm sure I had at least fifteen pounds on him. People had begun to notice our little fracas and were starting to whisper to each other about it. I saw that Frank, my newspaper friend, was keeping his distance but watching our argument. Dudley was ruining my night in so many ways. He leaned back smugly on the island, in a mockery of making himself comfortable. Kitty chose that moment to hop up on the island, and I swear she wrinkled her little nose at the sight of Dudley.

"The way I see it, Manners Girl, I'm in charge here. You are obliged to be polite or your reputation will be ruined, and I can do or say anything I want because . . . well, because I don't care what anyone thinks." And with that, Dudley grinned a weaselly grin and leaned back even farther onto the island.

I was silenced momentarily, thinking about what he'd just said. He was right—the room was full of media types. What would it look like if I made a scene and expelled someone from my party, even if that someone was evil Dudley? And by now half the party was watching the show.

The smoke show, that is. At first it was just a thin plume of smoke rising from the back of Dudley's head. Then actual flames. It made him look even more devilish than usual. When Dudley realized that he was on fire, he panicked. He was genuinely afraid for his life. The fire was spreading, catching onto a stack of paper napkins and lighting up the dried flower arrangement. Everyone around us froze. The fire alarm wailed. I grabbed a pitcher of water and emptied it onto Dudley's head. Elenor dumped the ice bucket onto the island to put out the fire there. Marshall grabbed a chenille throw and wrapped Dudley in it to further douse the flames.

"Are you okay? Let me see your back. I think it's all out," I said, checking Dudley's burned jacket. It was in tatters.

"You saved my life, Manners Girl." Dudley was breathing hard, still in shock.

"You're burned quite badly. I think you'll need to go to the hospital. Who can I call for you?"

Newspaper Frank came over then. "I'll take him to the hospital. But will you promise to call me tomorrow?"

"Okay," I answered. I hoped he wasn't going to try to turn this into another opportunity for Dudley and I to swing at each other in print. It wasn't fun anymore.

Frank must have read my mind, for he said, "It's not about a story. It's about a job. Call me, I'll be in early." And with that, Frank whisked Dudley, tatters and all, out of my home.

⣩ *Entertaining* ⣩

The Fabulous Girl will always be up for a good time, whether she's having a few friends over to watch a movie or attending another's eleven-course meal. An FG knows that preparation is key to entertaining well. She thinks—in advance—about what will please her guests and goes out of her way to make her parties stylish and fun. Even when she is simply a guest, an FG understands that she should be making a contribution. She arrives at the right time, dressed nicely and in the mood to socialize. But no amount of forward thinking can ward off the unexpected or even disastrous events that can occur at social occasions. There are times when an FG must cope with hostess high jinks at another's party, or entertain by the seat of her pants.

⣩ *Fabulous Girl as Hostess* ⣩

LAST-MINUTE ENTERTAINING

You're home after a long day at work. The suit is off and the sweat-pants are on. You're flaked out on the couch eating a bag of corn chips and thinking how nice your night will be. Your sweetheart will come home, get comfortable, and maybe the two of you will rent a movie and order in. And then the call comes: "I'm so sorry, I forgot to tell you I've invited my boss over for dinner. We'll be there in half an hour." Of course, at some later point there will be a conversation about how wrong it is to put a girl in this position. A long conversation. But for now you have half an hour to pull a dinner party out of thin air.

Tell Mr. Lucky-to-Be-with-the-Sweetest-Woman-Alive to bring home some wine. Then turn your attention to food. If your kitchen and pantry is even halfway stocked, you can do it. Pasta is the easiest route. Who has four steaks in the fridge? Nobody, that's who. Get a sauce going. Don't worry if you have to start with a bottle of prefab, you can jazz it up. Sauté some garlic and onion and whatever other vegetables (mushrooms, peppers, celery) you've got and have cut quite fine. Add the bottle of sauce. Throw in a bit of dried chili. While the sauce is doing its thing, look around your place. Clear the clutter, don't clean. Look more carefully at the bathroom; wipe down the counter, pull the shower curtain closed. Now get changed into something presentable in case they show up even a minute early. Put on some music. Light the candles. Pour them stiff drinks as soon as they walk in the door.

Hints for impromptu dinners: food

To pull off even a modest dinner party on next to no notice, you need a pantry stocked with the basics:

Garlic
Onions
Dry pasta
Rice
Potatoes
Butter
Milk
Canned tomatoes and mushrooms
Tomato and mushroom soups in cans
A jar of decent ready-made pasta sauce
Capers
Black olives
Lemons and limes (or even the bottled-juice variety)

Grated Parmesan

A pepper mill

Salt

Tabasco and Worcestershire sauces

A variety of dried herbs: oregano, basil, parsley, paprika, ginger, dried chili flakes, rosemary, and thyme

The drink

An FG knows the importance of a stocked bar. It allows her to be a more spontaneous hostess, since she's not starting from scratch with her liquor cabinet every time she thinks of having friends over. When you have the basics in your bar—red and white wine, vodka, gin, whiskey, vermouth, brandy, and bitters—it feels like less of an outlay when you want to start adding to it. You might be entertaining a friend who you know has very specific tastes. Your boyfriend may get an unexpected promotion. An FG starts to add to her basic bar with

Champagne

Single-malt scotch

Bourbon

Cointreau

Grappa (which may be kept in the freezer) and other liqueurs

Pernod

Port

UNDESIRABLE HOSTESS GIFTS

There is something special about receiving homemade gifts. The extra effort it takes to create an original card or prepare strawberry preserves says the receiver is worth it. And if you ask your guests to specifically bring a handmade offering to a potluck, they must try. If they are completely incompetent they may substitute store bought, but should explain this to you ahead of time. However, there are certain occasions and certain items when handmade is not necessarily desirable—especially wine. But other strange gifts—such as a the trout your boyfriend's pal just caught, or fast food that your guest sets out among the higher-end edibles on your table—can give a hostess a tense moment. You should remember that the get-together is supposed to be a happy one. Don't make fun of the person's gift (at least not in front of him or her); go with the moment. "Frank, I've never touched a whole fish; can you please prepare it for me?"

Wine

There are many people who find the whole process of making wine—be it grape stomping, bottling, or fermenting, we're not really sure—actually fun. Unfortunately, many friends—that is, victims— of the homemade vintner know that their pal's result, white or red, is often just plain grapy. So what to do when Bingo brings his best bottle of Spring 2003 to your dinner party? The Fabulous Girl will simply thank Bingo and let him know she intends to savor his brew at another, unspecified special occasion. If Bingo seems put out, then add that you've already selected the wine to accompany the meal, and hope that your pal Sally doesn't waltz in with her 1980 Barolo ten seconds later.

In the unlikely event that you, the FG, have actually made the wine yourself, you should still provide the "real" stuff as an option. While you may think that your wine is the exception to the rule and that this whole prejudice against homemade "moonwine" is misplaced, you should offer it to your guests as an alternative, not as the sole selection. "Would anyone like to taste my own label?" is polite, and your equally polite guests will of course concede. But do not then take this opportunity to poll the table on the success of your efforts, and don't be offended if guests do not finish their glasses or if they switch to the French pinot noir.

Of course, as the Fabulous Girl develops her culinary skills and as her pocketbook grows, she may become choosier about the wine she serves with meals and therefore not rely on her guests to provide the libations. (Many "sophisticated" social types wince at the thought of opening up a guest's bottle, but for many younger people, if guests don't bring wine, there may not be any at all.) If your guests do bring wine, you can add these bottles to your "cellar." The wine is a gift and you are not compelled to open it that evening. Even if a guest who fancies himself a connoisseur insists that the Reisling he bought is just a killer with rack of lamb, you do not have to open it.

SERVING VEGETARIANS AND VEGANS

More and more people are adopting alternative eating habits. Vegetarians are now common, and vegans, who don't consume any animal products, including things such as cheese and eggs, are also becoming more prevalent. Of course, this can mean some fancy footwork for a hostess.

If you invite either V type to your dinner party, ensure you have enough meat-free food for them. Do not ask them over and then insist that they bring their own dish so as not to inconvenience you. If it's dinner, feed them like the other guests.

Likewise, if you are a V girl, you should not accept a dinner party invite then get either (a) vocally squeamish at the meat or (b) self-righteous with the other guests about your choice. Understandably, however, many Vs prefer to not have their vegetable delight cooked on the same grill as meat. If your host has only one barbecue you must bring your own small Hibachi. As the host, please inform your V guests that they are welcome to eat animal-free but that you have only the one barbecue.

POTLUCK

This type of entertaining runs from the casual "having the girls over to watch *Breakfast at Tiffany's*" to the more formal "Cousin Claire is getting married again." We all know the rules: the host calls around and with pen and paper writes down everyone's contribution. The more organized will even give out the assignments: Jenny brings the salad, Bob the cheese plate, and so on. Invariably there will be those who turn up with a store-bought fill-in-the-blank. And those who have slaved over their bean salad will tsk-tsk the one with the frozen key lime pie. With everyone being so busy these days, we can safely cut slack to those who choose to shop not chop. It may not taste as good as your own homemade miracle, but as long as you all did your part it's okay. Especially since not everyone is adept in the kitchen— the shopper may actually be sparing you. And please refrain from making repeated jabs at the person who hasn't cooked. Just eat.

HOW TO HOST THE FAMOUS

If you know people who are well known (be it a Hollywood actor or the town's mayor), you may have occasion to integrate them with your more modestly accomplished friends. How you handle this situation depends on how well adjusted the famous person is to his fame. In the best-case scenario, the famous pal is well adjusted and has no trouble moving among civilians. It's easy to throw this kind of friend into any kind of entertaining. Your other guests may have a moment upon entering the room of "Oh, my God, is that really *the* Bingo Jones?" Then Bingo's relaxed manner will put them at ease and they'll soon be mingling comfortably. If, on the other hand, Bingo is self-conscious about his profile—which unfortunately can manifest in the deforming belief that everyone wants something from the well known—small groups may be a better way to go. A dinner party, say, where Bingo can become comfortable with a smaller group and no one is making any sudden movements to scare him. The only downside to this is that by the end of the night, Bingo will probably dominate the conversation and want to feel that the other guests are basking in his glow. A bit of a bore, but either way all your guests will remember it as a fascinating evening.

THE EARLY ARRIVAL

Being late for a party is considered rude. What is little understood however, is that being extremely early is equally ill-mannered. Yet, there you are, the Fabulous Girl hostess, two hours prior to your party, still preparing food, still not dressed, still ironing the table-cloth, and the doorbell rings. It's Patty; she's figured that you two would spend some quality time before the shindig. It would be rude to turn her away. Instead, exclaim, "Patty I wasn't expecting anyone so early; I'm not ready." If dear Patty doesn't take the hint, put her to work with all that slicing, dicing, and cleaning.

CONFLICT WITH YOUR COHOST

Entertaining is a stressful proposition, even for those with a lot of practice. You want to do it well, and so you have a lot on your mind. The last few minutes before the doorbell rings can be the most tense of all. Is the music on? The table set? The wine decanting? Even though this work is halved by the presence of a mate, somehow the potential for agitation is doubled. Be aware of this strange entertaining equation and make a decision to remain on the same team as your cohost/spouse. There's nothing worse for your guests than arriving at your door to feel the tension between the two of you. A good way to avoid getting on each other's nerves is to get out of each other's way. Divide and conquer the work. She sets and decorates the table, he oversees salad and main.

If your cohost is not your mate but rather a roommate or best friend, tension can still take over. If your friend has a competitive streak you could find her wrangling control away from you. Suddenly you notice she's deciding what CD to play, when to bring out the champagne, or just generally behaving as though she were the only hostess. You could try and outgun her by overcompensating. It may be better, however, to behave with grace and enjoy the extra freedom her self-enslavement affords. Use your time to chat up the handsome man or to pour drinks for guests. There is very little this sort of person can do to overshadow the Fabulous Girl in her cocktail party element.

He's gone too far

You love his quirks. You don't even mind his unsubstantiated diatribes on the superiority of Korean cars. But this time he's out of line. Yesterday's conversation about whether or not the two of you are going to have kids is suddenly bubbling up in the most unappealing way during dessert. It takes you a moment to focus on what he's saying to his dining neighbors, and then you hear it: "I don't even like children. I don't understand the desire for them—it's kind of sick to me, actually." Of course, this display of his is pure aggression toward you. It's nasty and childish. Nevertheless, you are the hostess of the dinner party where it is all unraveling and so you must buck up and get through it. Even in this extreme situation you may not start channeling a *Who's Afraid of Virginia Woolf?*–style aggression and throw crystal at his head. Hopefully your man will respond to the look of death that you are shooting at him from across the table—although he is showing himself to be a most insensitive sort—and shut up. If not, you must dive into conversation with the people sitting next to you and ignore him for the rest of the night. Well, at least until your guests leave.

Once you are alone with him, tell him straight out, "Quit with the passive-aggressive dinner banter. I know what you were trying to say; tell me directly, not the whole table." This will launch into an argument, which is what he was clearly asking for anyway.

Everyone's Talking Shop

When you're having dinner with colleagues, you probably do the same thing—everyone tends to talk shop. It's fun. You want to know what everyone is up to, who got which new job, who is about to get the sack, and so on. This is perfectly acceptable behavior—unless. Unless you are in mixed company. It is never polite to talk at length on subjects from which any one person in the social group is excluded. This isn't to say that a subject should be banned, but the way it's discussed must be considered. If you realize that Bingo is the only nondentist at the dinner party, you may draw him into the conversation: "When we were in school we had the most evil professor named Dr. Molar. Really, that was his name . . ." Even so, be aware of how long you are lingering on a subject that Bingo can contribute nothing to or cannot even ask anything about.

SQUABBLING GUESTS

Even after a lot of thoughtful planning, an FG can realize she's blundered once it's too late. As the guests are arriving, you spot a snarl at the coat rack. And then another guest lets you in on the problem: Tom and Yvette were once—years and years ago—a couple. Yvette had an affair, the end was messy, and Tom has never fully recovered. Now they are in your home with their respective dates and you feel bad. The only thing to do is to assume the best in your friends: that they will be able to handle the evening with a little support from you. Don't fuss over them or shoot them I'm-sorry looks all night. Quickly rethink whatever seating plan you had in mind. Obviously, you are going to want to separate them as much as possible. And make sure that during the cocktail hour you tell each of them how fantastic she and he looks.

BOORISH GUESTS

While the Fabulous Girl likes to think she has no ill-mannered friends, on occasion she may find that she has inadvertently invited a boor to her home. He won't introduce himself, he won't shake other guests' hands, he'll cut into conversations and not apologize. Either way, the FG knows he is off her future guest list. But for the moment she needs to try to teach the boor a thing or two about etiquette. When she spots him behaving rudely she should come to the rescue of the victim. "Samantha, I think Ralph believes you two have met before; let me introduce you." While you clearly cannot follow the boor around all night, intercepting wherever possible is about all you can do.

DRUNKEN GUESTS

You never knew how loud, opinionated, and generally gross your friend Sally was until she had one too many martinis. Boosted by liquid courage she's telling one of your guests that the guest's husband made a pass at her, she's grabbing another man's ass, or she's explaining earnestly to your nerdy coworker why he can't get laid. You must see to it that Sally is cut off from booze, and that a steady supply of water is poured down her throat. You will no doubt have to enlist help from another guest, preferably one whom Sally will listen to. Then call a cab and put her in it.

GUESTS WHO BREAK THINGS

Whether the klutz was drunk or sober, a Fabulous Girl cannot lose it on her guest because of a broken coat rack or glass. She simply accepts the forthcoming apology and cleans up the mess.

However, if what is broken during a moment of utter negligence is, say, her television or window, then the offender must pay up. If the klutz doesn't offer, the FG must contact the person within the week (having given the breaker a few days to come forward with the cash) and demand payment. "Fred, I understand you didn't mean to smash my DVD player when you threw it at Michael, but since it is now broken, I'm going to have to ask you to buy me another one."

SOMEONE CATCHES ON FIRE, CHOPS OFF A FINGER, AND OTHER DISASTERS

You have served a lovely meal. You know you've brought an interesting group of people together. You've made your apartment warm and inviting by covering every surface with candles. As the group gets up from the table to sip after-dinner drinks, Bingo leans back against his mantelpiece, resting an elbow there while telling a story. Then you notice the smoke. The arm of Bingo's shirt—no, actually, Bingo's arm—is on fire. Everyone freezes. Someone shouts at Bingo to roll on the ground. The fire is moving up his sleeve. Bingo is frozen in fear. The FG springs into action, grabs a bottle of sparkling mineral water off the table, and pours it over Bingo. The fire is out. If Bingo's burns are serious enough to warrant a trip to the hospital—and they probably are—the FG offers him her company while he waits in the emergency room. Whether or not Bingo takes her up on her offer, the FG follows up the next day to check up on his injuries and to thank him for coming to the party. Many people feel awkward in these situations and fear that Bingo may not want to receive calls after such an evening. But nothing could be further from the truth. The absence of such a call will be perceived as lack of concern for his health.

In such extreme situations, you as the hostess must take control—both during and after the catastrophe. See to it that your guests are reassured, delegate tasks to those who wish to help out, and call everyone the next day to make sure they're feeling all right, perhaps have a good laugh about the fiasco, and tell them how wonderful it was to see them despite it all.

DINNER IS RUINED

You read the recipe wrong. The oven was supposed to be set at 350 degrees for 45 minutes, not 450 degrees for 35 minutes. The chicken is now black on the outside and raw on the inside. And your guests have not even sat down yet. You need to quickly take stock of the situation. Can your first course be added to in a way that will make it a main course? A green salad could be turned into a niçoise with a tin of tuna and the potatoes that were going to go with the chicken. If no such shift can be made, then go ahead and serve the appetizer as you'd planned. But before you do, call up a good Indian or Thai restaurant and order in the rest of the meal. You needn't even say anything about it until the doorbell rings. Everyone will laugh and remember how unflappable you were in this little crisis.

FOOD POISONING

It may not happen immediately, but suddenly an hour or so after the sushi you and your guests are feeling unwell. You've served bad food and now everyone is going to pay for it with their stomachs. Of course you must apologize and telephone everyone the next day to ensure that all is better. Obviously you didn't intend to poison people, and if you had suspected anything was off you wouldn't have served it. As a nice gesture you can send your guests some flowers and a note. They should accept graciously, as this can surely happen to anyone.

❧ *Whom to Invite?* ❧

INVITING THOSE YOU DON'T KNOW WELL

The guest list is the most important ingredient for any successful party. Of course, you'll invite some of your close friends, but you should include those you don't know well. Perhaps they are friends of people you've chatted with briefly at an event; either way, don't be shy when extending invitations and don't worry that these groovy new people won't want to attend—just ask. You may feel awkward calling someone you've met only once, but most people are quite delighted by this sort of invitation. They'll be flattered that after such a brief encounter you want to know them better. Just be sure that when you call, you do it with the tone of someone who is regularly throwing interesting groups together—even if this is your first foray. Phone up and say, "It was so nice meeting you the other evening. I'm having a dinner party on Saturday and I thought you and your husband would really enjoy the people I'm having over." Invitations should feel like compliments, and even people you don't know well respond well to those.

INVITING COUPLES WHO HAVE SPLIT

You were close friends with both halves of the couple and you felt bad when they split. You don't want to have to choose which of them you carry on a friendship with, and you shouldn't have to. But you do have to be sensitive to how you handle invitations to them. Don't try mixing them together at parties for at least six months if your friends' relationship was a serious one. It's a rare broken-up couple who will want to be invited to a dinner party together but separately. Cocktail parties are the place where you can pull off simultaneous invitations. You should, however, warn your friends of your plans. Don't make a big deal of it, just let them know: "I'd love it if you could make it on Saturday night. Just so you know, I've also invited Nathan." You do have to be prepared for the possibility that your friend is not ready to be at a party with her ex and will therefore pass on your invitation. Don't give her a hard time. Never make a friendship contest out of an issue like this. It's not about you.

INVITING ONE HALF OF A COUPLE

A couple joined by love and/or marriage is not a single entity. However, within their social circle, they are connected for obvious reasons. So what do you do when you care for only one part of a couple? Even if you don't necessarily hate Bingo's wife, you may simply feel closer to him and prefer his company solo. Of course, you may actually loathe one half of said couple. While you're not obliged to become best buddies with Fifi, there are rules of etiquette for the treatment of a couple even if you care for only one of them.

Dinner parties

It is never acceptable to invite only one half of a couple to a dinner party. You can, though, seat the one you are less interested in at the far end of the table.

Cocktail parties or casual drink get-togethers

Again, you must invite both parts of a couple. A good rule of thumb when considering making this kind of half-invite is to imagine telling your mate that you'll be going out to a social function on Saturday but he's not invited. How well would that go over?

Except: Obvious exceptions to these rules must be made for work, club, or single-gender groups. If Fifi and her female investors' club go out once a month for dinner, she should not feel bad leaving Bingo at home. Bingo probably won't mind either.

Outings and activities

You and your good friend Bingo share a love of art. In fact, this mutual interest makes up a good deal of your friendship. You are not obligated to invite Bingo's wife along on your weekly gallery trips. Likewise, if you want Fifi to join your soccer league, you needn't feel you have to ask Bingo if he's never expressed an interest in the sport.

Conversation

You bump into your friend Fifi at a cocktail party and, unfortunately for you, she is with her boorish mate, Bingo. Although you could not care less if you never heard another sound from his mouth, you must take a stab at polite conversation with Bingo. It is childish and rude to address your party chitchat only to Fifi. Even if you only run into Fifi, you must ask after Bingo—pretending he doesn't exist is unacceptable.

Snubbing

If you do despise Fifi but for whatever reason maintain a relationship with Bingo, then you cannot snub Fifi in public. Greeting Bingo but ignoring Fifi is not acceptable.

You Are Invited Somewhere—and Your Beau Isn't

If you find yourself and not your mate invited to something that your mate really should be included in, you must either politely insist that your loved one join you or else decline the invitation altogether. Anyone who makes a point of excluding your mate from social events where he should be welcome is snubbing you both.

YOU ARE NOT INVITED

This one can hurt, not only in the scenario in which your boyfriend is invited and you are not, but if your best friend has a dinner party and doesn't invite you. You may not understand why you weren't included, especially if you learn that the other guests were all mutual acquaintances. You must remember that you and your friend do lead separate lives so she is never obligated to invite you to everything. However, if you suspect that she has snubbed you out of anger or such then you are free to ask her. "Jenny, I'm a bit hurt that you didn't include me last Friday night." You may discover that you were left out due to some perceived slight, or simply because of numbers. Accept her excuses and move on. If Jenny keeps excluding you then clearly she really isn't that close a friend.

Joint snubbing

If you are the victim of a snub, your partner should not go out of his way to be friendly with the snubber, as this only encourages the behavior. If you are the partner, be sympathetic and perhaps next time the ill-mannered lout selects you for the snub, employ the useful "nicing" tactic and force the snubber to say hello to both of you.

PEOPLE ARE RELUCTANT TO INVITE YOU BECAUSE OF YOUR EX

It may seem unreasonable, but it is quite possible that the FG may find herself with a dearth of invitations after a breakup. The more messy the breakup, the greater the chances of fewer invites. How do you handle this particular absence of invitations? Clearly mutual friends feel that they cannot have you and your ex in the same room, or worse, they've taken his side. You must decide first and foremost where you stand with your ex. Ask yourself: Can I stand to be at a party or dinner party with Fred? What if his new girlfriend, Fifi, is there? Do I really care that so-and-so have cut me off their cocktail list? If the answer to either of these questions is no, you must move on and begin to rekindle other friendships where your ex won't be an issue. If you answer yes to either question, converse with Fred to be sure he's also okay doing the joint party circuit. And then move on to the friends in question and let them know that they have no need to exclude you.

INVITATIONS FROM YOUR EX

It's perfectly acceptable to maintain friendships with someone you used to date, even if he and your current beau aren't crazy about each other. You do have to be careful about the kind of invitation you accept from this person, however. It's fine to meet for coffee or drinks one-on-one, and it's also fine to go out in a group with your ex as long as your boyfriend is welcome as well. You can't agree to go out with your ex and a group of people if your boyfriend is not welcome. And if your ex is so uncomfortable with your current beau, it may be time to reevaluate his friendship. Is your ex really over his feelings for you? Maybe you are quietly torturing him with your friendship.

∾ *Fabulous Girl as Guest* ∾

GETTING READY

A dinner party

We all know that it's worse to show up early than late to a dinner party. If the invitation was for 7:30, your hosts are almost certainly not ready at 7:30. And they are expecting to serve drinks before ushering everyone to the table. It's perfect to arrive about fifteen minutes late. If you have some legitimate reason for being much later than that (a car accident, an act of God), you must call to warn your hosts. Even if your hosts weren't planning to start serving dinner until 8:30, if you arrive at 8:25 you've just made the last hour an anxious one for them. If you are the hostess and one or two guests are quite late, you should only hold things up for them for a limited time. Never let the cocktail hour last longer than an hour—momentum will be lost, sobriety will be lost, and so on. Whenever it is that the stragglers arrive, they should sit down and just join the dinner at whatever point, be it first, second, or third course.

A cocktail party

When your beau comes to pick you up, pour each of you a quick drink. A shot of vodka (which you keep in the freezer) with a twist of lime will give you a bit of fire and can barely be detected on your breath.

A black-tie event

Choose and try on your gown at least forty-eight hours before the event. There may need to be alterations. There is nothing more vexing than to have a custom-made dress sent to your home hours before the party only to discover it's not what you expected and now you must attend the do looking like Cruella De Vil.

A sporting event

Don't try to one-up the rest of the hard-core fans and competitors by turning up at the horse show in stilettos. You may think you'll outshine everyone, but in fact you'll look silly. Research whatever type of sport you're going to see. Is it sailing? Hockey? Lacrosse? Polo? Surfing? And add your own brand of chic to the proper attire.

A work event

Chances are you're going straight from the office. Give yourself an extra half hour to freshen up. Take your FG-at-work supplies to the ladies' room, brush your teeth, reapply your lipstick, and fluff your hair. This break between your desk and whatever reception it is you're headed to allows you to switch gears. Even though this is a work-related party, you still want to have a bit more energy than the third-quarter report required. Once you arrive, head to the ladies' to give yourself a final look in the mirror, straighten shirts or jackets and so on, before entering the actual room. This five-minute prep will make you more confident and you'll appear unflustered. And remember not to drink too much!

YOU NEED A FABULOUS HOSTESS GIFT

No Fabulous Girl would arrive at any kind of gathering empty-handed. A wise FG also plans ahead of time what gift suits the hostess's particular occasion by enquiring ahead of time. Herewith a list of potential fabulous gifts:

1. Wine. A lovely bottle of wine is never unwelcome. If you're aiming for it to coordinate with a meal, you should check ahead of time with the hostess as to her preferences for color and taste.

2. Flowers. A grand gesture that is best made prior to the party. While flowers are lovely they can cause the hostess to be unsettled as she races around finding a vase and scissors, etc. at the same time as others are arriving. But calling a florist to have them delivered shows your consideration.

3. Chocolates. Few FGs can resist decadent chocolates to either share or to squirrel away for later.

4. Candles. A lovely pillar is often appreciated and can be used to create ambience on the night. If you know the decor or the hostess's favorite scent, you can definitely impress.

5. Books or CDs. If you know the hostess well and that she is just dying for the latest Martin Amis or Dido, this is very well planned. If you are only guessing, such a gift may very well fall flat.

All of the above gifts can be given with confidence (though #5 is high risk) on any occasion.

FAKE DINNER PARTY INVITES

The FG gets the phone call inviting her to a dinner party next week at a friend's. She arrives looking fabulous, bottle of wine in hand. Her hosts open the door looking less fabulous, the house not quite clean, and then sit the FG down on the sofa and casually offer her a variety of takeout menus. "We thought we'd just get delivery." This is a far-too-common occurrence.

There is absolutely nothing wrong about ordering in food. If you know that your Indian food is never going to be as good as your favorite restaurant's, then by all means call up and order their *aloo gobi*. Order in advance and decide when you'd like it delivered. Set a lovely table just as you would if you were making it yourself.

If you decide to go this route, the invitation should come with that caveat. Miscommunication is impolite. And as a host, if you choose to surprise your guests with takeout, be prepared to pay for it yourself. If you pay with a credit card over the phone, you'll avoid the uncomfortable moment when the food arrives and everyone reaches for their wallets.

Likewise, do not have people over for "dinner" and then announce that you'll all be walking over to the Italian restaurant down the street. People think that an invitation to dinner means you'll be cooking. If this is not the case, give fair warning.

If, as a guest, you're now poring over a Thai menu when you had imagined you'd be sitting down to a homemade meal, just go with it. Sulking does not become the Fabulous Girl. While it's not acceptable to chastise your takeaway-loving friends, it is fine to mention that you'll need to run out to the nearest ATM before the food arrives.

Badly Timed Meals

We have all had those dinner party's at which, despite the best-laid plans, nothing works. Or we've all been victims of hosts who insist that dinner will be served promptly at 7 p.m., only the incredibly elaborate dinner they've planned isn't ready until 10 p.m. Really, a guest cannot be expected to sit around for hours starving and drinking up a storm. All that leads to is a hungry, angry drunk. If this happens once, you can do little. However, the next time these same

people invite you for a dinner party at 7 p.m., you may want to inquire if they really mean 7 p.m. and offer to bring some appetizers
so that starving isn't an option. Once you are a guest, you cannot
leave because you are hungry, but you may ask for crackers and
cheese while you wait.

ODD GIRL OUT

If you find yourself the odd girl out at a dinner party—at a cocktail
party you can simply wander off to another conversational circle—
there are a few things you can do. First, assume that because you
come from a different field or background you are actually the most
interesting person in the room. This group is probably sick of having the same old conversation and is just dying to have someone
throw out a new opinion. You can either start with one of the people sitting on either side of you or take on the whole table. Granted,
this is a bold gambit, but it's one that could really make the party—
and your reputation as a desirable dinner guest. If you're going to go
for it, you should lead with something everyone will relate to or have
an opinion about. A book that's on the best-seller list. A film that
people are likely to have seen. A world event. "Is it just me, or is the
new show at the National Gallery the worst exhibit of the last ten
years? An obvious money grab!" Even if only half the people at the
table have seen the show, the ones who haven't will be drawn into
the new conversation.

DUELING HOSTS

You've heard that their dinner parties get lively, but you weren't expecting this. Bingo and Fifi have served up the main course and now

they're serving up the ugliest secrets of their marriage. You hadn't noticed, but maybe Fifi consumed rather a lot of wine during the first course and that jokey little back-and-forth during the cocktail hour about which of them was supposed to have picked up the groceries needed for dinner actually had more teeth than you had first guessed. Now they're bringing his parents into it, and that last family trip they took together. Who had paid for it in the end? Who? Well, Fifi had ended up putting down her credit card when Bingo's cheapskate father had choked. And there you are, a table of silenced ping-pong watchers.

Sometimes all that's needed is for someone to gently draw the couple's attention to the fact that they've crossed the line. "Would you two like some privacy?" should be enough. When this doesn't work, stronger measures are called for. The evening is pretty much shot anyway, so you may as well barge in: "Okay, you two, maybe you could finish this up a little later when it's just the neighbors who will have to listen?" If even this tactic doesn't stop the deluge, then you could suggest that the rest of the group pick up their drinks and move into the living room. Or you could simply get up and leave.

THE HOSTESS GETS SICK IN THE MIDDLE OF THE PARTY

You're having a lovely time at a dinner party. The meal is finished, and people are standing around the hostess's comfortable apartment. The guy you've had your eye on for months is telling you all about his trip to Paris—his parents have an apartment on the Île de la Cité and he goes at least once a year. Suddenly you notice your hostess bolt for the washroom looking a bit green. And she stays there. And stays there. Although you don't want to pull yourself away from the conversation you're in ("You should see this apartment, it looks right over Shakespeare & Co. . . . Do you ever get to Paris?"), you know you really should check on your friend. As discreetly as you can, extract yourself from the party, knock gently on the door, and inquire after her health. If she tells you she's fine, then leave her alone. Let her know, however, that you could fetch her some aspirin or a glass of water, whatever she may need in there.

If she's really ill—puking her guts out—then be willing to go into hostess mode yourself. Find out what she wants you to do and then just do it. Does she want you to just tend to her party while she pulls herself together? In this case you don't have to organize a game of charades; just listen for the end of the CD, refresh drinks, and so on. Or would she like you to clear everyone out of her place? Whatever it is, do it with the least amount of fuss. She probably feels ridiculous on top of feeling ill and so doesn't want a lot of attention drawn to the situation. If you do have to boot everyone out of her place politely, you should be the last person to leave. Make sure she has everything she needs—and make sure it's not so serious that she needs a trip to the hospital or for you to run out to an all-night pharmacy. Quickly stack up the dinner plates so she doesn't wake up to an utter disaster, and then be off. And, of course, call the next day to find out if she's feeling better. Assure her that in every other way, the night was a delight.

Of course if you are the hostess, right about now you are completely mortified. Grab your closest friend and explain the situation, give her instructions on how to either finish the meal or to kindly announce to everyone that they should leave. If one of the guests is a new guy you're into, don't be embarrassed; simply tell him the situation and suggest drinks later in the week.

QUESTIONABLE FOOD

FGs love dinner parties—it's the social occasion in which they shine most brightly. And hosts love FGs for the same reason. A host knows she can count on an FG to add to the conversation and fun of the evening. And an FG can handle almost any curveball that comes her way during a dinner party. Including a bad dinner. Obviously, not all dinner-party hosts are gourmet chefs, and most well-mannered people can make it through a bland pasta or an overly seasoned soup. But what's an FG to do if she bites into a mouthful of baby greens sprinkled with walnuts that have turned rancid? Or worse, if she's served a skewer of raw chicken?

It is not in the least ill-mannered to save yourself from food poisoning in these situations. If you know your hostess well and the group at the table is made up of good friends, you should just speak up. Be as friendly and light as possible: "Fifi, your timer must be broken because I think you meant to cook this chicken a little longer." And then immediately help Fifi—who will of course be mortified—deliver the chicken sushi back to the kitchen for a little more time on the grill. A good hostess would rather suffer a moment's embarrassment than send all her guests to the hospital. If you don't know your hostess well or if the dinner is a more formal one, do whatever you can to get her out of the room with you: "Fifi, could I trouble you for some aspirin?" Once you're out of earshot, you can gently let her know about the raw chicken.

YOU HATE THE FOOD

Perhaps the side dish or the main isn't rancid but just plain unpalatable. Try to stomach as much of the dish as you can, and try moving the food around your plate so it appears to have been eaten. Then simply put your utensils down. If your host asks you point-blank if you didn't enjoy her braised sweetbreads, say that they were fine but you're just full.

You Have a Food Allergy

If as a guest you know you'll have a nasty or unpleasant reaction to a certain type of wine or ingredient, you should inform your hosts in advance. In the case of wine you may let them know that you will happily bring your own bottle so as not to put them out. The host in this situation can, depending on his or her budget, decline this of-fer or accept it graciously. But if for some reason you've neglected to tell the host of your allergy or problems with migraines, you should graciously refuse the wine or food rather than suffer.

The Last Morsel

There always appears to be a strange kind of guilt that arises around a party or get-together when the last morsel of snack is left on the plate. Perhaps women don't want to appear piggish by eating the last spring roll or skewer of shrimp, but the Fabulous Girl knows this is silly. In fact, if the FG is eyeing that final canapé, she does the right thing by announcing to those around her, "Does anyone else want this before I indulge?" Then she will either split it or eat it. This is perfectly mannered.

The party broke up once the firemen arrived.

They looked around to make sure everything was okay and then headed out the door. Elenor asked if we could go for a ride on the truck, but you could tell that the firemen were used to dealing with frisky women. And off they went.

The buzzer rang again.

"Maybe the firemen changed their minds," said Elenor hopefully.

"Yeah, right," I said. "Hello? Nice? Hi, come up!"

I wasn't sure what to think. I was at once nervous and elated that Nice was at this very moment coming up to see me. The girls quickly got their things together and promised to call to check on me later. They both insisted that they'd had a really good time until the fire started.

When I opened the door, Nice looked a little nervous himself. I told him what had happened and showed him around.

"You were right, it's an amazing place. You did very well."

Which was very sweet, given the state of the place. There were puddles of water everywhere. Bits of burnt fabric floated in the puddles, and the general debris from the party cluttered the room.

"Thank you. I really wanted you to see it. It was so strange not to have you here tonight. It seemed wrong."

"I was wrong," said Nice. "I was wrong to push you about moving in together. I just felt hurt and insulted, and I thought you were sort of breaking up with me by getting this place on your own."

"I know, I know. And I can see why it seemed like that to you. But I wasn't. I just needed to do this. It felt really good buying this place on my own. Except I hate that you're gone."

"I'm not gone. I mean, I'm back. Can we go back? And we'll wait until you're ready to move in together."

And then there was the true housewarming.

Epilogue

WHEN LIFE IS FALLING APART

Every Fabulous Girl deserves a life full of happiness, love, and success. But even an FG, with her superior life skills, will have rough periods, when one thing after another falls apart, often simultaneously. Forget the bad hair day—it's the bad hair month. Your job sucks, you get dumped, you fall out with a friend, your landlord ups your rent, and to top it all off, you break the heel on your favorite (and very pricey) pair of shoes as you're hiking home from the subway in the pouring rain. Sometimes life bites, even for Fabulous Girls. The worst of it is not knowing when your losing streak is going to end. These are the moments (or months) when grace really counts. Because on top of having hardships to endure, a girl could find herself altered by them. Rather than becoming bitter and angry, an FG looks for ways to improve her lot and cope with the difficulties she faces. She knows that just as this hard time seemed to come out of nowhere, so too may it end. So, how do you weather such turbulent times with grace? Here are a few things for the Fabulous Girl to keep in mind in order to make the most of her great big life.

Don't whine

It is very easy to slip into complaint mode. Life can be very, very stressful and very, very busy. The little things can get to us—the too-slow checkout line at the grocery store, the skirt that has sold out of your size, the phone bill that's too high—even more than the bigger issues. But it is very unbecoming to be a whiner. Everything in life is going badly to this person, and even the teeniest deviation from her plan seems to her to be a personal attack. The Fabulous Girl will not allow herself to fall into this pattern—no matter how sticky things get—and if she does, she will take steps to curb chronic complaining. If she doesn't, people will get sick of her and be afraid to ask how she is doing.

Stand up

Of course, complaints do have their purpose. The Fabulous Girl prides herself on being civil to others, but "decorum," as we said, doesn't mean "doormat." If she's treated unfairly or not getting what she paid for, she speaks up. Politely, of course. It's all in the tone. An FG knows how to make her point in a direct way without sounding bitter. She knows it's the more civilized—and effective—way to assert herself.

Know when to walk away

A Fabulous Girl can be a real trooper. Her inclination is to stick things out no matter what. A bad relationship, a horrid job, a tricky family situation. Whatever the problem, sometimes it is smarter to give up. The FG does not relish banging her head against a brick wall. But being loyal, optimistic, and a hard worker, she may fancy that walking away from a problematic situation and admitting that something she cared for is over makes her a failure. It does not. It makes her wise. There will be times in her life when there is no other option. Her mental and even physical health may depend on her leaving a negative circumstance behind. As tough as this may be, the FG can look forward to the inevitable feeling of relief that is sure to wash over her when her newfound freedom finally sinks in.

Change your mind

At a certain point in her life, a Fabulous Girl may feel that she should have a comprehensive approach to life. Her life experiences will add up to a sensibility. She may know how much work means to her and decide how much to devote herself to it. She may find purpose in a rich family life and dedicate herself to that. But another thing can happen, too: she may change her mind. Her dream of getting married could be coming true when she realizes it doesn't feel like she thought it would. She may have clocked serious hours at her career but suddenly feel that all she wants is to be home baking pies. You've been planning to move to Rome for the past year but as the date approaches you are filled with dread rather than excitement. You probably feel as if everyone will think you're a loser or a coward by not following through. But it won't be them lying on a small bed in Rome crying from homesickness. Life's like that. It takes a great deal of courage to admit to yourself and the people close to you that you've changed your mind.

There's the old adage that it's a woman's prerogative to change her mind. The FG knows this is in fact true. So whether she decides at the last minute to call off her wedding or simply after six months of driving a compact car trades it in for a Jeep, she has the courage to make changes she knows to be right. The FG must stand up for herself and not let the opinions or perceived opinions of others guide her beyond her own carefully considered decisions.

Don't be afraid of wrong decisions

Actually, there is no such thing as a wrong decision. An FG will learn something valuable from every outcome. Part of being an adult is taking responsibility for your actions—even the actions that don't work out in your favor. You have to allow yourself to fail and not let the possibility of failure prevent you from taking chances.

Beware burnout

Too many FGs feel exhausted, stressed, and overworked. There comes a point in every FG's life when she must take stock and re-evaluate her priorities. Things such as getting a regular good night's sleep, healthy diet, and exercise should be no-brainers. But as any FG knows, work and other pressures can make these basics seem too time-consuming and she ends up neglecting one or all three. Don't work so hard that you haven't time for your friends and family, to see a film or read a novel, or just to walk the dog. If you find yourself answering "Busy" to the question "How are you?" every time it's posed, you need to take note. So much of an FG's sense of self comes from her accomplishments at work. Couple that with a busy social life and the whole thing starts to feel like a grind. It takes real effort to scale back. Back off on some commitments and find out what it means to really get a life.

Commit to fabulous fun

In keeping with avoiding burnout, every Fabulous Girl should commit to enjoying herself. When life hands you more than your share of lemons, seek out the simple remedies that will enable you to relax and forget your cares. A party, a vacation, or lunch with Mom—the FG should indulge herself in things that remind her of what life is in its best moments. After all, it's fun being a Fabulous Girl.

"*I'd love it if you'd come over to my place later,*" I said to Nice's voice mail. "I'm just meeting Miss and El for dinner, but I'm sure I'll be home around 9:30 or so."

As I walked into Dominick's, the girls—all the girls, Missy, Elenor and Olivia—were waiting at the table. This was a big night. Missy's divorce papers had been signed that afternoon. So understandably, she was relieved and sad and emotional.

We toasted the new chapters that we were all beginning. Frank had been as good as his word and had offered me a job. It seemed that the paper had such a strong response to my manners articles that the editiors had decided they wanted me to do a column each week. I was now officially Manners Girl. And since I could write on other subjects as well, they were going to hire me on full-time. I was elated. Working at *Smack!* had been a great experience, but it was obviously time to move on.

Elenor was feeling confident about single motherhood. She was going to be away from work for a few more months, but she'd started to interview nannies and seemed to have found a good one. Missy was happily ensconced in my old apartment and beginning to talk about dating again. Everything seemed pretty perfect.

"Well, at least I'm still rich," said Missy, taking a big gulp of her wine. Elenor and I raised our eyebrows at each other. "What? What's wrong with that? If it was my money when we were married, why shouldn't it be my money now?"

"I guess so," I mumbled. Just then Olivia started fussing. Not really full-on crying, but the whining that usually precedes it. Elenor was trying to get her used to being out in different situations. Sometimes it went smoothly; other times Olivia decided she'd had enough as soon as they arrived.

"I mean, I was supportive of Joe in our marriage. I threw dinner parties and stuff." Missy was getting defensive. Olivia was getting testy herself. Again Elenor and I just nodded. "Elenor, why is she crying? Is she hungry or something? Isn't there something you can do?"

Tears welled up in Elenor's eyes. "Sometimes I just don't know why she's crying. She just cries. She's a baby. I don't know what to do." Now Elenor was really crying. "Oh, don't you start being a baby," snapped Missy. "Don't you think she should take Olivia outside?"

"That's not fair, is it?"

I sat back and watched my two best friends bicker. Although I felt bad for El (and for Olivia and Missy, too), I had another thought. Given all my friends and their crazy lives and me and my crazy life, I was never going to run out of material for my new column. So at least I had job security.

Acknowledgments

We'd like to thank the incomparable Anne McDermid and also Nathan Whitlock and Kelly Dignan; the entire Broadway team, particularly Ann Campbell and Laura Pillar; Roxanna Bikadoroff for once again bringing the Fabulous Girl to life; to the staff at *Fashion* magazine for their friendship and support; to the staff of *Flare* magazine for their ongoing support, particularly Suzanne Boyd for her friendship and encouragement, and Ying Chu for rescuing the manuscript from behind locked doors one late night; the FGs for their extremely fabulous example: Lynn Creighton, Leanne Delap, Tammy Eckenswiller, Rebecca Eckler, Carole Hines, Victoria Jackman, Laura Keogh, Kate Mayberry, Leah McLaren, Jane Miller, Tralee Pearce, Elizabeth Renzetti, Martha Sharpe, Susie Sheffman, Alex Tigchelaar, Vivian Vassos, and Victoria Winter; Kim's mother and grandmother, Carolynne Nelson and Muriel Farrell; Margaret and Trevor Northeast, and David, Debbie, Dylan, and Gareth Marsh for their love and support; and those indispensable FBs: Angel David, Daniel Foster, Mark Kingwell, Claude Laframboise, Lindsay Mahon, Alexander Nagel, Doug Sanders, Russell Smith, Arlen J. Vranic, and Doug Wallace; and Richard Hay for his love, patience, and inspiration.

The little black dress of etiquette guides that's a must for fabulous girls everywhere.

Beauty is only skin deep, but when you're fabulous it goes all the way through. Now genuinely fabulous authors Kim Izzo and Ceri Marsh show you how to handle real-world situations like these with grace and complete unflappability:

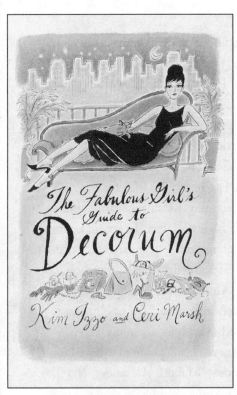

* **Coping with an office backstabber**

* **Hosting the perfect dinner party**

* **How to handle fair-weather friends**

* **Protocol for first-night sex**

With this smart, thoroughly modern book, you'll be fabulous in a flash and reap the rewards that come naturally to the charming new you.